Love Stories of Later Life

# Love Stories
# of Later Life

## A Narrative Approach to
## Understanding Romance

Amanda Smith Barusch

UNIVERSITY PRESS

2008

# OXFORD
UNIVERSITY PRESS

Oxford University Press, Inc., publishes works that further
Oxford University's objective of excellence
in research, scholarship, and education.

Oxford   New York
Auckland   Cape Town   Dar es Salaam   Hong Kong   Karachi
Kuala Lumpur   Madrid   Melbourne   Mexico City   Nairobi
New Delhi   Shanghai   Taipei   Toronto

With offices in
Argentina   Austria   Brazil   Chile   Czech Republic   France   Greece
Guatemala   Hungary   Italy   Japan   Poland   Portugal   Singapore
South Korea   Switzerland   Thailand   Turkey   Ukraine   Vietnam

Copyright © 2008 by Oxford University Press, Inc.

Published by Oxford University Press, Inc.
198 Madison Avenue, New York, New York 10016
www.oup.com

Oxford is a registered trademark of Oxford University Press

Library of Congress Cataloging-in-Publication Data
Barusch, Amanda Smith.
Love stories of later life : a narrative approach
to understanding romance / Amanda Smith Barusch.
p. cm.
Includes bibliographical references and index.
ISBN 978-0-19-531404-5
1. Love in old age.  2. Old age—Social aspects.  I. Title.
HQ1061.B374   2008
306.7084'60973—dc22      2007044673

9 8 7 6 5 4 3 2 1

Printed in the United States of America
on acid-free paper

In loving memory of my mother
Helen Henderson Smith
1931–2006

# Preface

As we stood sweltering in a neighbor's garden, my sister-in-law whispered, "Did you ever imagine this?" I had not. Not in my wildest dreams did I ever expect to participate in the wedding of two octogenarians, let alone be related to them. Yet my father-in-law was getting married. I had the usual reservations—she is after his money; he wants a caregiver; and how on earth are we going to blend these two families? But the bride and groom glowed and when the toasts were over they drove off in a well-decorated car for their honeymoon in the Sierra Nevada. I returned home to work on this book.

## About the Book

This book invites you to explore the romantic possibilities of later life. It is designed for anyone who is seriously interested in love and its manifestations, including students, researchers, teachers, counselors, lovers, and would-be lovers. It incorporates the theory and research of a wide range of disciplines, among them: anthropology, neurology, physiology, psychology, history, and sociology. Each chapter closes with a set of exercises designed to stimulate and expand your romantic imagination. Some of these may strike you as irrelevant to your experience, but I hope some will click for you, generating new insights into the way romantic love helps shape the person you are becoming.

The book has four parts. Part I explores what researchers and philosophers have learned about love and aging. Part II explores the early possibilities for romance in later life, showing how we create and negotiate illusion in romantic beginnings. Part III turns to love's more stable realities, celebrating commitment and recognizing the important role of family, friends, and culture in determining the shape of romance. Part IV turns to the darker side of love, exploring betrayal and loss to understand how older adults can cope with and grow through these experiences.

As you read the stories in this book, please keep in mind that all names have been changed to protect the privacy of respondents.

## About the Author

Upon turning 50, I was comfortable in a solid marriage and enjoyed my role as support person to our two teenagers. Though a secret fan of romance novels, I never considered romance a topic for serious research. My research focused on "important" matters, like Social Security and poverty. But romantic issues began to challenge my friends and family in our advancing years. After she turned 50, a colleague's lifelong search for romance took on new intensity, leading her to Internet dating and a disastrous marriage to an alcoholic. A woman I grew up with was forced to choose between her new lover and a long-awaited adoption. A determined bachelor fell in love and married impetuously (and happily) in his 70s. Meanwhile, friends and neighbors were having affairs that broke up marriages and traumatized our children's friends. When an intense infatuation disrupted my own sleep, I realized that love in later life was nothing like what I had imagined. It was time to get a grasp on this thing called love. True to academic form, I set out on a research project that would last for several years, surprise my colleagues, and enrich my life immensely.

## An Invitation

Launching a book is like putting a note in a bottle and tossing it into the sea. I hope you will consider sending a reply. I would love to know what meaning you found in these pages, what worked for you and what did not, or where you have taken this material in your life. Please feel free to email me at ASBarusch@gmail.com with "feedback on love book" in the subject line; or write to me at College of Social Work, 395 South 1500 East, University of Utah, Salt Lake City, UT, 84112. I look forward to hearing from you.

## Acknowledgments

Graduate students in the University of Utah College of Social Work helped in many ways. Those most involved included Troy Anderson, Jana Ballou, Mindy Calderon, Angie Charter, Mandy Cope, Marianne Evans, Holly Hamilton, Joelle Hazzard, Krista Horman, Alan Lowe, Cathe Madison, Hannah Miller, Debbie Olson-Morrison, Charlotte Richards, Joyce Starks, Marcos Uboldi, and Xin Xin. Ann Cederloft transcribed scads of interviews.

Robert Barth, dear friend and teacher, read early drafts and helped interpret complicated interviews. He taught me about Jung, about life, and about love. So did Ginny Richardson of Ohio State University. Her support and enthusiasm never fail to energize and inspire. Karen Huck teaches about love at Southern Oregon Community College. She offered helpful suggestions on several chapters. Mac Runyan helped me find an intellectual home for the work. Gudrin Mirin helped me focus on flow.

Maura Roessner and Mallory Jensen have been with this book all the way, helping me grow as a writer and editing draft after draft. I appreciate their talent and their patience. I am grateful for the suggestions from four people who anonymously reviewed the manuscript. It was great when they raved and even better when they did not. Jean Blackburn of Bytheway Publishing Services shepherded the book's production with care and skill.

Most of all, I owe a huge debt to the hundreds of people who shared their stories with me. Their generosity was tremendous and I hope this work does them justice.

The family brightens my days and gives meaning to my work. Ariana transcribed and interpreted interviews during a school break. Nathaniel thought the project was cool and invited me to speak to his high school English class. Larry Barusch has been my husband since 1983 and the love of my life since 1979. We enjoy long walks, and our open-air discussions have long focused on the myriad dilemmas of love presented in this work. The "old people" did not laugh when I told them I was writing a book on love. Maurice Barusch lost his wife of 63 years in 2003. While I was working on the book he married Barbara Langlois, expanding my sense of late-life romantic possibilities and offering a vivid illustration of the challenges of blending families at this life stage. Aunt Jean and Uncle Jack Knox provided support and inspiration, as did my father, Gilbert Smith, and stepmother, Carolyn Stallard. These family elders offer brilliant models of love and engagement in later life.

# Contents

Love Stories of Later Life

# Introduction: Love Stories of Later Life

Oh, the places you'll go!
—WITH APOLOGIES TO DR. SEUSS

"Grow old along with me! The best is yet to be, / The last of life for which the first was made." Robert Browning wrote these familiar words in 1864,[1] when *old* meant something quite different from what it means today. In nineteenth-century England life expectancy was under 45 years, and some thought the natural life span of mankind was 58 years.[2] The idea that many people would live—and love—into their eighth and ninth decades was unfathomable.

Yet throughout the world, millions are reaching advanced ages. Japan enjoys the world's greatest longevity, with a life expectancy of over 80 years, but the United States is not far behind, and in 2000 over 25 million Americans were 70 years or older.[3] As these elders chart new territory for those who will follow, they are redefining many aspects of the human experience, including romantic love.

The ranks of older adults now include members of my generation, known as the baby boomers. Born between 1946 and 1964, our generation has changed major social institutions as we have passed through life's stages. When our swelling numbers hit the educational system teachers were hired, classrooms were built, and curricula were revamped. (Remember the new math?) As we entered young adulthood, sexual norms were redefined. Over the years we adapted to the workplace with a complacency some found surprising. But our sheer numbers meant that competition for jobs and promotions was stiff. We had to buckle down. Now, in our 50s and 60s, we are redefining the latter half of life and expanding the possibilities in many realms, including romance. Of course, it will take the media and professionals a while to catch up.

3

Popular romance novels and daytime soaps still perpetuate the myth that only the young and unwrinkled can enjoy romance. For many, late-life romance is either comic or disgusting. Even the professional literature on love has little to offer regarding life after 20. Most love research studies the experiences of college students—a convenient population for professors, but hardly one that can illuminate the lifelong implications of romantic attachments.

While love researchers neglect age, gerontologists neglect romance. In 1973, Robert Kastenbaum chided the American Psychological Association's Task Force on Aging for neglecting love: "[W]e do not have a comprehensive gerontology unless we know something about this realm. . . . Loving is not encompassed by the frequency of reported sexual interests and activities. . . . All the 'dirty old men' jokes in the world do not dilute the poignancy of love and sex in later life."[4] In the 30 years since, professional priorities in the field have remained skewed toward the "gero-erotic," with literally thousands of articles published on sex and barely a handful on romance.[5] Like these scholars, most Americans acknowledge that sex is a possibility for older adults, but few can imagine that life's second half might bring the intoxication of infatuation or the agony of unrequited love.

Some people feel that romance after 80 is simply impossible. My father-in-law felt that way when his wife of 63 years passed away in 2002. He was 83 years old, and his grief was intensified by the expectation that he would spend his remaining years alone—an expectation that would prove false. On August 7, 2005, in a garden in California, two three-generation families gathered to witness his marriage to the longtime friend who became his soul mate and companion. Variations of this scene play out daily across the United States, as older adults discover the possibilities of late-life romance.

## About the Research

Seeking to describe the lived experiences of love among older adults, my students and I immersed ourselves in the topic. Our research method is described in detail in Appendix B. In 5 years, we conducted over 110 in-depth interviews, 91 of them with older adults living in nine states (California, Colorado, Georgia, Idaho, Maine, New York, Ohio, Texas, and Utah). We invited people to share their romantic narratives through focus groups, essay contests, workshops, and discussions. We read everything we could get our hands on. We spoke with people from all walks of life, from the independently wealthy to welfare recipients. We met with people of diverse ages, ethnicities, sexual orientations, and marital histories.

I chose 50 as the beginning age for inclusion in this study for three reasons. First, for women, the 50s usually bring the onset of menopause, a physical transition that can have significant ramifications for romance and sex. Second, though we do not all expect to live to be 100, centenarians are among the fastest growing age groups in the United States. In a few generations, living to 100 may become the norm. At present, by the time we reach 50 we are decidedly in, if not well into, life's second half. My final reason was personal. Issues of romance assumed urgency for me when I turned 50, and this seemed to be the case for the people around me.

Because of the great diversity among people over 50, I set out to ensure that we talked to people in each of the last five decades of life. Initially it seemed inappropriate to combine people in their 80s with those in their 50s. What could people of such disparate ages have in common? I kept looking for a natural cliff when romantic experiences became consistently different. I did not find one. Age 80 is different from age 50: Our bodies are more vulnerable; our futures are shorter and our pasts longer. But the possibilities for love and intimacy do not suddenly disappear. Personal characteristics and expectations are more important than age in determining our romantic futures. So, with a nod to their differences, this work integrates the perspectives of baby boomers and their parents.

The resulting interview sample included 91 people ranging in age from 51 to 97 years, with a mean age of 72. The group was pretty evenly divided across the sixth through ninth decades of life, with six participants who were over 90 years old (Table I.1).

Most of the people interviewed (63%) were women, and most (85%) identified as Caucasian. More were widowed (35%) than married (28%), and only seven reported that they had been single their whole lives. Most (87%) considered themselves heterosexual. Among the 12 people who identified as bisexual or homosexual, 7 were men; all were Caucasian; 2 were divorced, 5 were living with their partners, and 5 were single. Although this sample is

Table I.1.   Age Distribution of Interview Respondents by Decade

| Decade | Number | Percentage |
|---|---|---|
| Sixth (ages 51–60) | 18 | 20 |
| Seventh (ages 61–70) | 24 | 26 |
| Eighth (ages 71–80) | 24 | 26 |
| Ninth (ages 81–90) | 19 | 21 |
| Tenth (over 90) | 6 | 7 |

deliberately diverse, it cannot be considered representative of the general population.

When we were nearly through with our interviews, my students and I decided to attempt to reach a broader population by using the Internet. We posted a survey on a Website and recruited respondents by sending invitation e-mails to members of a range of professional organizations and inviting them to pass the e-mail along to people they thought might be interested. The Internet survey was anonymous, and it took 15–20 minutes to complete. We were astonished by the response. Over 1,000 people ranging from 19 to 86 years old participated in the survey, among them 343 who were over 50 years old. Respondents came from all 50 states, and many wrote eloquently about their romantic experiences. In fact, a few people under age 50 wrote so eloquently that I could not resist including their perspectives in this book.

The findings of this study highlight the variety and possibilities for romance after age 50, even as they underscore some unique issues and challenges faced by late-life lovers. The things we discovered surprised, delighted, alarmed, and sometimes disappointed us. We saw ourselves in some of the respondents. One day I glanced at an Internet survey and was surprised to see a woman in her late 50s from Kentucky whose long-term romance was challenged by the same problem I have, "differences in sleep patterns." My husband is an early-to-bed kind of guy, while I hate to miss those late-night hours.

We also learned some important lessons about love. We learned that love is not a single, static entity, but a complex, dynamic process incorporating biochemical events, emotions, decisions, and values. We learned that illusion plays an important role in romance and that the art of seduction is designed to sustain romantic illusions. We learned that people who report dissatisfying or disastrous love lives tend to see their parents as poor examples of how to love. We learned that romantic experiences of late life are influenced by a lifelong accumulation of lessons and expectations regarding love. Finally, we learned that romantic experiences shape our characters and our lives.

## Our Epistemology

This work is grounded in the phenomenological research tradition that seeks to describe, interpret, and understand complex human experiences. Our goal was to achieve critical subjectivity, described by Yvonna Lincoln, an expert on qualitative methods, as "an altered state of consciousness or 'high-quality awareness' for the purpose of understanding with great discrimination subtle differences in the personal and psychological states of others."[6]

This understanding is constructed through a complex reciprocal inter-action involving respondents, researchers, and ultimately the readers of this work. It includes three components: the lived experience of respondents, the survey as an expression of that experience, and our interpretation of the experience. In his insightful discussion of interpretive methods, Mark Tappan explained: "interpretation must take as its starting point the his-torical and psychological reality of the lived experience of both the subject whose expression of experience is being interpreted and the interpreter herself."[7] We therefore construct meaning in a dynamic process that inte-grates the perspectives of all participants.

Like all of us, I am influenced by my daily experiences. In this book, I have disclosed some that seem relevant to my interpretation of the data and the literature. This should help the reader understand where I am coming from and to evaluate the "truthfulness" of the material presented. Coming to the material with a unique life history, each person who reads this book will take away a different message. Nonetheless, a central insight has emerged from the array of romantic experiences reviewed here: love changes people.

## Love as a Force for Change

Romantic experiences define character in ways so subtle that they might go undetected and so varied that they defy generalization. Love opens the door to our potential and helps shape the people we become. The work reported here describes four ways that love shapes our lives and ourselves.

First, the intense unsettling experiences that come with romantic love create opportunities for personal insight. Coupled with self-reflection, in-tense romantic experiences can teach us about ourselves, our needs, our vulnerabilities, and our demons. As we will see in this book, these lessons can change a person's approach to life and to love.

Second, love is a training ground for relationship skills. We inevitably learn from interactions with our partners. Usually, these lessons are adap-tive, teaching the value of compromise and the importance of reciprocity. We also learn how to communicate our love. Particularly in late life, we confront the boundaries of our personal control as we learn about letting go. But damaging lessons arise when romantic interactions are marked by abuse, neglect, or manipulation, which can teach us to devalue our selves and retreat from engagement with others.

Third, love stretches us beyond our comfort zones, revealing capabilities we did not know we had. We see this in the uncharacteristic acts committed when we are deeply infatuated. Desperately in love, we discover personal capacities we never knew were there. Love can also stretch us by exposing us to different ways of being, as when we meet a person unlike anyone else we have ever loved and, in loving them, are transformed.

Finally, love changes the very course of our lives. Our choice of romantic partners can determine what jobs we pursue, where we will live, whether or not we have children. In midlife, people who have not experienced love as they have long imagined it may set out on a quest—some might call it a midlife crisis—to satisfy this burning need.

As a gerontologist, I have long felt the most interesting part of human development takes place in late life. Some changes are so gentle and slow that we do not notice them for decades. And most young people have too much on their plates to spend time in contemplation. Besides that, their reminiscences are awfully short. Late life provides the opportunity and the perspective to observe changes that romantic love has made in our lives and our persons. Then one day we turn around and realize that even in life's final decades some of us are still growing.

## Romantic Possibilities

Much of our interest in other people's lives stems from the hope of learning something that will expand our own possibilities. Psychologists Hazel Markus and Paula Nurius introduced the idea of possible selves, defined as the people we believe we could become.[8] One way that we learn about our possible selves is by observing the people around us, particularly those who are like us in some way. As Markus and Nurius observed, "What others are now, I could become."[9] Thus we observe others closely to vicariously monitor our own possibilities.

Based on the loving experiences of hundreds of older adults, this book offers an opportunity to expand your sense of late life's romantic possibilities. It affords a glimpse into love's adventurous and commonplace possibilities. Here are a few:

- Infatuation: It happens. Not just to the young, but to 50-, 60-, 70-, even 80-year-olds. It is just one of the possibilities of late-life romance. You may find yourself, like 88-year-old Ted, reflecting on a lifetime of inappropriate infatuations; or, like Barbara, you may be dancing in the street trilling "I'm in love!" at the age of 79.

- Pursuit: Looking for love can force you to look at yourself in new and sometimes uncomfortable ways. Like 62-year-old Candy, late life may be a time for you to seek the relationship in which you will finally get it right. Or, like 68-year-old Alice, you might find yourself cruising the Internet for a companion. Love might sneak up when you are not looking, like it did for Sandrine in her late 50s.
- Ecstasy: Long-term romance can be ecstatic. Like 87-year-old Marty, you may be able to say, "My whole life is a love story!"
- Complications: Late-life romances involve more than two people. You might find, like Barbara did at 83, that even after the romance is over you remain close to his children. On the other hand, when you fall in love in your 80s you might discover, as Ginnie and Saul did, that his children are a serious impediment.
- Loss: Grief happens, and life goes on (usually). You may lose the love of your life, like Susan did, and find that you are not looking for or even interested in love. This does not mean you will not find it, but it does mean the late-life experiences of divorced, single, and widowed adults can be rich and fulfilling even without romantic partners.

Awareness of these possibilities might change the way you think about love and about your own aging. Far from being a romantic wasteland, late life provides unique opportunities to experience love fully and intensely. Of course, these are just possibilities, not guarantees. Without paying attention, we may walk right past them on our way to something else.

More than anything, this book is an invitation to explore the romantic possibilities of later life so you will know them when you see them. It might also help you interpret your own romantic history and decipher the role love has played in making you the person you are today.

❖

**Try This**

The Road Not Taken: By the time we are 50, most of us have at least one romantic road not taken. It might be a relationship nipped in the bud, an infatuation stifled, or a rejection from a long-time lover. Starting with the premise that romantic experiences shape you—your habits, your personality, even your physical self—imagine for a moment what you would be like had one of those romantic roads actually been taken. Would you be sweeter? Happier? Bitter? Would you eat differently? Would you live someplace else? What might your children be like? In this exercise, you can use your imagination to enrich your life experience.

Married in San Francisco after 7 years together.

# Part I

# Love and Aging

Part I of this book reviews theory and research on love and aging. Here we will see how our conception of love has changed over the centuries and how our selves continue to evolve as we age.

Love is, in part, an idea, shaped by the culture and time in which it is expressed. Throughout history the idea of romantic love has changed radically, from a platonic ideal enjoyed by royalty to a biochemical phenomenon used to sell cars—with variations in between. Knowledge of love's history enables us to better understand various cohorts of older adults. Those in their 80s and 90s were raised with different romantic beliefs and aspirations from people who came of age in the 1960s. On a personal level, this knowledge liberates us from the tyranny of the present—from the notion that love has ever been and can only be as it is in America today. Love changes—over the course of history and of individual lives it evolves in surprising ways.

People change as well. For decades, aging was seen as an inevitable process of deterioration. Only lately have researchers discovered that maturation brings opportunities for personal development and growth. Love itself represents one of these opportunities. Indeed, when the dynamic force of love combines with the developmental potentials of age, the result can be a thing of surpassing beauty.

They met this week.
*Photo by Marianne Gontarz York*

# 1

## Understanding Love: Theory and Research

He who has been instructed thus far in the things of love...
will suddenly perceive a nature of wondrous beauty...beauty
absolute, separate, simple, and everlasting.
—PLATO, *Symposium*

*Valentine's Day celebrates the possibilities of romance. We see them
on display in a popular restaurant, where the action on this special day
revolves around couples. Intimate conversations merge into a gentle hum,
punctuated by the clink of silverware. Some are talking about love. But most
are just living it. Twenty-somethings sneak glances at the 80-year-olds,
wondering if they will make it that far and what "it" will be like. Old people
glance back, wondering how the time passed so quickly. Middle-aged
couples huddle close, grappling with problems from household finances
to their children's future. Two women hold hands openly, agreeing that
today's a day to order whatever they want. A gay man wonders why they
got the corner table, and his partner teases him back to good humor. Love is
in the air, but each one understands and experiences it differently.*

Those experiencing love for the first time feel as if they are inventing the
whole enterprise. Indeed, some of us spend lifetimes puzzling over the
intricacies of romance. We are not alone. Philosophers, theorists, and scientists alike have devoted their energies to questions of romantic love. This
chapter draws from their insights to illuminate the complexities of romantic
attachment. In this guided tour of love throughout history, we will see how it
has been defined and shaped by culture, science, and literature. We will also

hear stories and insights from hundreds of Americans who contributed to this book.

## What Is Love?

In magnitude and complexity, love is a little like the elephant and we are a little like the blind men, describing the parts we are able to perceive. Of course, love may be many things, and there may be many types of love. Definitions range from the grounded approach offered by a native Tahitian: "Love is, I want her. I desire her. I am happy with her and when I am not with her I miss her"[1] to the more esoteric version provided by Robert Solomon: "Love is a dialectical process of mutually reconceived selfhood."[2]

This book focuses on love in the second half of life—after age 50. Romantic love is captivating at any age. But in late life it can assume intensity and complexity seldom found in the young. From the charming 93-year-old philanderer puzzling over his wife's unwillingness to forgive to the devoted 77-year-old widow who never stopped grieving for a husband who died 35 years ago to the 76-year-old woman dancing in delight over her new love affair, older adults reveal puzzles and insights that fascinate and inform. And, as we will see in the coming chapters, their experiences can shatter our ageist stereotypes.

## A Brief History of Love

Each of us is a product, not only of our personal history but of the history of the human race. Evolutionary biologists would have us believe that the emotions and experiences we now call romance have their roots in the origin of our species. We all descend from winners in the great evolutionary battle; and so we are all hardwired to love. The experiences associated with romance may be mediated by human biochemistry and physiology. But what we make of those experiences—how we interpret and shape them— is determined by the culture and the era in which we live. Our romantic imagination is shaped by the ideals and myths of our culture, and some of the tensions that arise in contemporary romance were very much a part of historical efforts to capture the notion of love. These include the tension between spiritual love and physical desire, the struggle between sacrifice and self-interest, and the struggle to distinguish "good" love from "bad" or destructive love.

## Ancient Love

A reading of ancient Greek texts illuminates the role of culture in romantic love.[3] Ancient Greek culture recognized and accepted erotic love among men, particularly the attraction of a wise old sage for a younger pupil or protégé. (Yes, Greeks acknowledged passion among the old, although for them, *old* meant something different.) In *The History of Sexuality*, Foucault suggested that the ancient Greeks did not share our modern preoccupation with sexual identity and personal deviance.[4] So a man's love for a young boy did not fundamentally change the way he saw himself and certainly was not considered a form of deviance.

Instead, the Greeks grappled with what Juha Sihvola aptly termed the erotic dilemma, wondering how a powerful force like erotic desire can produce such disparate passions.[5] How, for example, can a lover in passion's thrall go in a relatively short time from seeking only to please his beloved to seeking to possess her regardless of her interests or desires? Perhaps, some concluded, this meant that there were two types of erotic desire. Ancient philosophers sought to distinguish "legitimate *eros*" from its destructive counterpart.

We see the beneficent side of erotic love in Plato's observation in the *Symposium* that an army made up of pairs of lovers would fight more bravely than any other. These warriors would strive to appear worthy in each other's eyes, so even the most average among them would achieve heroic feats. Perhaps the most vivid example of the Greek conception of the destructive power of *eros* lies in the tale of Semele, a mortal who caught Zeus's eye. The two enjoyed a passionate affair until Semele insisted on seeing the face of her lover. When she did, she was incinerated.[6]

Ancient myth and fiction offered intimations of the chivalry and passion that would later be associated with courtly love.[7] Wars and great deeds were the result of grand passions. The love between Paris and Helen sparked the Trojan War. Orpheus descended into the underworld to rescue his beloved Eurydice. In her grief over the death of Adonis, Aphrodite turned drops of his blood into a perennial flower, the anemone. Finally, of course, Psyche's trials as she sought to be reunited with her beloved Eros are legendary. As 76-year-old Harold said to me, "Love is an adventure!"

## Greek and Roman Definitions of Love

Ancient Greeks drew a clear distinction between love based on *eros* or *philia*, and that motivated by *agape*.[8] Long ago, the term *eros* had broader meaning than it has today. Where we understand it to mean sexual longing, the Greeks used it to refer to love based on need or desire. Love based on *eros* could stem from the desire for money, for art, or for transcendence. It had its roots in the lover's yearnings. The term *philia* was reserved for love between friends or brothers—affectionate, but usually not needy or sexual.[9]

By contrast, love motivated by *agape* (sometimes spelled *agapei*) is marked by self-sacrifice or the lover's desire to give or lose the self in the life of the beloved. This more charitable impulse may (or may not) be part of erotic love. It may be the reason so many people feel that sex is better when it is motivated by love. When *agape* is present the lover is doubly fulfilled— once by his own pleasure and again by the pleasure of his partner. Of course, *agape* can be present without erotic love in a parent's love for a child. In Christian theology, God's love for humankind is often characterized as *agape*.[10]

In the *Symposium*, Plato reported that Socrates emphasized the role of *eros* in love. Love is seen as the desire for something we do not possess, like beauty or goodness. In this respect, as A. W. Price so clearly pointed out, "Lacking is part of loving."[11] In this view, love is an endless succession of new desires and fresh accomplishments or possessions, with desire always managing to outstrip achievement. For Plato and other Greek philosophers, desire and generativity (both physical and intellectual) are manifestations of love.

We see the workings of *agape* whenever sacrifice is used as proof of love. For example, 54-year-old Abby explained that you know you love someone when "You would die for them." Plato would agree with Abby. He wrote of Pelias, who freely gave her life for her husband. The gods looked favorably on her action and allowed her to return alive to earth. Plato said, "Such exceeding honour is paid by the gods to the devotion and virtue of love."[12] Christian teachings emphasize the role of sacrifice in love. For many, Jesus is the personification of *agape*—love for the sake of the beloved. As Harold (whom we met before) explained, "God is love. The greatest love that was ever given was when God sent his love as a sacrifice. The atonement of Christ is the greatest thing that happened or ever will happen."

Caring and service remain central to most people's understanding of love. Time and again, interviewees referred to the agapic notion of love. It was the most common feeling mentioned by the 110 people interviewed for this book. The response from 63-year-old Dean was typical. When asked, "How would you describe love?" he replied, "When you do love someone there isn't enough you can do for them. When they hurt, you hurt, be there for them, comfort them."

Some despair that the spirit of generosity that stems from *agape* is no longer present in American culture. Mattie, a 68-year-old Latina, worried that today, "There is no love ... because love means to give everything to each other, don't be selfish."

Plato argued that we love an individual, not as a whole person, but as the symbol for a value such as goodness or beauty.[13] Several of the people interviewed for this book emphasized their admiration for specific traits or values in the beloved. In one charming example, 60-year-old Benjamin explained how love began for him:

> When you introduce yourself to that person, and you start talking, then you start to get feelings about that person that start to come across, you know. Ah ... aspects about them, and qualities, and attributes that ... ah ... that are interesting ... that's kind of fascinating to you, because you're not the same, you know, and you see qualities in that person that you really admire. You don't have 'em, necessarily, and so I think *that* kind of attracts you, too. You know, for instance, my wife noticing like a little ... cute little bird, or a little dog, or some kind of little animal ... she loves animals, you know ... deer, and so forth, and I think, "Gosh, why can't I be that way, you know?" I mean, I can walk down the street and I don't see the flowers. I don't see the birds. I don't ... you know, I'm just focused on going to someplace, and she'll say, "Well, didn't you see that back there?" And I say, "No. I didn't." "Well, where are you at?"

By contrast, the Aristotelian vision of love requires knowledge of the other and commitment to his or her uniqueness. The beloved does not represent an archetype or symbolize an ideal. Some of our interviewees emphasized knowledge or understanding of the person as an important component of love. For instance, 52-year-old Anna saw understanding as vital: "When you truly understand somebody, you cannot help but love [her]."

For many, love is divine. In the *Symposium*, Socrates quotes Diotima, his "instructress in the art of love."[14] She explains that love is a great spirit that serves as an "intermediate between the divine and the mortal."[15] For Diotima (and hence for Socrates), love is the vehicle by which the gods communicate with humans; and it is through love that humans approach the divine.

The rise of the Roman Empire expanded the reach of these ancient Greek concepts while leaving them virtually unchanged. Romans shared the Greek acceptance of same-sex love among men, and many Greek love myths were subsequently peopled with Roman gods. Ovid's erotic poetry offers a glimpse into the romantic aspirations (if not the experiences) of ancient Romans.

Ovid lived in Rome from about 43 B.C. to A.D. 17. His works include *The Loves (Amores)*, *The Art of Love (Ars Amatoria)*, and *The Cure for Love (Remedia Amoris)*. *Ars Amatoria* is especially informative. As a "tutor of love," Ovid advises where and how to choose a woman to love, how to bend her to your will, and how to ensure that love survives. Ovid's advice is timeless and specific: "Don't choose a woman by candlelight.... it's by daylight you should judge a woman's face and figure.... Above all don't go near her on her birthday or indeed on any day when you're expected to give a present." Ovid advises the would-be lover to begin his advances with a letter full of compliments and promises. He cautioned, "Don't, on any account, let her go to the theater looking her loveliest, without your being there to see."[16] His final advice was, "See to it that thy mistress grows accustomed to thee: nothing is so potent as habit. To win her heart, let no trouble be too great."[17]

A modern reading of Ovid suggests that the art of erotic love has changed little since Roman times. Unfortunately, Ovid's timing was off. Faced with a falling birthrate and obsessed with what he saw as moral decay, Emperor Augustus passed laws to protect marriage and prohibit adultery just before the publication of *Ars Amatoria*. Concluding that the popular work threatened his moral crusade, Augustus banished the poet and condemned his writings. Ovid died in exile.

Hundreds of years after the reign of Augustus, Constantine became the first Christian emperor. Christianity brought a focus on agapic love and disdain for eroticism. Nothing comparable to the eroticism of the Old Testament is found in the New Testament. The Song of Solomon vividly described the passion of two unknown lovers: "Let him kiss me with the kisses of his Mouth! For your love is better than wine" (1:2). "Sustain me with raisins, refresh me with apples, for I am faint with love" (2:5). Under Christian philosophy, religious adoration and marital love went hand-in-hand. We see this in Ephesians 5:25, where Paul exhorts, "Husbands, love your wives, even as Christ loved the church and gave Himself for it."

The end of the Roman Empire dated roughly from A.D. 476, with the arrival of Germanic invaders and the onset of the Middle Ages. Henceforth, Western European leaders would be Christian, and the church would dominate the popular imagination. But the medieval period hosted a romantic movement that would prove antithetical to the norms of the established church.

## Courtly Love

In the twelfth century a new approach to love appeared in the region of southern France known as Occitania. Courtly love or *courtezia* was celebrated by traveling minstrels known as the troubadours.[18] Their poetry and myths would spread throughout Western Europe.[19]

The troubadours described courtly love as a spiritual bliss not to be confused with sexual attraction, and certainly not to be sullied by the conventions of marriage. The classic prototype is Lancelot and Guinevere (seared into our minds by the popular musical *Camelot*). Lancelot conceived a passionate attraction to Guinevere who, to him, represented the perfect female. His spiritual commitment to her went beyond mere love or affection to a form of worship. Lancelot treated her comb as a holy relic because it contained a few strands of her golden hair.

Self-sacrifice for the beloved is central to courtly love, as it was to the Greeks' *agape*. Lancelot allowed his lady total control over his life. This was most evident when, at a public contest, Guinevere ordered the knight to fight poorly. This he did, to the point of humiliation, until his lady relented and commanded him to win the match.

The outcome of this legendary romance varies. In some accounts their passion set the stage for the collapse of Arthur's kingdom, whereas in Chretien de Troyes's version the future is left up to the reader.[20] That said, by no account did Lancelot and Guinevere ever marry. This separation between passion and marriage is a defining characteristic of courtly love.

The rise of courtly love has been linked to that of Christianity, with courtly love serving as a vital counterbalance to the religious tendency to demean sexual love in favor of spiritual attachment. Carl Jung identified the upsurge in Chrisianity with the defeat of the more organic "feminine" approach to spirituality, and argued that this created a pent-up desire for ecstatic experiences—a desire that would be satisfied among the upper classes through the exuberant practice of courtly love.

In the thirteenth century, organized Christianity set out to stifle the expression and impulses of courtly love. Pope Innocent III initiated a crusade against Occitania, effectively burying the poetry and romances of the troubadours.[21] Perhaps as a result, the Age of Reason would look with disdain upon the passions and excesses of courtly love. But the notion of romance was never completely suppressed. It had already spread throughout Western Europe and continues to inspire modern imaginations throughout the world.

## *Victorian Love*

Queen Victoria ascended to the British throne in 1837, following two remarkably different epochs. Two hundred years earlier, the crown was briefly overthrown and a Puritan republic established under the leadership of Oliver Cromwell. The republic was marked by severe repression of sensual appetites. Even Christmas was abolished as an unacceptable indulgence. Restoration of the crown (under the leadership of Charles II) would bring a backlash in the form of rampant debauchery, particularly among the aristocratic classes.[22]

These themes—repression of sensuality and libertinism—carried through the Victorian era. On the surface, Victorian morality strictly prohibited sexual expression. Indeed, a "language of flowers" was invented to permit expression of emotions that could not be discussed. Though much of this language has been lost, we see remnants in the use of roses to express emotions ranging from lust (red) to chaste admiration (white) or friendship (yellow). Upper-class Victorian women were supposed to be sheltered from the harsh realities of life and immune to passions of the flesh.

At the same time, Victorian literature and whispered conversations revealed fascination with and sympathy for the "fallen woman." Remember Little Emily in *David Copperfield*? Seduced by the incorrigible Steerforth, she descended into prostitution. Dickens's sympathy for the fallen woman is evident in Little Emily's rescue from a London brothel when she was allowed to emigrate to Australia. Dickens was less generous with Nancy, the mistress of Bill Sikes in *Oliver Twist*. Despite assisting Oliver, Nancy was destined for a brutal murder at the hands of Bill. Here we see the roots of a duality that would survive into the twentieth century: the Madonna and the whore. A woman could be chaste and respected (naive and passive) or she could be passionate and reviled (exciting and powerful). For decades this dichotomy persisted, exercising a powerful influence on the romantic aspirations of women.

One such woman was 97-year-old Emma. Born just 5 years after the end of Victoria's reign and a continent away, Emma offered the practical observation that if you have sex with someone who loves you, he is more likely to make you "an honest woman" by marrying you. "Well, if you don't love a man you better not have sex with him," she advised. "That's all I can say. Because if you don't know that you love them well enough before you marry them, you better not marry them." We interviewed seven people in their 90s, five women and two men, and while they varied in their understanding of the importance of sex in the context of marriage, they shared the Victorians' deep disapproval of sex outside of marriage.

The Victorian era also saw the emergence of psychoanalysis, which would shape the world's understanding of love for decades to come. Sigmund Freud and his successors—most notably Carl Jung and John Bowlby—each developed a unique approach to questions of love.

## *Freud's Definition: Love and Repression*

For Freud, the ability to love was a hallmark of adult mental health. *"Leben, lieben, arbeiten"* (to live, to love, to work) was his response when asked to describe the life of a healthy adult.[23] Love was central to his understanding of the human psyche. As Robert Fine explained, "Freud's total work should be looked upon as the greatest tract on love ever written."[24]

Freud's description of the role of the libido and the importance of sexuality in human development shocked many in Victorian Austria, and he was encouraged to use more subtle language. Freud's response was courageous: "I cannot see any merit in being ashamed of sex."[25] And so he argued that the sexual instinct or libido served as motivation for a wide range of human behaviors.[26] Observing the tension between sexual or libidinal energy and the ego's need for self-regulation—and no doubt reflecting on the criticism aroused by his theory—Freud argued that culture sided with the ego, demanding repression of primitive sexual urges.

This tension between the desires of the libido and the forces of repression has become a hallmark of Freudian theory. (It was a hallmark of the Victorian era, as well.) Ultimately for Freud, love was the healthy integration of passion and control; and human development was driven by the tension between these two forces. Freud shocked many with his description of infants and young children as sexual creatures. For him, human development proceeded through the successive erotic stages of anal, oral, homosexual, and genital sexuality. Ultimately, adult love objects and romantic experiences were largely determined by the traumas and satisfactions of childhood.

We saw this viewpoint reflected in the interviews conducted for this book. Several of the older adults we talked to attributed their ability to love in adulthood to childhood experiences of being loved. William was born in 1939, the year Freud passed away. Like Freud, he felt that childhood experiences determined the capacity to love:

> My parents were very loving. I always was made to feel like I was secure and loved and could do anything. I think they were unrealistic at times

about what they expected of me, but I never for a moment doubted that they loved me. And I think that's where you start learning about love is from your parents. And I think if you're lucky enough to have parents who are loving, that stays with you, and makes you the kind of individual who can have mature relationships when you grow up. I think if you have unloving parents, or no parents, or whatever, it damages you, probably, for life. Maybe not irrevocably, but it makes it harder for you to establish meaningful relationships with depth.

Freud identified three types of love: anaclitic love, narcissistic love, and oedipal love. Some psychoanalysts argue that men are most likely to experience anaclitic love—affection for the person who provides care and support. Women, on the other hand, may be more likely to experience narcissistic love, in which the beloved is idealized, representing what the lover wishes to be. Oedipal love stems from the childhood love triangle, in which the same-sex parent became a competitor for the affection of the opposite-sex parent. The resulting emotional response is a complicated love that integrates a bit of hatred and can serve as a model for future love relationships.

### Jung's Definition: Love as Projection

Jung worked closely with Freud until 1913, when his understanding of the psyche began to depart from the master's views.[27] Rejecting the "pansexual" aspects of Freudian theory, Jung felt the urge toward meaning and wholeness was innate and powerful, and argued that this served as the impetus for romantic love. Like Freud, he was a critic of Western culture. But his criticism focused on organized religion. He argued that the rise of Christianity reduced opportunities to experience spiritual ecstasy and attributed the intensity of modern infatuation to a pent-up need for spiritual expression.[28]

Jung shared Freud's appreciation for the role of transference in romantic love. But where Freud saw the beloved as a projection of a parental figure, Jung saw it as an idealized version of the lover's self. As Jungian therapist Robert Johnson explained, "Romantic love always consists in the projection of the soul-image. When a woman falls in love it is *animus* that she sees projected onto the mortal man before her. When a man drinks of the love potion, it is *anima*, his [feminine] soul, that he sees superimposed on a woman."[29] Unlike Freud, Jung devoted considerable thought to the transition from infatuation to "mature" or "true" love.

Jungian psychologists suggest that the Western version of romantic love treats a person as a symbol. We have incorporated the worshipful aspect of courtly love to the extent that the beloved disappears as a human being.

Instead, he or she represents something perfect and nearly divine—a mystical vision. As romantic worshippers, we experience love with almost spiritual intensity. Infatuation's emotional roller coaster gives life an intensity that in previous eras came only from religious experiences. Often we have no knowledge of the person. It is as if we have drunk a magic potion and become possessed.[30]

## *Bowlby's Definition: Love as Attachment*

Although not a student of Freud's, John Bowlby attempted to ground his work in psychoanalytic theory. He departed from major tenets of the theory to articulate his popular theory of attachment and separation, also known as object relations theory. Like Freud, Bowlby emphasized early childhood experiences as determinants of later relationships.[31] But where Freud used retrospection to infer the impact of parent-child interactions, Bowlby's "prospective" approach was based on detailed observation of infants interacting with their mothers. Bowlby then speculated about the future implications of these interactions.

Based on his observations of infant behavior, Bowlby argued that children learn to love through processes of attachment and separation from caregivers.[32] A secure and well-loved infant will emerge from his mother's reassuring hug to tentative exploration of his environment. When the exploration generates anxiety, the infant returns to mother for comfort and security. This serves as the basis of childhood development, with the child's explorations taking him further and further but always premised on his understanding that mother will be there to comfort and care for him. Bowlby suggested that this process was instinctive.

Mary Ainsworth expanded on Bowlby's theory, introducing the now widely accepted idea that people develop attachment styles based on their early childhood experiences.[33] Based on observational research, Ainsworth and her colleagues identified three attachment styles: secure, insecure-avoidant, and insecure-ambivalent. The foundation of a secure attachment style is what we might think of as a healthy relationship with the caregiver, such as the one William described. An insecure-avoidant attachment style is associated with rejection by the caregiver. In this case, a child seeking physical contact or emotional comfort would be actively rebuffed by the caregiver. In adulthood this style might manifest as a tendency toward detached and aloof relationships. The insecure-ambivalent style results from inconsistent parenting. If the caregiver's concern and empathy for the child are unpredictable, but not overtly rejecting, the child is expected to develop

an ambivalent approach to relationships. These children tend to be preoc-
cupied with monitoring caregiver emotions and trying to predict caregiver
reactions. In adulthood the style might be characterized by intense, unstable
relationships. Ainsworth and others try to avoid evaluating these attachment
styles. Still, there is a tendency for all of us to see secure attachment as
healthier than the other two styles.

Bowlby felt the capacity for attachment (or love) was inherent in human
nature. Unlike his psychoanalytic predecessors, Bowlby was interested in
the evolutionary value of interpersonal attachment. He saw the adaptive
value of attachment in its capacity to ensure an infant's survival and argued
that the infant's response to separation was similarly adaptive.[34] Expanding
on this theory, some have argued that adult attachment styles also serve to
promote reproduction.

Clearly, a secure attachment style can promote the birth and survival of
children; but recent thinking has focused on the insecure attachment
styles.[35] Combating the tendency to view these as pathological, scholars in
this area have begun to explore the possible evolutionary value of insecure
attachment. Noting that these attachment styles are more common among
groups (such as the poor) who experience financial stress and personal
instability, some have argued that people have a psychological switching
mechanism that allows us to form secure attachments when the environment
is stable and insecure attachments when it is not. According to this view,
secure and stable relationships demand supportive, stable environments.
When the environment is stressful or unstable, short-term intense romantic
relationships better serve the purpose of human reproduction. In essence, a
stable environment allows the potential breeder to put all his or her eggs in
one basket, investing deeply in relationships and offspring. But in times of
danger or instability, humans might hedge their bets by mating frequently
with different people. A leading proponent of this view, James Chisholm,
argued that "the capacity for romantic passion is a human universal, but that
its manifestation may depend, in part, on socio-ecological or political economic contingencies affecting men's and women's opportunities for 'secure'
attachment relations."[36] Chisholm's thesis suggests that America's relatively
high rates of divorce and infidelity may be due, not to moral or individual
failings, but to the rapid pace of change and lack of social stability.

## Love as Commodity

The twentieth century has seen what we might call the commodification of
America. Everything is for sale for the right price, and the rules of supply

and demand govern even the most intimate human relationships. Our enthusiasm for the free market has extended to romantic love through a theory known as the marriage market theory.[37] This theory applies market principles to understand how people enter into and remain in relationships.

In this view, an individual who is interested in a relationship enters into a "marketplace" possessed of certain positive attributes (physical attractiveness, intelligence, and wealth feature prominently) as well as specific desires. The laws of supply and demand, coupled with the strength of an individual's assets, determine how well a person will fare in this market. When the supply of possible partners is low, a buyer may have to compromise and settle on someone less desirable than he had in mind. If the supply is high, he might hold out for something better.

I saw an example of this perspective when I asked 51-year-old Bruce whether he had ever fallen out of love. He explained that he had, and that it hurt the woman badly. But he was looking for "something better." He said, "I really liked her, enjoyed being with her, had a lot of good times. But to think that I might be in this forever . . . And I don't know. It's unexplained. I don't know why. It ought to be better than this . . . it should be better than this—waiting for something better. That's not quite right. It wasn't quite good enough." He didn't say that she was not quite good enough. But I had the sense that given his attractive attributes Bruce felt that he could do better in the love market.

Those interested in watching the relationship market in action might find the personal ads in major newspapers, or the profiles in dating Websites like Match.com of particular interest. As we will see in Chapter 4, these settings provide a relationship marketplace in which those seeking love can present themselves and shop for partners in an efficient, if somewhat flat, setting.[38]

## Modern Love: The Sexual Revolution

Literary, scientific, and economic developments in the middle of the twentieth century set the stage for what Wilhelm Reich famously termed the sexual revolution. The revolution was about freedom—a value near and dear to the American psyche. As Hugh Hefner put it, "In this century, America liberated sex. The world will never be the same."[39]

Academic and popular literature challenged the repression of passionate and sexual impulses. Alfred Kinsey and his collaborators published their first work on human sexuality in 1948 and were credited with bringing sex into the public discourse. His work debunked popular myths about sexuality and triggered great controversy. Masters and Johnson followed in the Kinsey tradition, publishing *Human Sexual Response* in 1966. Prohibitions on extramarital sexual activity were questioned in several popular works, including Helen Gurley Brown's *Sex and the Single Girl* and Betty Friedan's *The Feminine Mystique*. These were followed by practical manuals such as David Reuben's 1969 work, *Everything You Always Wanted to Know About Sex (but Were Afraid to Ask)* and Alex Comfort's 1972 classic *The Joy of Sex: A Gourmet Guide to Lovemaking*.

The development of antibiotics and contraceptives reduced some of the risks associated with sex. The discovery and mass production of antibiotics allowed for effective treatment of sexually transmitted diseases like syphilis and gonorrhea. In 1960, the U.S. Food and Drug Administration approved oral contraceptives. Other contraceptive devices such as condoms and intrauterine devices were improved and mass produced. Modern surgical techniques and the 1972 Supreme Court decision in *Roe v. Wade* reduced the hazards associated with abortion.

Meanwhile, women who had entered the labor force during World War II learned they could succeed outside the cloistered domestic settings to which they had been restricted. Wives and mothers returned to the labor force in record numbers, achieving a measure of personal and financial independence.

These trends converged to radically change sexual attitudes and practices throughout much of the world. To the dismay of most of the 80- and 90-year-olds we interviewed, the double standard that had held that "nice girls don't" while "a guy's gotta try" was replaced by a popular philosophy that celebrated "free love" and the beauty of sex.

Some, like Rollo May, were concerned that the lack of sexual prohibitions would delete romance from the lexicon of love, and that passion would be traded for sterile, unemotional sexual experience.[40] Other scholars like Albert Ellis and Ira Reiss actively debated the relative merits of recreational ("body-centered") sex and affectional ("person-centered") sex.[41] In the midst of their debate, Ellis proposed the following "Confucian-like" precept: "Sexual congress is good in, of, by, and for itself and should under no circumstances be disparaged; however, most human beings who have sufficient sex experience and who gain a good degree of intellectual-emotional maturity find that affectional sex relations are more rewarding than non-affectional relations and devote more of their time to the latter than to the former."[42]

The sexual revolution was not just about sex. In conjunction with the women's movement, it changed women's views of themselves, opening up a range of alternatives beyond the Madonna–whore dualism. This is readily apparent in the popular literature of the period. Romance novels have been mass produced in the United States since the early 1970s. In her 1987 examination of the heroines in these novels, Carol Thurston argued that the dualism persisted until the early 1980s. In her contemporary state, the romantic female persona is no longer split between two archetypal female characters: the plain-naive-domestic-selfless-passive-chaste heroine and the beautiful-sophisticated-worldly-selfish-assertive-sexually active other wo-man. Instead, the new heroine is both good and sexual, and she has a strong drive for self-determination and autonomy.[43]

In this postrevolutionary world, most Americans (92% in our Internet survey) feel that sex does not define love, but it is an important part of a romantic relationship. People sometimes resorted to metaphor to explain this. One woman responding on the Internet said, "Sex is the glue that holds relationships together." A man wrote, "Sex is the oil that keeps the romantic flame alive." Food metaphors were popular. Eight respondents volunteered, "Sex is the icing on the cake." One woman disagreed. For her, "Sex is like the decorations on the frosting on the cake." Another woman argued that sex and love "go together like ham and Swiss," while yet another woman suggested that "it's the whipped cream and cherry on top." Overall, most feel that sex is the physical manifestation of romantic love and that it enhances relationships and "completes the circle." As one 86-year-old woman explained, "Love and making love are intermingled if you truly love someone."

Our in-depth interviews permit a more nuanced examination of the link between love and sex. For some of the people interviewed, the link represents a moral imperative, with love a necessary prerequisite to sex. For example, 57-year-old Marian explained this clearly: "I don't feel that you should have a sexual relationship with somebody unless there is love there."

For some in their 80s and 90s, the connection between love and sex is associated with the prohibition of sex outside of marriage. We saw this earlier in 97-year-old Emma's remarks. Cynthia, a 63-year-old woman of Asian descent, was somewhat more flexible. Rather than an outright pro-hibition on premarital sex, Cynthia felt, "People should have sex if they are sure they will get married to that person."

Others argue that sex and love together offer a richer, better experience. For example, 72-year-old Hal explained, "To have sex with someone you love is beautiful. To have sex for sex is sheer physical. I want sex to be beautiful." Groping for words, 58-year-old Henry suggested that the agapic character of love can improve sex: "Because it's that . . . that . . . what's the word I'm trying to think of? Um, when you, you know the feeling that you want to help do something for the other person. They want to do something for you and it's not because they have to, but because they want to and so it's the feelings that you get that come about." Wilson, a 62-year-old Native American, said, "If you truly love someone and you have sex with them, oh boy there is a difference! . . . Because you love that person. You just feel them. And they feel you."

A few of the people we interviewed saw love and sex as separate experiences, though 80- and 90-year-olds were conspicuously absent in this group. As 59-year-old Daniel explained,

> I'm trying to figure out what a gay relationship is. I don't believe the traditional model of relationships fits. It's much more a voluntary thing. There's no reason for gay people to get together other than the bond between the two. There's no societal norm that says you have to get married. There's no reason you have to get together to have kids. There's—you don't have to do it. So when gay people get together it's truly not because of sex. . . . It's totally based on choice. . . . I'd like to be in a long-term relationship that's not bounded by sex. That's not bounded by anything. You're separate. You're yourself. But you form an entity that's different from the two.

Similarly, 75-year-old Mathew said, "I think that sometimes sex is just a recreational thing. And I think there can be love and no sex. And if you're lucky enough to have both then that's good too." Finally, 49-year-old Patrick explained, "I don't really equate love and sex in the same breath. I think sex is something you end up giving and taking when you get married. It doesn't necessarily mean that you love each other. I could go out and pay a hooker for sex, but that doesn't mean I love them. To me sex is a physical act that ends up giving pleasure."

## Modern Love Taxonomies

Whereas the laypeople we interviewed tended to view love as a complex whole, some scientists and academics understand love by examining its components. Robert Sternberg, a psychologist at Yale, has written extensively on his theory that love is a triangle. Based on his observations of the problems experienced by married couples, Sternberg concluded that romantic love has three components: intimacy, passion, and commitment. He argued that relationships can be understood by knowing the relative strength of each component.[44]

For Sternberg, intimacy describes the feelings of closeness or bonding that arise in loving relationships. It consists of sharing, empathy, and high regard for the beloved. Passion is associated with desire, physical attraction, and romance. Commitment includes both short-term and long-term aspects (subdivisions). In the short term, commitment involves the decision or realization that we love. In the long term, it consists of a promise to sustain the love. As Figure 1.1 illustrates, Sternberg argued that "consummate love" represented the perfect balance of these three components.

Sternberg's triangulation theory also illustrates a second approach to understanding love—categorizing different types of relationships. After developing his theory, Sternberg went on to suggest that love could be understood as a story. In his 1998 work, *Love Is a Story*, he identified 25 prototypical stories that described both experiences and ideals regarding love. Examples include "The Sacrifice Story," in which one or both of the lovers sees himself as constantly making sacrifices for the sake of the

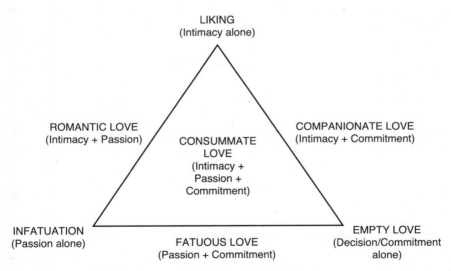

Figure 1.1.   The kinds of loving as different combinations of the three components of love. (From Robert J. Sternberg, *The Psychology of Love*, © 1989 Yale University Press. Used with permission.)

relationship or the beloved. In "The Sewing and Knitting Story," a loving relationship is based on the active construction of love itself. Love, in essence, is what those involved make it. Sternberg noted that stories can change and suggested that the story metaphor is a useful tool for understanding and improving love relationships.

### Love as Color

John Alan Lee used color as an analogy for love. He observed that while it is relatively easy to compare different colors, it is difficult to define the concept of color, and argues that this is also true of love. Lee suggests that, like color, love comes in different styles that can be mixed and matched. The three primary love styles, *eros*, *storge*, and *ludus*, can be combined with the secondary styles, *mania*, *pragma*, and *agape*.

Drawing his labels from ancient Greek, Lee adjusts their definitions to fit contemporary realities. So, for example, erotic lovers associate love with powerful physical desire. They know and seek out precisely the physical type that turns them on. Storge, on the other hand, refers to a more gentle and affectionate love that develops over time. A storgic lover has no ideal physical type and never consciously selects a love partner, instead choosing to allow love to grow on her. Ludus describes a playful, noncommittal style of love. The ludic lover might be promiscuous. He or she can be described by the lyric "if you can't be with the one you love, love the one you're with."

The secondary styles are similarly framed. So, a manic lover plunges energetically into love relationships with inappropriate partners, eagerly projecting exceptional qualities onto the partner that most people can see are not really there. By contrast, pragmatic lovers are, if nothing else, practical. They have a clear idea (perhaps even a list) of the qualities they seek in a love partner. The pragmatic lover would probably be quite comfortable in the marriage market described previously. Lee suggests that the *agape* love style is least common in modern America. This love style is based on altruism and duty. Even in the absence of enjoyment the agapic lover will continue to love and to sacrifice for love.

Most of us will find each of Lee's major love styles as we contemplate love relationships we have experienced or observed. Perhaps this reflects Lee's scientific approach. He began by studying those who observed love, as he put it, "from Plato . . . to the most recent psychologists."[45] His taxonomy was based on this material, then tested through interviews in the field.

## *Love as a Verb*

We tend to believe that emotions cause behavior. But some psychologists and philosophers suggest that the reverse is true: We behave in response to external stimuli in the environment and then conclude that we must be feeling a certain way. In the nineteenth century, psychologist William James argued that action precedes emotion; that fear does not make us flee.[46] Instead, we infer that we are afraid of something because we run away from it. The rise of behaviorism strengthened this focus on behavior, and cognitive psychologists continue to argue that behavior determines emotion, rather than the other way around. Under this view, emotion is as much a cognitive as a physiological experience. We observe our behavior and conclude how we feel on the basis of that. So if I consistently behave as if I love someone, I will eventually conclude that I must be feeling love.[47]

Of the people we interviewed, 20 described love with reference to actions. For them, four types of behavior defined love: expressing affection, offering services and gifts to the beloved, sharing projects or activities, and refraining from hurtful activities.

Laughing, 73-year-old Callie, from Idaho, described the expressions that constituted love for her, saying that love is "a smile and a wink across the room. Like a hug." But a disconnect between expressions and behavior can erode trust in expressions alone. As 90-year-old Dale, from Utah, explained, "My mother would always tell me 'I love you.' But at the same time there was this absence. She wasn't really present. So the expression of love is more in actions than in words."

Actions and gifts for the beloved are widely seen as unambiguous indications of love; 64-year-old Rosie certainly thought so as she described her fiance's loving behavior. "His love for me—he cooks meals and serves me with a tray and everything. He does all my laundry for me and he folds it just like a woman would fold it and brings it to me. He vacuums for me. He surprised me with that plant right there. See all those teddy bears and everything? He bought that. Every month that we're together he gets me a gift of some kind." Several respondents shared Rosie's appreciation for tokens of affection.

Service was important, both as an expression of love and as a way of developing love. Some respondents expressed love through caregiving. This was true of 83-year-old Eunice, who said love was "caring for him as I did. And I said, 'That was only a privilege.' That was my privilege to do that. He was sick for 10 years." Two specifically mentioned that caregiving generates loving feelings. We interviewed 72-year-old Mary shortly before, then after her husband Tom died of Alzheimer's disease. Reflecting on the definition of love, she focused on caring service. Mary explained, "I think that service is the best way to develop a loving kind of relationship or feeling for other people. And that includes my husband. I have served him for 50 years and I have chosen to."

Mutual activities featured in several respondents' definitions of love. As 91-year-old Jim put it, love is when "two people agree on things and do things together." Reflecting on the shared labor of raising a family and establishing a home, 97-year-old Emma described how love grows, saying, "You just work together and you get to liking more. Get better acquainted with them all the time."

Finally, a few respondents felt that when they refrained from doing things that might be hurtful, this was an indication of their love. After her husband's death, 80-year-old Justine could not bring herself to attend dances at the senior center. She said, "A lot of good dancers [were] there, you know, a lot of good men, and I had a couple of fellows that maybe I could have dated, but there's no way. I just couldn't do that because I just had too much of a feeling still in me for my husband."

The notion that love is a skill or a set of behaviors is manifest in Eric Fromm's classic work, *The Art of Loving*. This view may also be found in a plethora of how-to books in this area. As I was researching this chapter, I came upon yet another advice book. This one, called *Love Is a Verb*, argues that couples with relationship problems should focus on their actions rather than their feelings.[48] Christian authors often use the phrase "Love is a verb" to admonish readers to behave in a way that is consistent with biblical statements. A friend of mine uses it to get his son to mow the lawn.

How do we know we are loved? Behavioral psychologists argue that we never really know the content of a lover's heart or mind. In this view, love can be seen as a theory. Events over the course of relationship tend to confirm or disconfirm the theory that we are loved. This notion applies to our own love as well. We carefully observe our emotions and behaviors and conclude, voilà, we are in love. Over time our confidence in the theory may wax and wane, but love survives as long as the behavior of both partners supports the theory.

### Love as Limbic Resonance

Consider what your presence today means in evolutionary terms. Each of us represents an unbroken line of successful lovers that stretches deep into the

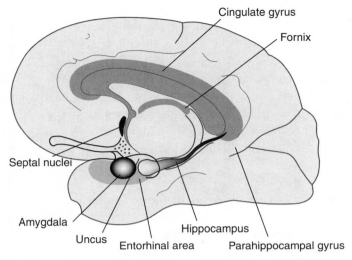

Figure 1.2. The limbic brain structures, shaded darkly, are considered the biological home of love. (From Per Brodal, *The Central Nervous System*, © 2003 Oxford University Press. Used with permission.)

origin of the species. From this perspective, we represent the romantic (or at least sexual) successes of untold ancestors.

Like philosophers and psychologists, evolutionary biologists have concluded that love—not just sex, but love—is a vital and adaptive part of what it means to be human. And not just human—as Thomas Lewis and his colleagues argued, we share the capacity for love with other mammals.[49] Indeed, mammals share many emotions such as anger, jealousy, and affection, and when we look at other mammals we can often tell what emotions they are experiencing. Anyone who has played with a dog understands this transspecies communication, which, biologists argue, is due to our limbic brain.

The limbic brain is the seat of advanced emotional activity—the biological home of love (Figure 1.2). It enables us to interpret and send subtle emotional cues and directs the hormonal and parasympathetic responses we experience as emotions. Ever tried to figure out what a lizard was feeling? Reptiles do not have limbic brains.

Biologists argue that the development of this brain represented an important evolutionary advance for mammals. Through a phenomenon known as limbic resonance, mammals become emotionally attuned to each other. A mammal can look at another mammal, know what emotional state that mammal is in, and adjust his or her physiology to respond appropriately. This resonance has been described as "a full-throated duet, a reciprocal interchange between two fluid, sensing, shifting brains."[50] When our children, friends, or lovers walk through the door, the process of limbic resonance makes us emotionally prepared to greet and interact with them.

This limbic response is not something we learn. Biologists argue that we are born with an emotional vocabulary that is vital to our survival. This may explain a newborn child's response to his mother's feelings. There is evidence that babies regulate their heart and breathing rates to be in sync with their caregivers.[51]

Over time, some of us learn to ignore or refine our limbic responses. We wall ourselves off so that we do not detect the emotions of others—at least, not on a conscious level. Or we can fine-tune our emotional receptivity to the point where some think we have magical powers of intuition. Like many women, 50-year-old Shannon reported being hypertuned to cues that her husband had become angry: "He might be talking in a quiet tone, but if he's angry it feels like he's shouting at me; then, when I say 'Don't yell at me!' he'll tell me he's not. Really, he's not. It just feels like he is." Biologists would argue that Shannon's limbic system has become tuned to cues of anger—a trait that could be lifesaving for her (or her ancestors).

### Mars and Venus: Do Men and Women Love Differently?

Many people believe that men and women experience romantic love differently. This is celebrated by some—"Vive la difference!"—and bemoaned by others: "What do women want?" Lord Byron clearly thought of gender differences when he wrote, "Man's love is of man's life a thing apart; 'Tis woman's existence." And John Gray, author of the popular *Men Are From Mars, Women Are From Venus* series would certainly agree with him. Similarly, Simone de Beauvoir argued that "the word love has by no means the same sense for both sexes, and this is one cause of the serious misunderstandings that divide them."[52] Later, radical feminists of the twentieth century would argue that, in a culture marked by male privilege and control, men are incapable of loving.[53]

Yet modern research has demonstrated few gender differences in the experience. Helen Fisher developed a 54-item questionnaire on romantic love. It included statements such as: "I have more energy when I am with ____." "My heart races when I hear ____'s voice on the phone." Then she and her colleagues surveyed over 400 American and Japanese adults about their current or past love relationships. Their findings suggested the experience of love was similar across age, gender, sexual orientation, religious affiliation, and religion.[54]

Men and women may experience love in ways that are more similar than we imagine. When we are socialized into distinct gender roles, we learn to express ourselves and structure our time somewhat differently.[55] Along with other relationship functions, romantic love has traditionally been "women's work." So the differences celebrated by famous authors are not inevitable, but the result of a social and economic system that relegates intimacy and family to women while committing men to productive external functions. If this is true, we might expect to see gender differences in romance diminish in future generations.

Late life may reduce gender differences in love. With advanced age we are freed from some of the constrictions of traditional gender roles. Women are less immediately concerned with child rearing, and men often have been released from the workforce. Several gerontologists have observed that the freedoms of later life can cause a blurring of traditional gender divisions.[56] We may find, for instance, that men in their 60s are more concerned with the emotional quality of their romantic relationships than they were in their 20s.

Comments from older men we interviewed do suggest a change in perspective with maturity. We asked whether their experiences of love had changed with age. Like 58-year-old Henry, several found their romantic interests shifting away from sex and toward a deeper emotional intimacy with their partners. Henry explained, "The first thing is, you know, of course, that physical thing, and then, 'Yeah, we can go out and have sex. This is great. Hey, I've waited all my life for this.' [Then, with age] all of a sudden you find out, 'Well, you know, that's okay. But, you know, there's a lot more that's more important in an individual, than that.' Anyway, to me it is."

Other men reported that the emotional depth and intimacy of late-life relationships made for fantastic sex. Harold, age 76, explained that in late life he and his wife had discovered the pleasures of cuddling and holding. He shared his view that "the whole body is a sex organ." Hugh agreed. At age 79 when we interviewed him, Hugh said, "Well, I think without love sex is just in your mind, you know. But with love you enjoy each other before and after, let's put it that way.... And our sex life was good all the way through even up until the time she died and she was weakened. We had a good sex life."

Several couples in their 60s confirmed that their sexual experiences were excellent. Some commented on the absence of time pressure and interruptions. One man in his 60s enthused that he could take hours for foreplay with his new partner.

Like older men, older women emphasized improvements in the emotional character of relationships in later life. Some agreed with 97-year-old Emma that "the more I lived with him, the more I loved him." Wilhelmina, age 92, attributed this to the accumulation of shared experiences: "I think that makes us feel closer, and if we love someone that we share those experiences with, I think that's what makes our love deeper and truer."

Some discovered a new level of sexual passion in later life. The experience of 64-year-old Evelyn is illustrative. Evelyn was widowed in her 50s and fell in love a decade later. She had been with her lover for several tumultuous years when we met. Evelyn said, "He brought me to a level of passion that I don't think I even experienced with my husband." She feels that this experience has changed her: "and when I say that to him, he'd say, 'No.' He said, 'You already had it.' He said, 'I just helped you open it up to that.' "

There's no arguing the differences between men and women, and some of them play out in the romantic arena. Many of these differences can be traced to the traditional division of labor between men and women. But this division is less relevant to later life—a time of greater freedom when men can focus on emotional intimacy, while women may enjoy sex as they never have before. Free of the pressures of children and jobs, older adults may enjoy greater romantic possibilities than the young.

## Conclusion

As mammals, we humans are biologically equipped for love. Manifestation of our romantic potential is shaped by our selves and the families, communities, and cultures in which we live. But ultimately our romantic experiences are bounded only by our imagination. We can liberate the romantic imagination by probing the origins of beliefs we take for granted.

In the light of day, you may find that the inherited prohibitions of your Victorian ancestors are irrelevant or that the fantasies of the troubadours ring false. You may wake up agreeing with Socrates that love is the link between humans and the gods, and go to bed convinced that love is just an excuse for sex. Understanding love is like understanding ourselves, a life-affirming process with no fixed end point. The wonderful gift of this twenty-first century is that most of us will have more years than ever before to participate in this process. In the next chapter, we will probe the implications of these extra years.

## Try This: Exploring the Romantic Imagination

1. Love's Lessons: Reflect on the lessons you have learned about love during the course of your life. What did your parents teach you about love? Did you learn that people punished you because they loved you? That they gave you presents to prove their love? That even if they did not display affection they must love you because they pay the rent? That you are loved when you are good or when you win or when you accomplish something? That people who love you leave? Do not apply judgments to your insights. These lessons about love are not good or bad, and they are not indelible. They just are, and through them you can understand the origins and content of your romantic imagination.

Now consider the lessons learned at other times in life. Did they contradict what you learned as a child? Has your understanding of love changed as the result of adult experiences? How would you define love today?

2. Time Travel: Consider the effect of history on your romantic expectations and values. What would they be like had you been born 50 years earlier or 50 years later? This might be a fun exercise to share with a friend or partner.

## Suggested Reading

Fisher, H. (2004). *Why we love*. New York: Henry Holt. A very readable work by a renowned anthropologist. Dr. Fisher has done work for Match.com. Here she synthesizes a wide range of literature to shed light on many facets of the romantic experience.

Hopkins, A. (1994). *The book of courtly love: The passionate code of the troubadours*. San Francisco: Harper Collins. I found this delightful little book on a library shelf and fell in love immediately. With illustrations from medieval tapestries, paintings, and poetic interludes, the author deftly introduces the history and themes of courtly love. She uses the words of Andreas Capellanus, Geoffrey Chaucer, and Chrétien de Troyes to describe its features.

Illouz, E. (1997). *Consuming the romantic utopia: Love and the cultural con-traditions of capitalism*. Berkeley, CA: University of California Press. In this academic work, a sociologist from the Hebrew University argues that romance has been "colonized by the market." Illouz draws the link between romantic rituals and consumerism in a book that is insightful and thought-provoking.

Lewis, T., Amini, R., & Lannon, R. (2000). *A general theory of love*. New York: Random House. This delightfully readable book by three psychiatrists from the University of California at San Francisco introduces the physiology and evo-lution of love.

Mclaren, C. (2002). *Aphrodite's blessings: Love stories from the Greek myths*. New York: Anetheum. Three Greek myths (Atalanta, Andromeda, and Psyche) reveal the character of Aphrodite, the ancient goddess of love. Told from a woman's perspective, this is a pleasant read.

Petersen, J. R. (1999). *The century of sex: Playboy's history of the sexual revolution 1990–1999*. New York: Grove Press. This book is not easy to find. At our university they keep it under lock and key because, as the librarian explained, "It gets stolen otherwise." I bought a used copy and treasure it in part (I confess) because of the lovely illustrations, but mainly because it offers an informed and sympathetic view of the sexual revolution.

Just turned 90 and ready for college.

# 2

## The Aging Self

Those who love deeply never grow old. They may die
of old age, but they die young.
—SIR ARTHUR PINERO

*The senior center nestles midblock in a neighborhood of small shops, res-
taurants, and historic homes. The parking lot is tiny. (Most people walk or
take the bus.) The landscaping is meticulously groomed, with a profusion of
plants. (Senior volunteers have their way with it, and the staff respect their
gardening expertise.) Just before lunch, the foyer bustles with arrivals. Some
cling to walkers, a few sit in wheelchairs, but most people move briskly.
Announcements litter an overstuffed bulletin board, and newspapers and
magazines are free for the taking. A placard near the sign-in sheet pro-
claims, "Old age ain't for sissies!" The activities schedule reveals a lecture
Wednesday by a local professor on the roots of terrorism; the tai chi class
meets three times a week; this month's service project is collecting books for
the school in the homeless shelter; and bingo is not even offered. The caf-
eteria is noisy, and loud greetings echo off the walls. The crowd is mostly
female, with hugs and pats for everyone. The afternoon chef (a young,
overwhelmed staff member) comes out for her applause, then everyone digs
in. Those who are diabetic skip dessert, but the rest of the food disappears.
The room empties quickly as people head off to the afternoon's activities. An
ancient man naps in the corner.*

As we age we experience life—not to mention love—in ways we could not
have imagined when we were younger. Growth spurts are not just for

teenagers. Adults continue to develop, but only lately have researchers begun to examine how late life shapes our relationships and our selves. Their work suggests that many aspects of life, including love, improve with age. Randy, age 86, explained this simply: "I find that love gets better as we get older."

The chapter begins with a brief consideration of physical changes that come with age before turning to some of the fascinating new research on cognitive and emotional development in later life. We then consider diverse theories of psychological maturation before touching on the role love, particularly a kind of love I call transformative, can play in adult development.

## Physical Aging

Unlike emotional and even intellectual maturation, physical aging is both inevitable and relatively predictable. Cosmetic changes serve as harbingers. One day, we look in the mirror and see our parents—or the version of our parents that tormented our adolescence. I never wore the big hair that was so popular in the 1950s, so went through life confident that I did not resemble my mother. This happy fantasy persisted until one day at a ski resort I caught a glimpse of myself wearing a wool cap. There, in that crowded women's room, was my mother's face. Most women can share a similar moment: the first gray hair glimpsed in a hotel mirror, the tooth that broke while chewing lettuce, or the worry line that somehow became a fixture.

In an interesting study of vanity, Mary Harris asked Americans of all ages about the effects of aging on their appearance.[1] Both men and women reported that balding was the most negative aspect of aging, but only when it happened to women. Yul Brynner benefited from the general view that balding in men can be distinguished. Neck wrinkles were also seen as problematic for women, suggesting that Nora Ephron is not alone when she says, "I hate my neck!"[2] Although Harris's respondents did not generally object to gray hair or wrinkles, over a third of women and 6% of men reported that they colored their hair, and a quarter of the women used wrinkle creams. Harris reported that her respondents had negative opinions of people who used these artificial measures to alter their appearance.

And yet Americans spent over $4 billion in 2006 on antiaging "cosmeceuticals."[3] We have mixed feelings about battling the signs of age. On one hand, like those Mary Harris interviewed, we do not approve of these measures. On the other hand, we do want to look younger. We just want to look that way naturally. Mariene Goodman reported that women who had cosmetic surgery had higher self-esteem than those who did not—even before their procedures.[4] A quick perusal of the popular press reveals that men are turning to these products in growing numbers. Creams, potions, and yes, even procedures can help us feel better about ourselves, and feeling better about ourselves can make us more responsive to new relationships and more effective in social situations. Other physical changes accompany aging, and some have implications for romantic and sexual relationships.

## Chronic Illness and Disability

Most people over 65 do not experience severe disability, and each successive cohort of Americans has had a lower risk of disability.[5] Nonetheless, we tend to associate old age with illness and disability, and advanced age does bring increased physical vulnerability.

When Bernice Neugarten entered her seventh decade, she suggested that those over 65 be divided into the "young-old" (those 65 to 75) and the "old-old" (those over 75). More recently, the term "oldest old" has been applied to people over the age of 80. Some day, centenarians (one of the nation's fastest-growing age groups) might be termed the "incredibly old." These separate groups have distinct experiences with disability.

Many Americans cope with disability and chronic illness in their later years. According to the Census Bureau, about half (42%) of those over age 65 have some kind of disability and 29% have a physical disability that might impair their ability to engage in activities. Of course, most people with disabilities are very old. A vast majority (84%) of those over 85 experience some kind of disability, with half requiring assistance with daily activities.[6] The litany of chronic illnesses that affect us in late life is a tad depressing: Arthritis is common, while heart disease, cancer, and stroke are the greatest killers.

The prospect is daunting and can discourage anyone from taking on a new commitment late in life. A 52-year-old woman I interviewed explained that she was only interested in dating younger women. "I have to say it's kind of weird. There is a point where, well, I dated a woman who was 62, and she didn't look her age and certainly didn't act her age, but I kept thinking, when I'm her age I could be doing hospice or caretaking. You start thinking of the caretaking side of that and maybe you want someone younger, someone who can take care of me. Then again, you just never know."

An older respondent offered clear advice. Marty, age 87, explained, "People that are over 75 or older, and they lose a companion, by and large, they should not remarry. [chuckles] Because one or the other of 'em is gonna have to take care of the other one. And they're taking care of a person with which they don't have a long relationship of love."

Marty has a point. Caregiving exacts a toll on long-term relationships. Several of the older women we talked to had cared for dying husbands. For example, 80-year-old Judith explained how she coped: "I often think right now how Mary set and washed Jesus' feet. That's what I'm doing with Carl now." For some, widowhood brings an element of relief, as 92-year-old Justine exclaimed: "When my husband died, I didn't feel anything but relief. Isn't that awful?" Often these widows resolved to avoid relationships with older men for fear of another difficult bout of caregiving.

There were the indomitable few who did not hesitate to become involved far into their later years. Viola, age 87, buried three husbands, each more lovable than the last. She explained that the relationships just kept getting better. "The feeling—of course with my last husband he was so perfect that my love for him was as great as it could possibly be. I don't think I could ever love anyone else. That's the way I feel now. I think there isn't any more perfect men out there. There isn't any more my age." Viola married Howard when she was 79. He had multiple health problems, but she was happy to care for him. They had "eight wonderful years" before he died of complications from diabetes.

## Sexual Changes

Physical aging can change the way we experience sex. Illness and medications may also interfere with the experience. For some, diminished sex drive offers a welcome relief, and for others inability to perform becomes a source of anxiety. The young man going through life perpetually aroused may find it impossible to imagine that after age 40 his sexual experience will be much different. Older men can take longer to become aroused and to ejaculate. These days we cannot watch television without being reminded that erectile dysfunction can be fixed with a little blue pill. Women experience more subtle changes. After menopause, thinning of the vaginal walls and decreased vaginal elasticity and lubrication can result in discomfort with intercourse. Personal lubricants and regular sexual activity usually alleviate this problem.

Ten of the people we interviewed reported that physical problems had affected their sex lives. Most, like 64-year-old Vera, found other ways to experience physical intimacy: "It's just his age. There's other ways to have sex—oral sex—I just love to be held and told that I'm loved. I like it. When I'm out with him he puts his arm around me and makes me feel like I'm number one in his life." Those who experienced sexual problems usually reported that they coped by talking about the problem and finding other ways to achieve physical intimacy. Nonetheless, 58-year-old Jim's advice to women was, "Don't always have a headache every night, you know."

Some people—particularly in their 80s and 90s—reported their sex lives were over. In these cases, cultural norms and personal preferences probably have as much influence as physical changes. In her early 90s, Vera said, "There ain't no sex. I want that recorded. There's no desire. I've had it, kid." Ted, whose wife found sex in the 60s so satisfying, was worried about his ability to replicate the experience with another woman after her death: "That was 60. At 65 . . . at 70 . . . at 75 . . . at 80 . . . I might still be able to perform. But now [at 88] I would be embarrassed to find out that I couldn't."

By contrast, some of the people we interviewed discovered new heights of sexual pleasure in their later years. After her husband's death, Evelyn, age 64, became involved with a married man. She said, "When my husband got sick, too, I really . . . we didn't have sex for a long time, because it was difficult, so I just figured I was asexual. But [with her lover], probably in the first, maybe 6 months or so, you know, that we had been together sexually. It was like, 'Oh, my God! I can't believe how I feel.' . . . The way he pleasures . . . he's a totally unselfish lover."

Also in his mid-60s, Dean discovered the potential of late-life romance when he was reunited with his high school sweetheart. "I just can't get enough of her, mentally and physically. She's so free with affection and love. She's always telling me that we have so many years to make up for. We have sex just about every other day and it's so physically and meaningfully better now. Our life experiences seem to have matured and mellowed us. Sex is a deeper passionate feeling and we linger afterward by just relaxing, caressing, and talking." Vastly improved sex was not restricted to new relationships in late life. Ted, age 88, said, "My wife, incidentally, said, 'You know, here we are 60 years old, and I'm getting a better charge out of our sexual relationship than I ever have."

C. S. Lewis discovered the comic aspects of late-life sex when he married for the first time at the age of 58. His book, *The Four Loves*, was published 2 years later. In it, he suggested that the god of love must have a sense of humor:

She herself [Venus] is a mocking, mischievous spirit, far more elf than deity, and makes game of us. When all external circumstances are fittest for her service she will leave one or both of the lovers totally indisposed for it. When every overt act is impossible and even glances cannot be exchanged—in trains, in shops, and at interminable parties—she will assail them with all her force. An hour later, when time and place agree, she will have mysteriously withdrawn; perhaps from only one of them. What a pother this must raise—what resentments, self-pities, suspicions, wounded vanities and all the current chatter about "frustration"—in those who have deified her! But sensible lovers laugh. It is all part of the game; a game of catch-as-catch-can, and the escapes and tumbles and head-on collisions are to be treated as a romp.[7]

Sex in late life can be both fun and funny. People vary in their experiences of late-life eroticism. Some rediscover their passionate selves, while others let go of "the physical aspect." Loss of a sex partner can end a person's sex life, while negative attitudes about aging bodies can make sex embarrassing. Here we may see cohort differences between baby boomers, who came of age during the sexual revolution, and their older counterparts.

## Cognitive and Emotional Maturation

Like the rest of our bodies, our brains change as we age. While some of these changes may result in declines, there is solid evidence that the experiences of a lifetime can lead to improved cognitive functioning. Age can also improve our emotional lives.

### Cognitive Aging

New technologies have allowed researchers to observe our brains at work, and a new field known as the *cognitive neuroscience of aging* has emerged.[8] Research in this field suggests that our brains are marvelously adaptive and flexible. Most of us were probably taught that brain cells do not regenerate or grow—that, after a peak sometime in our mid-20s, the brain goes through a steady process of cell death until we "lose our marbles."

Nothing could be further from the truth. The denizens of senior center workshops and classes know that learning is both possible and enjoyable in later life. Even scientists now understand that the process of brain development can last a lifetime and that learning results in actual physical changes in the brain. The process of neurogenesis (production of new brain cells) can continue throughout our lives. Further, in a phenomenon known as plasticity, brain cells change in response to stimulation. Early animal studies in the 1960s documented this process in rats. Marion Diamond, a professor of anatomy at the University of California at Berkeley, found that when rats were placed in a stimulating environment the neurons in their brains grew and changed, as did the chemical climate of the brains.[9]

Today, the use of brain imaging technology has enabled researchers to document the physical impact of learning on the brain. For example, in the past few years researchers in London have demonstrated that taxi drivers have an enlarged hippocampus. As it happens, this is the part of the brain used for navigation.[10] Generally speaking, as Gene Cohen explained, "neurons that fire together, wire together."[11] So the learning and experiences of a lifetime determine the physical structure of our brains. And that structure is constantly evolving. Our brain cells continue to grow and change regardless of our age.

In another intriguing development, researchers have used positron emission tomography scans and magnetic resonance imaging to demonstrate that high-functioning older adults actually use more of their brains than younger adults. In these studies, people are asked to perform a cognitive task, like remembering a word, while researchers examine their brain activity. Young adults usually rely solely on the left side of their brain for this task. In contrast, older adults doing the same task tend to use both brain hemispheres. Robert Cabeza at Duke University, who is responsible for most of the work in this area, calls this "hemispheric asymmetry reduction in older adults."[12] This finding suggests that with age we become more efficient and more flexible at using our cognitive resources.

The complexity and quality of cognitive functioning can both improve with experience, and the lessons of a lifetime may enhance our judgment and reasoning. Indeed, older adults generally have superior judgment on problems that require complex, relativistic thinking. Further, with age we become better at reasoning tasks that demand recognition of diverse perspectives, the synthesis of contradictory information, and the anticipation of potential problems.

Of course, anyone who has spent time with older adults is aware that brains function more slowly in later life. We process information more slowly, and increased reaction times can make us terrible drivers. Further, poor health, depression, environmental deprivation, and other factors can deprive us of the cognitive improvements described in this section. Enhanced reasoning abilities can be seen as a potential of late life—one that requires cultivation.

## *Emotional Maturity*

Researchers have also observed emotional changes associated with age. It seems that emotional intelligence increases with age. Older adults report that they experience more positive and fewer negative emotions than young adults.[13] For example, a friend of mine was an angry young man. He experienced intense frustration at home and in the workplace. But as he entered his ninth decade, he told me he was finished with that destructive emotion. "I just don't get angry anymore," he said. "It's as if I can't be bothered."

Our respondents reported similar experiences. Harold, age 74, was asked whether love was different for him now. He replied, "It's more placid—more settled—there are not so many ups and downs. Like a mountain range but at a nice soft plateau of feeling." I asked whether he preferred this, and his answer was, "Mad passion—one kind of wishes one time that you could do it. But theoretically I think it would be incongruous or almost demeaning at my age."

What brings us to this new plateau? Researchers believe that with age we become skilled at emotional regulation.[14] That is, we learn to manage our emotions, optimizing those we find enjoyable and minimizing unpleasant feelings. As 64-year-old William pointed out, "I think that people have more control than they think they do, sometimes, as far as who they have feelings for. Or maybe that's—maybe the older you get, the more you think that. You know, I think when you're younger it's harder to control that sort of thing. . . . It's different in that it's not as painful and it's not as—how you let things go, that maybe would have bothered you more when you were younger. You're not led as much by emotion."

Improved judgment and skill at emotional regulation may be part of the wisdom many associate with advanced age. As 62-year-old Wilson explained, "When you're young you're foolish. You think life is a game. As you become older, you become wiser. You do your best to make the best of it." Reflecting on the loss of his late-life lover, he said, "I didn't feel that extreme. As you get older, you learn to condition yourself. I'll get over it."

A fascinating body of work suggests that age also improves our ability to manage interpersonal conflict. Several researchers have observed that older adults experience less interpersonal conflict than young people. Laura Carstensen and her colleagues at Stanford offered the theory of socio-emotional selectivity to explain this phenomenon. In essence, it holds that older adults minimize their contact with irritating people.[15] In addition to this reasonable approach, older people may be more constructive in handling interpersonal tensions. Kira Birditt, at the University of Michigan, studies what adults do when faced with interpersonal conflict. Her results suggest that older adults are more likely to use loyalty strategies (remain calm and wait for the situation to blow over, or do nice things not related to the problem), whereas younger adults were more likely to use exit strategies (argue, end the relationship, leave, call the person names, yell).[16]

Finally, older adults demonstrate greater emotional complexity.[17] Through the use of daily diaries, researchers have learned that older adults report experiencing more different emotions in the course of a day. They also experience some emotions that are virtually absent from the daily life of young adults. These are the more poignant feelings associated with reminiscence. This might reflect yet another skill that comes with age, the ability to distinguish subtle changes in our emotional lives. Greater emotional complexity may be the reward for learning to pay attention to our feelings.

Taken together, these cognitive and emotional changes seem to improve the quality of loving relationships. Respondents in our research consistently reported that love improved with age. For example, 92-year-old Wilhelmina explained, "I think as you get older it's more of a mature love, and maybe a little bit more genuine." Candy, age 83, agreed: "Love has gotten stronger as I've gotten older." Reflecting on her parents, 80-year-old Theresa recalled, "My parents loved more when they were older. He would give her a kiss and pat her on the 'you know.' I expect to be loved like he loved her." Similarly, 56-year-old Anna said, "My parents and grandparents had real love. They became gentler and more compassionate."

The potential for agapic love may increase with age. Theresa continued to reflect on her parents' relationship: "There was give and take. Not just all take, take, take. You've got to give to receive." Similarly, William said, "I think as you get older, my personal feeling is that love becomes more of an outgoing thing, rather than just an incoming thing. So, as you mature, love becomes less selfish. That is, if you mature at all [laughs]." Anita, age 83, from the Philippines, reflected on the joy of serving her beloved: "When younger, I didn't serve him. We had maids and only saw each other at night. Older is better. Love has a stronger impact. I served him. Mature love is so sacred. More time together. No distractions. Everything for him. Mature love has more involvement."

## Theories of Psychological Maturation

Physical aging is readily apparent and can obscure some of the less visible changes shaped by decades of experience. We have seen that some cognitive and emotional processes can improve with age. Age can also bring deeper psychological maturity. Several major psychological theorists have sought to describe the process of psychological maturation.

## Erikson

Apart from his 1935 comment that healthy adulthood consisted of love and work, Freud wrote little about adult development. But Erik Erikson did address adulthood in his theory of human development. Erikson's understanding is based on a developmental process in which people struggle with opposing traits or tendencies. The synthesis of these traits results in development of an underlying ego strength or capacity. Like most developmental theorists, Erikson spent most of his efforts describing stages of development through childhood and adolescence; however, three of Erikson's eight ages of human development take place in adulthood.

The first of these adult stages is characterized by a struggle between intimacy and isolation.[18] With resolution of this dialectic comes the capacity to love. Erikson described intimacy as "a true and mutual psychosocial intimacy with another person, be it in friendship, in erotic encounters, or in joint inspiration."[19] But such intimacy is not always possible. Erikson argued this might result from previous failure to develop a clear sense of identity. In this case, Erikson said a person might "settle for highly stereotyped interpersonal relations and come to retain a deep sense of isolation."[20] In time, the resolution of the struggle between intimacy and isolation results in the capacity to love.

Erikson's seventh stage of life involves the struggle between generativity and stagnation or self-absorption. Resolution of this struggle results in the ability to care, which Erikson describes as "the widening concern for what has been generated by love, necessity, or accident."[21]

The final stage for Erikson comes with growing awareness of mortality and interest in evaluating events and accomplishments that make up a life. This stage is characterized by the struggle between integrity—a sense that one's life has been meaningful—and despair, an existential sense of failure or waste. The result of this struggle is wisdom, described as "the detached and yet active concern with life itself in the face of death."[22]

For Erikson, healthy development through the life span results in a greatly enriched human experience. The wisdom of age along with the capacities to love and care result from sensitive engagement in life's paradoxes. Erikson pointed out that the sequence of these stages is neither fixed nor immutable.

Instead, we cycle back and forth among them as we grapple with the conflicts he identified—resolving each tentatively, only to revisit the issues when life presents new challenges.

While his work has been criticized for reflecting a male perspective, as well as a bias toward Western values and expectations, Erikson's theory remains one of the most nuanced and articulate descriptions of psychological maturation available today.[23]

## Jung

Where Erikson focused on stages, Jung emphasized the process of human development called *individuation*. He argued that we have an inherent drive toward fulfillment and meaning, and that psychological maturation requires the integration of conscious and unconscious aspects of the self into an authentic and unique individual. This frees a person from slavish adherence to social conventions and sets the stage for personal fulfillment.[24]

Jung favored living life to its fullest, suggesting that "the art of life is the most distinguished and rarest of all the arts." He argued that "for many people all too much unlived life remains over . . . so that they approach the threshold of old age with unsatisfied demands which inevitably turn their glances backwards."[25]

## Expansion of the Self: An Eastern Perspective

In Eastern philosophy, the Vedic tradition serves as the intellectual root of major schools of thought, including Buddhism, Vedanta, and hatha yoga. Arthur and Elaine Aron, psychology professors from Santa Clara University, drew upon this tradition in their theory of love's role in the expansion of self.[26] Just as Freud posited a life instinct and Jung suggested an inherent drive toward fulfillment, Aron and Aron argued that humans have an inborn desire for self-expansion. We seek to experience, to know, and to understand an ever-increasing range of phenomena. Self-expansion increases our efficacy or ability to engage in and affect the world.

Loving relationships help satisfy this expansive drive because we incorporate the experiences, resources, and sometimes even possessions of our beloved. We identify with the other person, and vicariously share his or her experiences. We have access to his or her material and intellectual resources, almost as if they were our own. So, for example, a wife need not learn to prepare a tax return because her husband—an extended part of herself—has mastered that skill. Or a person might vicariously experience the thrill of his partner's mountain-climbing adventures, freeing himself from the need to put forth the effort and take the risks.

In this view, healthy adult development requires optimum self-expansion. But expansion is not a constant, linear process. Instead, periods of expansion alternate with periods of *integration*, where we process new experiences and knowledge. A person can only take so much growth before he or she needs to rest and regroup.

## Midlife Crisis

The pursuit of meaning and fulfillment may be essential for healthy adult development. But it is not without risk. People change in later life. Long-dormant traits and desires may surface to disrupt established customs and relationships. The popular term *midlife crisis* is sometimes used to describe existential changes of this type. The person experiencing radical midlife change may not see it as a crisis. Instead, this is a frame that others tend to place around the new realizations and behaviors. With slightly pejorative overtones these days, the term midlife crisis can be used to belittle the vitally important process of psychic renovation. Some psychological theorists have incorporated the notion of midlife crisis into their notions of normal adult development; however, research does not consistently support this idea.[27]

Is midlife crisis inevitable? Several psychological researchers tangled with this question, and the result of their studies is a resounding no.[28] While radical change is certainly possible in midlife, it is by no means inevitable. Researchers disagree about the proportion of individuals who experience a major change in midlife. Daniel Levinson reported that as many as 80% of men in his study experienced a midlife transition. On the other hand, George Vaillant reported that very few men in his longitudinal study experienced radical change in midlife. Florine Livson followed a small group of women and concluded that those who were "nontraditional" tended to experience important changes in midlife. In her study, "traditional" women showed a less varied trajectory.

Among the 110 people we interviewed, only one mentioned a midlife crisis: 52-year-old Sandra, of Japanese ancestry, used it to explain her ex-husband's behavior. Due to a midlife crisis, she said, he deserted Sandra (his wife of 21 years) and their daughter. The transition was brutal. But Sandra eventually forgave him and went on to fall in love and marry a man of artistic temperament.

Of course, change and the value of change are in the eye of the beholder. And much depends on time. Had we asked Sandra to evaluate her first husband's midlife crisis right after it happened, she would have told us the results were disastrous. Looking back from a safe distance of 12 years, she sees it as one of the best things that ever happened to her.

## Daniel's Story

Daniel experienced a dramatic change in his sexual identity in his 50s. Although he never described it as a midlife crisis, his wife clearly experienced it as such. During 32 years of marriage, he and his wife Cindy had become pillars of the community and raised four wonderful children. Then at 4 o'clock one morning, Dan told Cindy he was gay. His statement was the result of decades of introspection and secret exploration.

Dan met Cindy in college and soon was at her home every Sunday night for roast beef. He never talked to her about feeling he might be gay, but the marriage was not particularly happy. Cindy "was a little bit critical," and inclined toward depression.

Dan began to explore the gay community. "I've always been a planner, so I made lists. . . . On the list of 'not to do it' there was, well, I'm going to hurt everyone I know, the kids, and she'll have a severe depression and I'll hurt everyone I love. I'm in the church; everyone looks up to me and how can I do this? . . . How do I do that? I don't know how to date. I'm 50 years old. How in the world will I find anybody to be in love with? So that was all on the don't list. And on the do list was just, 'Well, I get to be what I am.'" He laughed and said, "That's it!"

So Dan woke Cindy up to tell her. For a couple of years they went through agonies of indecision. Cindy alternated between attempts to be sexually attractive and emotionally supportive and periods of barely repressed rage. They sought counseling. Cindy blamed Dan for lying and accused him of not loving her. Dan explained, "She doesn't understand that there were different kinds of love in relationship to our marriage. She says I was deceitful. But I wasn't trying to be deceitful. It wasn't deceit, unless I was deceiving me. I was trying to be everything everybody thought I should be. It was a sincere effort!"

More than anything, Dan wanted the experience of being wildly in love. Since leaving Cindy, he has had that experience three times. He is currently in love with Jeffrey, a 62-year-old he met through friends. When asked what it is like, he said, "Oh, it's exciting because you love to eat together, and you talk forever about things. He doesn't like all my friends around, calls them 'nincompoops.' That's kind of a bad thing. But I am in love with the guy. He makes me smile. He's absolutely gorgeous."

Cindy doesn't understand. "Cindy says, 'How could you love me and do such a thing?' And I say, 'But I love you still.' I love her now just like

I've always loved her. And that's an affront to her. But I really wasn't in love with her. It really hurts her to think [that]."

Many Americans know at least one couple that has experienced this kind of transition. Like Dan, men who are at last free to experience their true sexual orientation can find the change deeply fulfilling. Like Cindy, women left behind typically find the experience devastating.

Seven of the women who responded to our Internet survey reported that their husbands had told them they were gay. In this sample, the experience was limited to people between 50 and 65, who experienced the event as a betrayal. Norma, age 65, from Georgia, described her experience simply: "We were married for 34 years when I found out he is homosexual." Also, 54-year-old Connie, from Nebraska, explained, "My husband of 25 years left me for his 30-year-old boyfriend after several years of secret gay affairs." Meg, age 52, from Wyoming, said, "My ex-husband had a *boy-friend* for 3 years before I found out. Very heartbreaking and traumatic." Finally, 51-year-old Catherine, from Utah, explained, "After over 20 years of marriage he told me that he was a woman trapped in a man's body, that he had never really loved me, and that our whole relationship was part of a 'cover' for who he really was." None of these women remarried, and none of the men who completed the survey reported a similar experience.

Few midlife changes compare in magnitude to those experienced by Dan and Cindy. But the difference in their perspectives is not unusual. To the person who is changing, radical midlife change can feel like discovering a true self who has been hidden for decades. But the people around that person can be—at least initially—profoundly disturbed and hurt by the change. Again, we should remember that radical midlife change is not inevitable, and midlife crisis is often in the eye of the beholder. Love can be part of these changes, as people enter and leave romantic relationships. But love can also transform us in more subtle and gradual ways.

## Love's Contribution to Adult Development

As we have seen in this chapter, people change physically, emotionally, and psychologically over the course of a lifetime. In a 2006 *New Yorker* article, Calvin Trillin described the "transformative power of pure, undiluted love."[29] Indeed, love can be a catalyst for personal transformation. A bitter experience with love may lead some to focus their energies in other areas, or to withdraw from potential partners. A healthy love life can set the stage for resilience and satisfaction that extends for generations.

One of the nice aspects of late-life love is that many older adults have been shaped and improved by love's lessons. Our respondents reported subtle changes and realizations as a result of their experiences with love. Some of love's most important lessons involved the distinction between illusion and reality. Abby, age 54, learned to interpret her intense love affairs, saying, "I'm the kind of person that falls in love very easily, and I realize that so much of that experience is tied up in fantasy." Anna, age 52, also learned to separate fantasy from reality. Of her current relationship, she said, "We took time to get to know each other and be friends before and that's been really good. So what I have come to realize in looking for relationships—looking for that perfect person who had everything. That's a big conversation. But do they have everything? No. That's just a fantasy. Nobody has everything."

At 68 years of age, Alice learned that she was not responsible for everything that happens in her relationships. Reflecting on her husband's choice to leave their 32-year-old marriage, Alice learned not to blame herself. She explained, "You know, when I was divorced I felt like I was a failure because I did blame myself. And so it took me a while to realize that it wasn't me. I had a good marriage. I put a lot into it."

Sometimes the very intensity of love teaches us that we can do more, survive more, than we had ever thought. For example, 66-year-old Edmund experienced an epiphany when his partner left him:

> Anyway, I, these emotions welled up in me and I went for a walk on one of the hills of San Francisco. You could actually see the bridge and you could see this bank of fog coming in, and I was thinking what am I going to do? I'm going to die out here? And I kept walking and just put one foot in front of the other, gravel under my feet and eventually the mist from the bay had overcome me and I was in such torment that I finally just fell on my face and I can remember the gravel in my nose as I fell on my face. And I lay there and I said, "I just can't do it anymore." And a voice said to me from inside, just as clear as day, "It's OK. I'm here. Just go." And I nodded. I didn't realize until later that what had happened to me was something that came from inside, that it was OK to go on.

In this process Edmund discovered an inner strength that would sustain him through later challenges.

Finally, 83-year-old Emma offered the insights of a lifetime when asked what advice she would you give to a young person about love:

> Not to take it lightly. To realize that a lot of love that you give for a lot of things is, well, that you enjoy doing it, that you are making them happy. But it doesn't always end in a beautiful bridal gown. That's not what love

is all about. Love, to understand it, can hurt, because people are human and they don't think before they speak. It's not like a little girl playing with a doll [makes kissing noises] pat pat pat. There's so much more to love than that . . . but that's the thing. Not to expect rewards for love. Not to work to have someone love you. Love yourself, and be for them what you . . . it's just the golden rule, you know, "do unto others." . . . You can't love everybody, but you don't have to reject them. . . . Along with the love comes sadness. Don't look for love. Just feel love. And don't be too quick to judge. . . . We learn to say, "I love me even though I did this and this and this and this. And I love this person in spite of . . . " This usually happens after you think you love someone and they disappoint you.

Lessons from earlier romances can improve our capacity for love in later life, and sometimes love transforms us.

### Transformative Love

Transformative love changes individual and family lives. We are all changed by love, but transformative love is revolutionary. It provides an opportunity to rewrite life histories and reverse patterns that have stifled or warped relationships for generations. For some, transformative love begins in young adulthood. For others, it comes with the reflective opportunities and skills of late life. As 58-year-old Henry explained, "Love brings a whole different meaning to you."

Evelyn experienced transformative love. She was 54 years old when her husband died, and figured, "That was it. I would not have any opportunity because he was gone and I was old. I wouldn't have any opportunity for love. But I missed the companionship of someone to be with, and I didn't even think of it in a sexual context . . . and then [2 years later] this man walks into my office and knocks me for a loop. I haven't been the same since." Evelyn fell head over heels in love, and she says the experience has transformed her. As it turned out, her lover, a man 17 years younger than she, was married—not separated, as he had told her. "But I really love him." Before meeting him Evelyn thought of herself as an "ordinary old person." When asked how the experience had changed her, she enthused, "It's changed me infinitely. I will never, ever be the same because of knowing him and I don't hesitate to tell him that. He's given me the gift of knowing who I am—my passion and my zest for life." I spoke with Evelyn 3 years after our original interview and learned that her zest for life and her love affair remained intact and ongoing.

A retired trucker, 78-year-old Jim, experienced a more subtle, healing transformation. He met his first wife at a dance when he was 17. She was pretty, and he wanted to marry before going into the military. When he returned from duty, he realized the marriage was a big mistake. But he hung in there, sticking with the marriage from 1944 to 1970. They raised four children, despite high levels of conflict and mistrust. When he finally left the relationship, Jim felt disappointed and defeated. His second marriage was brief. Jim felt that he was reliving the conflict of his first marriage all over again.

Then, in his mid-40s, Jim met Betty. She was divorced from an abusive husband and had 10 children. His friends thought Jim was crazy to take on so many kids. But he was in love. In fact, the two of them went on to have a child together when Betty was 42 years old. Today their small home is papered with pictures of children and grandchildren, and Jim credits Betty with saving him from the bitterness of failed love. Jim believes their relationship has served as a model for their children, helping to heal the effects of previous relationship failures. As evidence of their love, Jim says they do everything together, even shopping, and they never have any real fights.

## Conclusion

Late life can be a time of growth and discovery—a time when relationships are enriched by wisdom and experience. We will probably retrieve facts more slowly, but we can make more nuanced and practical judgments about them. We will probably experience more positive emotion and less conflict than in earlier life stages; and our daily emotional lives are apt to be more complex. We may be better able to detect and manage our emotions and more skilled at handling interpersonal tension. Love might be deeper, less physical, and more altruistic. But even as it changes, romantic love continues to shape our lives and our selves.

As we have already seen, late life can bring passionate surprises. There are more to follow in the next chapter when we turn to one of love's most powerful illusions: infatuation.

## Try This

Personal Ageism: Watch your use of the expression, "I am too old." Are you using it to avoid something you do not want to do? Or as an excuse to avoid taking a risk that might help you grow? Does it stop you from doing things you want to do? Does anyone else ever tell you that you're too old to do something? How do you respond to these age-based prohibitions? Do you "act your age"?

## Suggested Reading

Butler, R. (2002). *The new love and sex after 60*. New York: Ballantine. Written by a Pulitzer prize–winning physician, this valuable book offers detailed information and suggestions for enhancing sex in later years.

Cohen, G. D. (2005). *The mature mind: The positive power of the aging brain*. New York: Basic Books. Gene Cohen is a psychiatrist who has treated thousands of older adults. In this book, he brings together the latest research on the aging brain in a readable and upbeat presentation.

Juska, J. (2003). *A round-heeled woman: My late-life adventures in sex and romance*. New York: Villard. The memoir of a semi-retired English teacher who put an ad in the *New York Review of Books*: "Before I turn 67 next March, I would like to have a lot of sex with a man I like." You'll love the ending.

Latham, A. (1997). *The ballad of Gussie and Clyde: A true story of true love*. New York: Villard. A monograph, written by Clyde's son, this delightful piece tells the story of an aged widower (Clyde) who found love with a similarly aged widow (Gussie).

Marnham, P. (2006). *Wild Mary: A life of Mary Wesley*. London: Chatto & Windus. Mary Wesley became a best-selling novelist in her 70s, and was a lifelong iconoclast. In later years she was not averse to younger men, sometimes describing a handsome man as one who could put his slippers under her bed anytime. At her insistence this authorized biography was published after her death. It offers a wild ride and an intriguing glimpse of late-life passion.

Sheehy, G. (2007). *Sex and the seasoned woman: Pursuing the passionate life*. New York: Ballantine Books. This is typical Sheehy with categories and phases. If you can get past that, Sheehy's case studies are interesting and the book illustrates the wide range of romantic possibilities that older woman are exploring.

They fell in love at a senior dance.

# Part II

# Love's Illusions

American culture fosters romantic illusions. Through novels, movies, television shows, and advertisements, we are bombarded with misleading messages about love—messages like "unless your body fits a specific model of physical attractiveness you will not be loved" or "love is a magical and mysterious feeling that is beyond our control" or "love and marriage go together like a horse and carriage."

In her 1969 song "Both Sides Now," Joni Mitchell reminded us of the power of illusions. We cherish them. They bring excitement, hope, and joy as they lure us into life's major decisions (to marry, to have children, to establish a career). The people around us cultivate these illusions and before we know it, we are committed for life to someone who farts in bed, or we are trying to ignore our 2-year-old's tantrums in the grocery store, or we are sitting through staff meetings that seem to last for eons.

Eventually reality takes off its mask and reveals its true nature, leaving some with the feeling that we have been deceived or cheated. But let's hold reality in abeyance for a while. In this part of the book, we focus on love's illusions, seeking first to understand the dynamics of infatuation and then to illuminate the process of looking for love.

You may be wondering what these experiences have to do with later life. After age 50, shouldn't we be immune to love's illusions? No. People over 50 experience the thrill of infatuation and the anxiety of meeting potential partners, probably in greater numbers than ever before. And some of us never quite let go of the illusions that seduced us in our early years.

Their infatuation blossomed into a lifelong love affair.

# 3

## Infatuation: A Madness Most Discreet

Love is a smoke raised with the fumes of sighs;
Being purged, a fire sparkling in lovers' eyes;
Being vex'd, a sea nourished with lovers' tears;
What is it else? A madness most discreet,
A choking gall and a preserving sweet.
—SHAKESPEARE, *Romeo and Juliet*

*At the age of 88, Ted is the picture of health. Tall and slim, he swims regularly and has demonstrated his yoga abilities on television. Located in a quiet residential neighborhood, his home speaks of neglect. There is a sadness about him too—an air of lonely regret, sometimes disguised by a frenzy of thought and movement. When painful topics came up, Ted dashed to his piano to play a tune. We met for two 3-hour sessions, and he never seemed to tire. The story that unfolded was one of repeated infatuations.*

*Ted met Ruth through a mutual friend, and remembers that within 30 minutes of meeting she began talking with him frankly about her interest in learning what an orgasm was like. Ruth was the daughter of a judge, and her wedding to Ted—the son of a single woman—was an important event in their small town. The marriage would last 53 years, until Ruth's death. The couple had four children.*

*For Ted, sex and love are intertwined. He thrills to remember his early years of marriage when they had sex every day. "But never twice a day," he adds wistfully. After the birth of their first child, the couple moved so Ted could take a job in his father's clothing company. They manufactured uniforms for the military. Ted's father had left the family when Ted was 3 years old. He was not heard from until he blew into town to offer Ted the job. So, as we might say, there were issues.*

*One day a woman he worked with said, "Why don't you learn to talk to your father as if you're just as important in the conversation as he is?" Ted explained that her words produced an immediate and powerful sexual attraction. "I would have left my wife and the three children." Ted pursued this romance long enough to irritate his wife. He gave the woman roses on Valentine's Day. When she found out, Ruth told him she would never accept roses from him again. I asked Ted how she found out. "How did my wife find out? I told her. I said, 'Ruth, I got to tell you something. This girl has gotten to me in some way.'"*

*Ruth's sisters urged her to "leave that SOB." But the affair ended on its own when Ted had the opportunity to take his first teaching job out of state. He said, "Ahhh . . . that's what I need," an opportunity to, as he put it, "Deal with my feelings about my father." The second incident arose after the couple's return. At a book club meeting, Ted was describing an encounter he had at church. A minister was trying to show Ted the error of his ways. Listening to his description of the encounter at the club meeting, April, one of his wife's cousins, said, "You don't have to take that from him! What does he know?" Ted said her comment went straight to his sex chakra and led to a disastrous affair.*

*When I asked Ted whether he told Ruth about the relationship, he said, "Of course." To end the affair, April's husband arranged a church mission in Vietnam for himself and his wife. They were both killed trying to evacuate children from the war zone. Later, Ted told me he had visited April's son and apologized for his role in their deaths. The son forgave him and explained that their decision to go to Vietnam was complex and not entirely due to the affair.*

*And so it went, through three extramarital romances that Ted describes in the same way: instant attraction—total openness—abrupt end.*

*Ruth died when she was 81, and since her death, Ted's feelings about her have changed. It was hard to love her while she harbored resentment about his affairs. She never forgave his infidelity, and she never let him give her roses; but now Ted says, "Her mind has access to every second of our relationship." So he is sure Ruth has forgiven him and would welcome his roses. In retrospect, he thinks that during the marriage he and Ruth focused on "the 5% that was problematic, taking for granted the 95% that was perfect."*

*Ted has considered remarriage three times. The first woman was too religious for him. The second died before he could broach the subject. The third is still in contention. Ted says that he hears a faint hint in her voice that makes him worried. He thinks she might want to "put me down." But he is considering a visit. He explains that he would stay at her house for several days, and if by the second she had not crawled into bed with him he would forget about marrying her. Of course, Ted worries, "to put it frankly," whether he can "get it up."*

*But this is only one of the barriers to love after age 80. Ted called me the Saturday after our interview to say that he had found a friend's obituary in the paper and it made him realize that he is reluctant to love again because the person might just die on him. He said he might not even bother to visit "the widow."*

Listening to Ted, it was easy to become frustrated at his lack of personal insight. Wouldn't it seem, after the first or second experience of extramarital infatuation, that he would learn something? Clearly Ted was not in a position to embrace the growth opportunities presented by his intense romantic experiences. This does not mean he never will. One advantage of later life is that many of us acquire the maturity to reflect on infatuation and hear what it is trying to tell us about ourselves, our values, our needs, and our capacity for love.

This chapter begins with the physiology of infatuation, before turning to the factors that trigger this powerful experience. It then considers the course of infatuation in individual lives and the role of culture in its trajectory.

## Infatuation: A Powerful Experience

Infatuation is a multidimensional experience of rare power. It has an ecstatic, almost spiritual intensity. The infatuated lover becomes obsessed with the beloved. The lover loses sleep, cannot eat, thinks of little else, and rides an emotional roller coaster that goes from peaks of ecstasy to the depths of misery in nanoseconds. Schopenhauer pondered the intensity of infatuation, wondering if "it is merely a question of every Hans finding his Grethe," why would such a little question carry such ferocious emotions?[1] His conclusion was that romance is not simply about two compatible individuals meeting, but that its ultimate end is "the composition of the next generation." Infatuation determines the very content of future generations. For Schopenhauer, infatuation's powerful attraction represented the next generation's will to live. This "World-Will" has been described as "blind, irresistible, indescribable, irreducible, and ultimately uncontrollable."[2]

## The Physiology of Infatuation

Emerging research on brain structure and chemistry provides insight into the physiology of infatuation. In Chapter 1 we learned that biologists see the limbic brain as the home of love. This mammalian brain communicates with the rest of the brain through billions of neurons, or nerve cells. Chemicals known as neurotransmitters facilitate the movement of impulses across these neurons. One such chemical is PEA or phenylethylamine. PEA is a natural amphetamine present in large amounts when people are experiencing infatuation.[3] When neurons in the limbic system of the brain are saturated with PEA, we experience a natural high. The feelings associated with infatuation may be the natural result of a deluge of PEA and other neurotransmitters that alters our sense of reality and leaves us intoxicated.[4]

## An Infatuation Continuum

While the exact biological mechanism is unclear, most researchers in this area believe that the neurochemicals explain why people seem to have different appetites for infatuation. Human appetites for infatuation vary along a continuum, with "love junkies" at one end, who skip from infatuation to infatuation, sometimes in the space of days.[5] Michael R. Liebowitz is a professor of clinical psychiatry at Columbia University and author of a widely used book, *The Chemistry of Love*. He studied people who were addicted to infatuation's high. In the rush to experience this high, infatuation addicts subject themselves to a horrible cycle of ecstasy and despair as they go from one unsuitable love object to the next. Not only does this lifestyle effectively preclude meaningful or long-term relationships, it can interfere with other parts of life, such as friendships and work. Liebowitz suspected that these people suffered from low levels of PEA and were essentially self-medicating by using infatuation to artificially maintain an acceptable level. When he prescribed antidepressant drugs known as MAO inhibitors, the baseline levels of PEA went up and many of these patients were liberated from their infatuation addictions.[6]

My mother may have suffered from this affliction. From my childhood to her death I watched, helpless, as she bounced from one destructive love relationship to another, trapped in an alternating cycle of infatuation and depression. With each new partner the object of her affections took center stage, consuming her life's energies. She wrapped herself around each new man and disappeared in an ecstatic haze—until he tired of her attentions or she discovered his fatal flaw.

At the opposite end of the continuum are those who suffer from "love blindness." People in this rare situation never enjoy the intoxication of infatuation. Jim, a 69-year-old man from Georgia, explained to me that he had never fallen in love. He never experienced "this kind of nutty love, I would call it" and conversely had never been brokenhearted. In fact, Jim suspected that the whole notion was a fairy tale. When we met, Jim had been married for 42 years to a woman he loved deeply. She had chosen him as her husband, and he cheerfully went along with her decision. Jim's wife developed a bipolar disorder after their first 20 years of marriage, so the last two decades had been, as he said, "a wonderful hell." Still, he understood love as "the great friendship of your life" and was deeply committed to the relationship.

Love blindness is sometimes associated with hypopituitarism, a condition in which the pituitary malfunctions and the patient experiences hormonal problems.[7] While it is probably less disruptive than love addiction, the inability to experience infatuation might be experienced as a loss or a personal deficit. For Jim, this was not the case. He crafted his own definition of love—one that (like Dante's) emphasized the transformative power of being loved.

Most of us fall somewhere between the extremes of love addiction and love blindness. Some of us experience infatuation at inconvenient times with inappropriate people. Others are fortunate enough to move smoothly from a whirlwind romance to a lifelong commitment unimpaired by a misjudged infatuation. Though our love lives are hardly ruled by biochemistry, understanding the biology of attraction can help us make sense of our feelings—and perhaps even discover what might spark an infatuation.

## Infatuation Triggers and the Science of Attraction

The tremendous energy unleashed by infatuation focuses on one special other in an experience that some call *limerence*.[8] Suddenly this beloved soul becomes the center of our universe. But just what is it that disrupts our sleep, distracts our thoughts, and strips us of rationality? Scientists have tackled the question head-on and come to some tentative conclusions.

### *Physiological Triggers*

The brain's capacity for learning is one key to infatuation's triggers. As we saw in Chapter 2, our brain structure changes with experience. Each time a stimulus or an experience is repeated, it strengthens the relevant neural pathways. Each time a loved one hurts us, it becomes easier for us to associate love with pain. Soon, the mere thought of loving someone becomes painful. Alternatively, pleasant loving experiences prime the brain for more love experiences.[9] So repeated happy experiences with dark-haired men might incline a woman toward infatuation with this phenotype. Of course, if it were this simple we would find infatuation less magical and mysterious. Other factors must also be at play.

Physical arousal increases the probability of love at first sight. People who are in states of fear or excitement are more likely to experience attraction to potential romantic partners in the vicinity. In one classic study, researchers took male volunteers to a tourist site with a deep gorge. Two bridges crossed the gorge: one a perfectly safe concrete contraption and the other a flimsy suspension bridge that swayed in the wind. Half of the subjects were randomly assigned to cross the safe bridge, while the other half had to make their white-knuckled way across the suspension bridge. A female research assistant met each man at the end of his bridge and instructed him to write a story about the experience. Then she gave him her phone number, casually inviting him to call if he wanted to discuss the experience further. As you might guess, the men who had the terrifying experience were much more likely to call the research assistant later.[10] This and similar studies may have helped increase the popularity of adventure dates.

The study of attraction further suggests that men and women seek different attributes in a love partner. David Buss, a psychologist at the University of Texas, suggested that women focus more on men's ability and willingness to provide support, weighing a man's wealth, personal strength, and competitive abilities heavily. Men, on the other hand, focus more on a woman's physical attractiveness or reproductive abilities. So for men a woman's shape, youth, and vitality are important. This seems to be the case even with men and women who are not consciously seeking a partner for childbearing. His prediction has received some support from experimental psychologists.[11]

## Psychological Triggers

Like the neuroscientists, psychoanalysts emphasize the importance of early experience, in this case with parents, in setting our infatuation triggers. Freud's theory of human sexuality began with the erotic connection between a child and an opposite-sex parent, which would become the basis of future romantic attractions. Indeed, psychoanalytic theory treats infatuation as transference.[12] In its popularized forms, psychoanalytic theory might suggest either that we are constantly seeking to reestablish the connections we had with our parents or that we are driven to establish antithetical connections. According to this view, we might be attracted to or repelled by people who in some way remind us of a parent or of the way we felt about a parent. This belief in the centrality of parents in determining love objects has become part of the popular understanding of attraction.

Infatuation triggers may also relate to psychological or developmental needs. After giving a workshop in a senior center, I stood in the hall waiting for a ride home. A 60-something woman approached me and said, "I found your discussion of infatuation very interesting. I've been married for 45 years and for a while I kept falling in love with men who weren't my husband! Each time it threw me into panic. Then one day I figured it out. I kept falling in love with powerful men who were in a position to help my children—Scout masters, school principals, and the like. Once I figured this out, my infatuations stopped!"

Infatuation triggers are mysterious because they are unique and unpredictable. It can take decades to sort them out. Ted's infatuations were triggered when attractive women defended him or his opinions from powerful others. Indeed, power seems to figure prominently in infatuation. Yet most people spend so much energy stifling their attractions that they never learn what has triggered this overpowering experience.

## Infatuation's Trajectory

As anyone who has experienced infatuation knows, its beginnings are magical and its manifestations powerful. A quick read of popular love poetry might lead to the conclusion that infatuation is all about the beloved. But this is deceptive. Infatuation is all about the lover. The beloved is little more than a placeholder—someone who was in the right place at the right time with the right characteristics to trigger this powerful response. From a Jungian perspective, the essence of infatuation is projection. I like to think of the process as projection through a mist. The beloved is little more than a screen onto which we project an idealized image. Mist facilitates this process. It blurs our perceptions and allows us to deceive ourselves into believing we have found the perfect partner or soul mate.

In time the mist clears. According to neuroscientists, this typically happens between 12 and 18 months following the onset of infatuation.[13] As it lifts, the lover finds it increasingly difficult to maintain the projection.

Reality intrudes, and the true characteristics of the beloved emerge. During infatuation, we are too busy nurturing our projection to see the qualities of the person behind it. Ecstasy is impossible to sustain, and it mixes poorly with mundane aspects of life like housekeeping, bill paying, or child rearing. Many of us are seduced into believing that the image projected through the mist is reality. We abandon promises made in marriage and other settings to chase the chimera until it dissolves in the light of day. Then we rationalize the chase, saying, "the marriage was doomed from the start."

The faded projection signals the end of infatuation and reactions can vary. For some, the ending is an intolerable loss. Addicted to its heady intensity, these people blame the beloved for changing or for concealing his or her faults. One respondent in our survey reported over and over that her lovers had misrepresented themselves, failing to acknowledge the self-deception inherent to early infatuation. Some try to prolong infatuation or recapture its delights.[14] Many self-help books on marriage offer advice on recapturing the thrill of infatuation. Others find relief in infatuation's end. As one man explained to me, love is at its best when "you don't have to worry about farting in bed." Still others find that the end of projection signals the beginning of love.

From a physiological standpoint, the trajectory of infatuation is akin to that of intoxication. Our brains are saturated with stimulants, with nerve impulses traveling at amazing frequency and speed to and from the limbic brain. But this natural high cannot be sustained. Eventually, either our nerves become habituated to the neurochemicals that have saturated them or the levels of PEA and other stimulants begin to drop. As Michael Liebowitz explained, "If you want a situation where you and your long-term partner can still get very excited about each other, you will have to work on it, because in some ways you are bucking a biological tide."[15]

While all humans (and perhaps other mammals) share the potential for infatuation, our cultural beliefs about love and commitment determine how we interpret and respond to this biological and psychological experience.

## Infatuation and Culture

Infatuation threatens social conventions and institutions. Who can focus on the rules while engulfed in this intoxicating drama? Over time, divergent cultures have engineered various approaches to managing this universal human tendency. Some either ignore or tolerate infatuation but do not allow it to serve as the basis of marital commitment. Others strictly regulate contact between the sexes in an attempt to eliminate the impetuous behavior inspired by infatuation.

For decades, infatuation was seen by Westerners as a Western invention with its origins in courtly love. But more recent work by anthropologists (and any reading of love poems from other cultures) reveals the experience is much more universal. Far from being limited to Western Europe, infatuation has been observed in cultures as diverse as the Mangaia of the Cook Islands, the Fulbe of North Cameroun, the Taita of Kenya, residents of the People's Republic of China, and Australian Aboriginal communities.[16] This widespread distribution has led evolutionary biologists and others to suggest that the capacity for infatuation must be innate. As Helen Fisher suggested, "Perhaps love at first sight is no more than an inborn tendency in many creatures that evolved to spur the mating process."[17] With the force of millions of years of evolution bearing down on us, what choice do we have? We are hardwired for infatuation.

Cultures differ in the value they place on infatuation and the sanctions imposed for inappropriate attractions. Infatuation plays a central role in the American approach to romance. We idealize a relationship trajectory that begins with infatuation and results in lifelong commitment. We expect people in committed relationships to forsake all others, which in this culture means that infatuations outside of committed relationships are widely condemned. Jung argued that this approach can be destructive, that the American focus on personal—as opposed to collective—fulfillment leaves us vulnerable to the dark side of infatuation's power.

Some cultures organize long-term relationships around family compatibility rather than personal infatuations. A respondent from Japan, another from Italy, and two from India indicated that their parents had had arranged marriages. Heena, age 60, felt that her parents loved each other because they were caring and respectful. She had fallen in love with her husband but would only marry with her parents' permission. Born in America, Heena's children did not have arranged marriages, but both son and daughter married Americans of Indian descent from families they had known from childhood. For Heena, the primary advantage of an arranged marriage was that parents carefully selected brides and grooms for compatibility with their family, which ensured family and community support for the match. She felt that her children had enjoyed the best of both cultures by falling in love with people the family could approve of.

Harsh disapproval of extramarital infatuation, while not unique to America, is not universal among the world's cultures. Anthropologist Helen Fisher described cultural differences in the response to extramarital infatuation and sexual liaisons.[18] Along the Adriatic coast in Italy are several towns in which extramarital liaisons are, as she says, "the rule rather than the exception."[19] Public discussion of these affairs is taboo, but the relationships themselves are not subject to disapproval. Living in a small village in Brazil, the Kuikuru people routinely take lovers, called *ajois*, sometimes within months of their weddings. While they do not discuss their *ajois* relationships with their spouses, the liaisons are generally public knowledge and only subject to criticism if they interfere with marital obligations. These are just two examples of cultures in which extramarital infatuations do not threaten marriages or the social fabric of the community.

## Infatuation in Later Life

Physiology plays an important role in infatuation. Given that, we might wonder whether intense infatuation is compatible with the physical changes of advanced age. Ted argued that it was not. When I asked whether he thought he might ever fall in love again, his answer was clear. "No. Not in the same way I was before. 'Cause it's part of, people of our age. You're not going to feel [the same way] about love all your life."

Do people become too old to experience infatuation? Certainly, older adults describe themselves as being in love. Does that mean the same thing? Previous researchers identified three key aspects of infatuation: a cognitive aspect (obsessive thoughts about the beloved), an emotional aspect (roller coaster in response to real or imagined acts of the beloved), and a physical aspect (changes in appetite or sleep). In the course of this research, my students and I set out to determine what infatuation looked like in later life.

We began with Loli and Billie Joe Banes. They met when she was 66 and he was 71. The director of the housing facility in Georgia where they met described them as a Valentine's couple who had met, fallen in love, and recently married. Both Loli and Billie are heavyset and inclined toward immobility. Our halting conversation about infatuation went like this:

> LOLI: He was up on the third floor and I was on the first floor and that's how we met. We just started going together and then got married.
> INT: Really! So when you met him the first time, what did you think about him?
> LOLI: Well, I liked him from the very beginning. His disposition and all, I liked him.
> INT [TO BILLIE JOE]: How about you?

BILLIE: Same way.

INT: You liked her from the beginning?

BILLIE: Uh-huh.

INT: Did you fall in love immediately?

BILLIE: Yup.

LOLI: After we started going together, I fixed just about all his meals.

INT: How nice. Did you . . . were you . . . obsessed with him? Were you thinking about him all the time when you first met?

LOLI: Uh-huh.

INT: Did you lose sleep?

LOLI: No [laughs].

INT: You slept okay?

LOLI: Sure.

BILLIE: I did too.

INT: Did your appetite change at all when you met him?

LOLI: Mine didn't. [To Billie] Did yours?

BILLIE: Uh-uh. Ate like I always did.

INT: Was there anything else that attracted you?

BILLIE: The way she does things . . . talking and listenin' to all that stuff, I guess.

In other interviews, older adults indicated that their experiences of infatuation, while enjoyable, lacked the intensity young people experience. Our Internet survey allowed us to consider whether age is generally associated with less intensity. Selecting only the 644 individuals who reported that they were currently in love, we compared those who were over 50 with those who were younger. The results indicated that people over 50 experienced significantly less intensity on nearly all of our 15 questions regarding their love experiences. These are summarized in Table 3.1.

A simple comparison of older and younger adults can be deceptive, however, since older adults tend to have relationships of longer duration. Perhaps the reduced intensity we were seeing was due, not to age, but to the longer duration. To test this possibility, we created four groups among those who said they were currently in love: those under 50 with new relationships; those under 50 with long relationships; those over 50 with new relationships; and those over 50 with long relationships. We compared these groups' mean scores on general measures of romantic intensity. This time the results were quite different. Adults over 50 who were in new relationships (for less than 4 years) reported the highest overall romantic intensity. This group also scored highest on measures of physical and emotional intensity. These results are summarized in Table 3.2.

Table 3.1.  Intensity Measures Among Internet Respondents "Currently in Love"

| Measure of Intensity | Over 50 Mean Score | Under 50 Mean Score |
|---|---|---|
| Emotional intensity | | |
| Think about the person all the time** | 2.30 | 2.52 |
| Emotional highs and lows | 1.88 | 2.12 |
| Wake up thinking about the other* | 1.96 | 2.09 |
| Feelings of personal insecurity** | 1.31 | 1.47 |
| Feelings of personal well-being | 2.56 | 2.63 |
| Physical intensity | | |
| Loss of appetite** | 1.13 | 1.20 |
| Weight loss** | 1.07 | 1.14 |
| Sleep disturbance** | 1.24 | 1.33 |
| Focus on beloved | | |
| Admiration of the other person | 2.74 | 2.80 |
| Sexual attraction to the other person** | 2.67 | 2.80 |
| Desire to take care of the other person** | 2.77 | 2.85 |
| Empathy and understanding for the other person | 2.85 | 2.91 |
| Sense of personal improvement | | |
| Increased energy and vitality** | 2.27 | 2.41 |
| New lease on life** | 2.12 | 2.29 |
| Greater self-confidence* | 2.45 | 2.57 |

*Note.* Question: Please indicate how often you experience each of the following in your current relationship. $1 =$ Not at all; $2 =$ Somewhat; $3 =$ Very much.

*$p < .05$; **$p < .01$.

Table 3.2.  Age, Relationship Duration, and Romantic Intensity ($n = 653$)

| | Under 50 Means | | Over 50 Means | |
|---|---|---|---|---|
| | Short Duration | Long Duration | Short Duration | Long Duration |
| Overall intensity* | 11.96 | 11.21 | **12.27** | 10.73 |
| Physical intensity* | .88 | .46 | **.90** | .34 |
| Emotional intensity* | 3.15 | 2.88 | **3.48** | 2.57 |
| Focus on beloved | 4.98 | 4.98 | 4.93 | 4.97 |
| Sense of personal improvement | 2.98 | 2.88 | 2.90 | 2.78 |

*Indicates a significant effect.

It seems that older adults in new relationships were experiencing romances every bit as intense as younger adults. This was confirmed when I came across 64-year-old Rosie on the verge of her wedding to 72-year-old Hal. A petite, well-dressed woman, she conducted the interview while applying makeup in preparation for a party. Rosie was giddy with emotion. Sometimes tears of joy messed up her mascara. She said she felt just like a teenager as she gushed:

> We went together 3 weeks and 3 days and got engaged. That's his ring. It's about 2 carats. And he's the nicest guy I ever met in my whole life. Now I am deeply in love for the first time. . . . I'm his first really deep love. He was looking for a girl who's kind of country—small and petite and skinny. Not like his wife. She was large. . . . It's something I never experienced in my life. . . . My one girlfriend had her arm around him and I was a little bit jealous. Usually I don't get jealous about men. I usually figure I could go get somebody else. I was a little bit jealous here. I felt like I was losing him and I was a little bit jealous. . . . I'm always hugging and loving him and kissing him. . . . A girlfriend said to me . . . "You can see Rosie that you're in love. You've got a smile on your face. You're bright and happy." I don't have that stress, you know? And my back didn't go out for 4 months!

My hunt for infatuated elders took me to Los Angeles, where I met 82-year-old Ginnie and 76-year-old Saul. Ginnie is a tall, stately woman with a well-groomed head of white hair. She gave me a blow-by-blow account of "the spark" that led to her involvement with Saul. It reminded me of the detailed conversations friends and I shared about our high school crushes where we explored every nuance, recalled every glance, and dissected every phrase:

> Our table's oblong . . . holds six. There was an empty seat to my left and this gentleman, one day, came over and wanted to know if he could sit in that seat. . . . So it went on, and we talked and nothing special. . . . So then he started helping me with my sweater or coat, whatever I had, after our meal. And of course, I had to stand up to put it on, and all the eyes in the dining room were on us. But when we left, he went his way and I went my way. He always had to stop and talk to all of his ladies. . . . Everybody liked him. . . . He'd catch up with me in the breezeway on the way to the elevator, but he'd always call, "Hey, wait for me!" Okay, this went on for about a year. Then one day, I was in the elevator and he was the other one.

Two of us. He was on one side, I was on this side, and we get to his floor, and he says, "I'm gonna kiss you on the cheek." Well, I didn't say nothing. [He kissed her.] The next day . . . same thing happened. In the elevator again, and we're always alone. We always managed that we were alone. So then the third time, I said to myself, "Now, if he says that again, he's gonna kiss me on the lips!" And sure enough, he started to pucker up and I turned like this and that was the spark! From then on we got very lovey dovey. So we just got very close, and then it got so the help, they'd see us coming hand in hand, and they'd start humming or singing, "Here comes the bride," and they tried pushing us getting married, but we decided to just be good friends.

Ginnie's spark took place a year before our interview. She reported that while she did think about Saul first thing each morning, she did not obsess on him. She did not experience an emotional roller coaster, though she did sometimes wonder whether he really cared about her. And she had no sleep or appetite changes. Ginnie may have cause to wonder. When I asked Saul whether he was in love with her, he said, "I like her very much. She's a very funny companion. But to say I'm in love with her. No."

Like Ginnie, 83-year-old Barbara experienced an intense late-life infatuation. Barbara radiates vitality. In conversation, she said she was so deeply in love at the age of 79 that she found herself one sunny California day, skipping down the street with him singing, "I love you! I love you! I love you!" I immediately asked for an interview. It began with her experiences of being madly in love. Barbara said:

Someone brought him to one of the dinners here, in this condo, and I guess I sat at the same table and I was attracted to him and then I assumed he was not only her date, 'cause she spoke about being to his house and all, but that they had a relationship. So all I did was ask him if he played bridge and subsequently we played bridge together for 6 months. And it's interesting because it was a nonromantic interaction. I felt completely comfortable. Because usually as strong and together that people think I am, I get very scared when I'm interested. So he saw the best of me, in a way, and the thing that I really liked about him, aside from being physically attracted to him, was that he had a marvelous sense of humor. Anyhow, he finally called and we went out. I think the first night we went to a party, to the theatre, and then he called again and then I called him.

What happened was, his sense of humor, I was laughing all the time. Sometimes I wet my pants from laughing, so funny.

Barbara thought about him all the time, even though she was seeing him almost every day, and the experience was something of an emotional roller coaster. She lost sleep over him, and when things were going poorly she cried a lot. But Barbara didn't lose her appetite. "It wasn't that bad actually. Later it did get bad but it was like being on the same roller coaster when I was 19. . . . But in some ways I felt more relaxed with him, more able to be myself eventually."

From these and other interviews we concluded that, at least up to age 80, some of us retain the capacity for infatuation. Though older adults report experiencing the cognitive and emotional aspects of the experience, the physical aspects are less common.

## One-Sided Infatuation: Unrequited Love

Unrequited love is one of life's cruelest romantic experiences, from which we seldom emerge unscathed. In the throes of one-sided infatuation, we do and say things so out of character that we do not recognize ourselves. Many of us remember these experiences decades later with pain or embarrassment.

While the most virulent examples of unrequited love typically involve younger adults, one-sided infatuations can happen in the later years. Jim, a 55-year-old man who lived outside the United States, explained in our Internet survey that he was recovering from an unrequited infatuation with a woman 30 years younger than he. He said, "At times it's been difficult, but mostly, I have never taken it too seriously because of the age difference. However, at one point, two friends, both of whom are quite responsible people, encouraged me to disregard the age difference and make my feelings known. I did, but was rebuffed, at least in part because this young woman said her parents would never ever feel truly good about their daughter involving herself with an older man." Jim reported that he was over the rejection, and explained that his recovery "happened pretty quickly, for the most part. Although I certainly did want to spend as much time as possible with this young woman, I was undeniably relieved too, when she said no. Despite what my friends had said, I felt quite clear that the age difference was too much. At the time, for her to be 23 and me to be 54 might be acceptable, but in 10 years' time, she would be 33 and I would have been 64. And what about in 20 years' time? No. So some mature part of me was able to let go pretty easily. I still spend time with this young woman as a friend, and enjoy it."

An older adult's approach to love is informed by the lessons of unrequited love experienced at younger ages. Some have learned to approach love with courage and vigor, secure that their self-esteem can weather rejection. For others the lesson is more damaging or the rejection more painful. These individuals may shrink from any hint of infatuation, nursing their wounds in splendid isolation. In-depth consideration of just what happens in unrequited love will illustrate why the experience has such lasting ramifications.

## The Course of Unrequited Love

In its most recognized form, unrequited love happens when a person becomes infatuated with someone who does not share his or her interest.[20] In this one-sided infatuation the lover experiences the ecstasy and misery of infatuation, and the beloved (sometimes called the rejecter) does not.

Psychologists Roy Baumeister and Sara Wotman asked college students to write stories about their experiences with unrequited love, collecting and analyzing over 200 tales.[21] Their results suggest that both lover and beloved suffer during one-sided infatuation.

The would-be lover has more at stake than the beloved. He or she may suffer the agony of rejection but, on the other hand, if the love is returned, a life of bliss lies at the end of the rainbow. So at least in the beginning, the lover faces a heady gamble. The challenge is to attract the beloved's attention and affection, and nothing less than self-confidence and self-esteem are at stake. Sooner or later comes the denouement: either a confrontation in which lover confesses and beloved rejects, or a slow fade through which the lover incorporates the realization that the beloved does not and will not share the affection. In either case, the lover is left with a sad message of possibilities lost and personal inadequacies.

The role of the beloved is less clear and probably less exciting. Some have called it scriptless, arguing that we know how to behave when we are infatuated, but there are no clear rules on how to break someone's heart. The target of unwanted affections has nothing to gain, as this role offers only losing possibilities. No one likes to hurt another person, and if the couple has shared a platonic friendship, the beloved faces the prospect of losing a valuable relationship. Facing the challenge of rejecting affection, the beloved person usually tries to do it in a way that causes as little pain as possible, using phrases like, "I just don't feel the same way" or "You and I are not compatible." Of course, these phrases disguise more hurtful feelings, like "I wish you would leave me alone!" or "I find you physically repulsive!" The attempt to be kind often results in confusion, with the lover asking, "Why?" or arguing vigorously.

We see these themes—obsession, unattractiveness, and failure to communicate—when one-sided infatuation is memorialized in literature and drama. In a classic nineteenth-century French play, the great swordsman and poet Cyrano de Bergerac pines in secret for his lovely cousin Roxane. Possessed of an extremely long nose, Cyrano cannot imagine a woman finding him attractive. Eventually he finds some relief, writing love letters on behalf of the inarticulate (but extremely handsome) Christian. The play ends tragically, to leave us wishing Cyrano had found the courage to tell Roxane of his love. The more ridiculous side of unrequited love is beautifully described in Cervantes's seventeenth-century novel *Don Quixote*. Victor Hugo presented a feminine experience in *Les Miserables*, in which little Eponine falls hopelessly and fatally in love with the unattainable Marius.

Given its exquisite pain, we may wonder why people would ever subject themselves to unrequited love. Even if we assume that this behavior is inexplicable on an individual level, we must wonder what sort of perverse chemistry is at work on the species. The "love economists" (also known as equity theorists) have offered an explanation.[22] These theorists suggest that in the marriage market, we strive to get a partner with the best possible array of assets and resources. Marriageable men and women are positioned on a hierarchy of attractiveness, with their relative value based on a composite of physical beauty and other assets such as wealth, charm, or intelligence. The ultimate result of multiple interactions in this market is couples who are roughly equal on the attractiveness scale. In one-sided infatuation, the would-be lover is, as Roy Baumeister and Sara Wotman put it, "falling upward," in love with someone ranked higher in attractiveness. In Jim's case, falling upward may have meant falling in love with someone younger and (in our youth-oriented culture) more attractive. In other cases, it might mean falling for someone with better looks or higher status.

Unrequited love leaves the lover vulnerable to exploitation. Regardless of gender, a would-be lover who seeks romance and finds only sex is likely to feel violated and exploited. The same might apply to an older woman who married the man of her dreams only to find that he was looking for a housekeeper and cook; or to an infatuated man whose beloved takes his money and fails to return his affections. So in a sense, rejecters who tell it like it is are displaying integrity, respect, and perhaps restraint when they forgo the opportunity to take advantage of the besotted.

## The Lover's Misery

From the lover's perspective, one-sided infatuation can be an intense roller coaster. Beginning with dawning awareness of romantic and sexual attraction, it goes on to demand careful attention to every word and gesture made by the beloved. In times of uncertainty, some obsessively tug petals off daisies to unravel the mystery. Carefully arranged chance meetings provide the beloved with opportunities to notice the gasping lover's wonderful attributes. Frustrated with the failure of these tactics, the lover may confess, upsetting the apple cart and laying himself or herself open to rejection. "I like you, but ... " or "I care for you, but ... " Then comes self-reproach, bitter agony, and embarrassment.

In unrequited love, the boundaries between normal and pathological blur. Would-be lovers experience obsession, fantasy, and emotional intensity well beyond that of daily life. They do things that are out of character, sometimes jeopardizing jobs, schooling, and even their health. At times they imagine the object of their affections returns that affection. At other times they descend to the pits of despair anticipating rejection. The fundamental difference between those for whom unrequited love is an illness and the rest of the population is that healthy adults move on. They may have scars, and they may have insights, but they do move on.

## Moving On and Looking Back

It is particularly important for older adults to understand their experiences with unrequited love. Studies find that lovers and rejecters differ in their recollections of the events.[23] It seems that rejecters recall the experience with greater negativity than the lovers. In Baumeister's seminal study, some would-be lovers remembered the experience fondly, despite the agony and embarrassment they experienced at the time. On the other hand, the rejecters had nothing positive to say about the experience. They reported feeling guilty that they had hurt the other person through their rejection, and sometimes feeling angry at the other person for forcing them into the situation.

Our Internet survey focused only on would-be lovers. In fact, they displayed considerable resilience. The vast majority (87%) who had experienced unrequited love reported that they were "over it" at the time they completed the survey. We asked what it took for them to get over it, and those results are summarized in Table 3.3.

Most offered a clear formula for recovery: "allow time to pass" or "find someone else." One 53-year-old man from Virginia was typical in his

Table 3.3.　What It Took to Get Over It

| Response | Men (n = 97) (%) | Women (n = 388) (%) | Total (n = 485) (%) |
|---|---|---|---|
| Time | 61 | 40 | 44 |
| Another lover | 23 | 24 | 22 |
| Realization/perspective/ understanding | 9 | 21 | 18 |
| Maturity/personal growth | 8 | 14 | 13 |
| Mental discipline, focus, resolve | 9 | 4 | 5 |
| Distance and unavailability | 5 | 5 | 5 |
| Friends | 1 | 2 | 2 |
| Talking it out with the person | 2 | 2 | 2 |
| Therapy | 1 | 2 | 2 |
| Self-indulgence | 2 | 1 | 1 |
| Prayer/God's help/Jesus | 1 | 2 | 1 |

response: "time, friends, and prayer." Similarly, a 52-year-old woman from Hawaii attributed her recovery to "time and a new man." A 52-year-old African American woman from Mississippi credited her recovery to "another meaningful relationship." Another staunch advocate of new love, a 52-year-old Latina from New Mexico, explained, "The best thing for a broken heart is a new love. I just found another person that could love me."

Understanding and maturity were also highly recommended, with 18% of the sample attributing their recovery to a new perspective, realization, or understanding, and another 13% explaining that maturity and personal growth were key. Women were somewhat more likely than men to mention these factors. A woman from Missouri who described herself as "single and celibate" explained: "I grew up. I learned to love myself. I realized that I'm addictive to being loved so I have avoided getting into relationships with men because I don't think I handle them well. Most significantly, being 57, overweight, and by normative standards not appealing anymore, it's pretty easy to avoid 'love' entanglements and I find my life is of a much higher quality now." A woman from New York who reported that she had just started a new romantic relationship said she got over her one-sided passion by "deciding to get on with my life. When you're looking 60 in the face, life's way, way too short to 'f' around with negative feelings." Finally, a 58-year-old who wished she were in a relationship explained, "Getting older and more mature takes care of this rather nicely."

Sometimes recovery depended on distance or the person becoming un-available. As an 86-year-old woman from Texas explained, "He married someone else and that did it for me immediately. My feelings for him at that time were over and done with . . . and I went on with my life and am so thankful now that I didn't marry him although one doesn't ever forget their first love." Similarly, a 62-year-old man explained that he got over it when "she got married to someone else after I asked her to marry me three times over 4 years."

### Does Unrequited Love Have a Purpose?

Is it really "better to have loved in vain than never to have loved at all"? As we have seen, practically no one seriously describes unrequited love as a pleasant experience. A mountain of human suffering has been laid at the feet of this phenomenon. Viktor Frankl suggests that humans cope best with suffering when we can find some meaning in the experience.[24] With this in mind, we can look at unrequited love from several perspectives.

From the marriage market perspective, the species benefits when each of us mates with the most attractive partner we can find. In cases of falling upwards, the lover simply overreaches—a small mistake in support of a generally adaptive evolutionary principle.

From an existential perspective, the intoxication of infatuation may dis-tract us from the reality of our situation. Some may use the fantasy of un-consummated love to anesthetize themselves from the tensions and bore-dom of everyday life.

From a developmental perspective, unrequited love helps us learn what we are capable of. As we have seen, one-sided infatuation leads us to behave in ways that are out of character. A man who is ordinarily shy is compelled to aggressively promote himself before the object of his affections. A con-servative woman throws caution to the wind as she pursues opportunities to bask in the presence of her beloved. Is it possible that this outside-the-box behavior is good for us? Perhaps the experience of unrequited love expands our possibilities and teaches us that we are capable of things we never imagined. Later we may be chagrined by our lack of restraint, but in the process we have expanded our possibilities.

A few (19) of the people in our Internet survey described unrequited love as an experience in which they either learned or realized something. These lessons varied. For most, the experience offered insight into the nature of relationships. Tamara, age 54, from New Hampshire, saw it as a lesson in life's priorities: "It is a good lesson that life is not fair. But it was also a good building block. A person does not always get what he or she wants and life goes on. There are other things that merit more attention and grief."

Psychologists Baumeister and Wotman specifically asked people whether they were changed by their experiences of unrequited love. Some of their young would-be lovers reported becoming more cautious and slower to enter into new romantic involvements. Some mentioned they would be more careful about where they placed their trust. Others reported lessons learned that might help them in future relationships. For example, one woman who had experienced sexual exploitation in her unrequited love experience said that she "was much more perceptive in seeing the signals. I have not gotten to the point of paranoia or total mistrust of guys—in fact I think I'm just better at reading people and what they want. I can use all my experiences to learn. Believe me, it helps."[25]


## Conclusion

Reflections on the intensity of infatuation have inspired philosophers and psychologists. Schopenhauer sought to explain the power of infatuation with reference to an all-encompassing World-Will. Freud saw it as a life-giving libidinal energy. Jung saw it as a pent-up need for spiritual ecstasy. We saw a hint of that intensity in the experiences reported by Ginnie and Barbara.

Paradoxically, this magical, intense, biologically destined experience has a bad reputation. Psychologists, self-help professionals, and many others see it as an inferior cousin to "true love."[26] As we all know, infatuation can be destructive, destroying marriages and lives.

On the other hand, infatuation's very intensity makes it a powerful catalyst for personal growth. Through careful reflection, the besotted lover can find a rationale and even meaning in the experience. Infatuation can teach us about ourselves—what we yearn for and what we assume to be good. Though we cannot always control the waves of emotion that infatuation sends our way, we can certainly control our behavior. We can channel infatuation into a tool for personal insight, not as the basis for organizing our love lives. We can harness the energy and joy of infatuation to create pleasant memories and experiences that need not threaten our commitments.

Infatuation is nature's great motivator. It hurls people of all ages in pursuit of connection. In later life, less powerful motivators like loneliness, desire, or social convention send some in pursuit of romance. In the next chapter, we consider the process of looking for love.

**Try This**

1. Infatuation's Trajectory: Take some quiet, private time to consider the infatuations you have experienced. You may want to make a list. With a sense of compassion for yourself and others, consider the following questions for each one:

    a. What was going on in my life at the time the infatuation began? Was I in the midst of an important transition? Was I stressed, anxious, or bored? Most infatuations feel like a bolt out of the blue, but in retrospect we sometimes find that they served a need we had at the time.

    b. What did I see in this person? This may not be reality based. What did you imagine about the person that sustained the infatuation? Did you fantasize about your life together? What was that like?

    c. How long did this infatuation last? When did it end? How was life different without the infatuation? Did you miss it?

Once you have developed a chronology of infatuations, look for themes and similarities. Can you identify your triggers? What function has infatuation played in your life? This is not a time for judgment, but for reflection and learning.

2. The Target of Unrequited Love: If we think about it, most of us can remember a time when we were the object of unwanted affection. In this role, we may have inadvertently hurt our would-be lovers. Ask yourself these questions about your experience:

    • Did the other person's affection cause me to feel differently about myself?

    • Did I feel flattered? Here was a person who found me attractive and fascinating.

    • Did I bask in the attention? Or did I dismiss the opinion of someone I found unattractive?

Now, write a letter to that person. (It might not be a good idea to send it.) Do you feel a need to apologize? Are you angry at him or her? Do you wish you had done anything differently? Are you grateful for any aspect of the experience? Is there anything else you would like to say? Dispose of the letter in a safe and respectful way. You might keep it in your private journal, bury it, or burn it. In the process, let go of the experience of being a rejecter and allow yourself to take something positive away from the experience of being the object of affection.


## Suggested Reading

Baumeister, R. F., & Wotman, S. R. (1992). *Breaking hearts: The two sides of unrequited love.* New York: Guilford. This highly readable academic book reports on a study in which college students wrote about their experiences, both as would-be lovers and as rejecters. The students' stories are fascinating, and the authors do a great job of pulling out broad themes and linking them to psychological theories.

Jankowiak, W. (Ed.). (1995). *Romantic passion: A universal experience?* New York: Columbia University Press. Despite its heavy academic tone, this book is utterly fascinating. It offers a collection of anthropological studies of how passion manifests itself in diverse cultural contexts, as well as some mind-bending theory and research chapters.

Lowndes, L. (1995). *How to make anyone fall in love with you.* Chicago: Contemporary Books. Some people find this book massively irritating. Based on an exceedingly manipulative model, it promises "85 techniques based on scientific studies" to make absolutely anyone fall in love with you. Women are deemed "huntresses" and men "hunters," all out to generate as much infatuation as possible. Still, it is a fun read, and does offer some good pointers.

Rostand, E. (1897). *Cyrano de Bergerac.* Anyone in the throes of unrequited love will enjoy this classic French tragedy. Or, for a good cry, rent the movie. Speaking of movies, *Loves Me, Loves Me Not* offers an intriguing look at erotomania from the perspective of the deluded lover.

Taken when she was looking for love. She found it!

# 4

## Looking for Love

*Candy is a tall, energetic 62-year-old, retired from her job and deeply involved with gay and lesbian organizations in her community. For the first time in her life, she is actively looking for a balanced, "50–50" relationship. "I would love to be in love. Have dinner with somebody, go to a show—I have an idea that if love comes again, which I pray that it will, it's going to be much more low key." Her early love experiences were anything but low key.*

*At 16, Candy experienced her first grand passion. "The first person I had a mad crush on was a fellow in high school. . . . I was madly attracted to him and then one day he persuaded me at school to forge a note purportedly from my mother to give to my homeroom teacher and we walked from the high school to his family's home, which was not far, and he, uh, we attempted intercourse but I was not ready at all and it was god-awful. I mean it was very painful and it was real bad. And after that he stopped being interested in me. And I was very hurt and I realized what had happened, which is a story, this is well known. I am sure that he was really only interested in whatever that was. And before that act of intercourse ended the relationship, I was really really infatuated and I just thought he was very glamorous and very attractive and very sexy. I was unprepared. I mean, I was 16. . . . For me to discover in retrospect how really uninterested he was in me as a long-term even dating partner was certainly the cause of a low. And I think I started drinking seriously that summer."*

*A couple years later, Candy found another love. "Again," she said, "it was a huge infatuation. I had just graduated from high school and I fell in love with this guy . . . that summer romance was grounded in lust and alcohol. And I was drunk the night I conceived that child and he disappeared at the end of the summer. There was a rumor that he had impregnated another girl in the valley. I don't know if that's true, but anyway, he did me." Candy left town to stay with relatives. She gave her baby girl up for adoption and returned to community college spinning tales about the baby and her husband away in the Navy.*

*Next Candy married "an alcoholic, surprise surprise. And he was a very gifted artistic man—a play writer and novelist and songwriter. And he had many many gifts and he was an alcoholic. My husband and I thought of ourselves as Dashiell Hammett and Lillian Hellman. Because both of us were brainy people, we said, 'Work hard, play hard.'"*

*Ten years into what she describes as a codependent marriage, Candy fell in love with a woman—one who was "very emotionally damaged by her own upbringing." Though she has no memory of the event, Candy evidently came out to her husband. "I'm a blackout drinker. That means I don't remember things I do when I'm drinking and apparently at some point near the end of our not-so-successful marriage I told him that the reason I couldn't love him was that I was a lesbian. . . . He says that is what I said."*

*For 2 years Candy was "just madly in love with this woman, but I wasn't telling anybody." In the early 1980s she came out at work, a process she describes as "terrifying. You can tell if somebody is glad to see you and you can tell if they're not, and I would watch people turn off and go around the room to avoid me. So that was hard. It was painful." The relationship ended in disillusionment, and Candy joined Alcoholics Anonymous.*

*Now that she is confident in her ability to remain sober, Candy is looking—and longing—for love. "I would be much happier if I had a lover. I've been talking about having a fuck buddy but I would much rather love the person that I'm with—that I have sex with. I, uh, I would like to try having an unequivocal relationship with somebody—in every respect. And I have never had one, but I would like one. Because I love eating with somebody. I love physical contact. I love just, you know, driving along and sharing something. Looking at a beautiful scene. Many many times I've wished that I could share something with somebody I cared about—right there next to me."*

*Candy has told family and friends of her interest in finding a romantic partner, and has had several dates with people they recommended. She has also met people through her community activities. She has not tried the Internet or personal advertising, and does not expect to.*

*She remains hopeful, if not optimistic, about her chances. "I do believe that a healthy person can love. I think I'm in a state of loving relation to a lot of people at this point in my life and it's very helpful to know that." But the process is daunting for several reasons. At 64, Candy is afraid she does not have much time to find a partner. She worries that her expectations are too high. "I want to find somebody who's interested in the life of the mind. And it's not easy to do. All the women I've met in town here are lovely and they're just delightful and they're not. That's one reason I'm in a hurry. See, that worries me a little because Ms. Right may never come along and it might be because of my failure to see the qualities that I could value and love in somebody that doesn't fit my requirements. This does worry me." She also struggles with insecurities. "I do struggle with self-hatred and self-esteem issues. But—and I think that's one of the things that keeps me from being present and open to the possibility of love."*

In late life Candy has worked through many of the problems that complicated her youth. She did not speak of regrets but of lessons learned, and, in her 60s, she is poised for an intimate relationship. Filled with hope, Candy is looking for love—maybe for the love of her life. In this respect, Candy is like many older adults.

In this chapter we begin with a look at the supply of potentially available older adults in the United States before turning to a theme that colors the pursuit of love: objectification, treating people as means rather than ends. With that done, we consider the experience itself, examining older adults' experiences in the dating scene and on the Internet and touching on the "over 50s personals." The chapter closes by considering an alternative to looking for love: letting love find you.

## The Supply Side

As of the 2000 Census, the U.S. population included 31 million adults over age 50 who reported that they were single, widowed, divorced, or separated. Among them, over 5 million have never married at all. While some of these may be romantically involved, this gives a rough indication of the size of the potentially available population.

As we grow older, the number of available partners goes down, as does the number of men. This is illustrated in Table 4.1. Among those aged 50 to 54, there is less than one man (.85 of a man) for every woman. By the time we reach the 85 and older group, there are four women for every available man.[1] But even in this rarefied age group, there are over half a million

Table 4.1.   Composition of the Available 50-Plus Population

| | Widowed | Divorced | Separated | Never Married | Total | Male/Female Ratio |
|---|---|---|---|---|---|---|
| **Men** | | | | | | |
| 50–54 | 112 | 1,582 | 278 | 1,064 | 3,036 | .85 |
| 55–64 | 323 | 2,005 | 266 | 1,030 | 3,624 | .62 |
| 65–74 | 621 | 867 | 151 | 350 | 1,989 | .45 |
| 75–84 | 936 | 325 | 46 | 177 | 1,484 | .31 |
| 85+ | 429 | 43 | 4 | 46 | 522 | .24 |
| **Women** | | | | | | |
| 50–54 | 421 | 1,901 | 323 | 947 | 3,592 | |
| 55–64 | 1,540 | 2,868 | 387 | 1,041 | 5,836 | |
| 65–74 | 2,631 | 1,235 | 142 | 391 | 4,399 | |
| 75–84 | 3,989 | 531 | 56 | 247 | 4,823 | |
| 85+ | 1,990 | 87 | 13 | 83 | 2,173 | |
| **Total** | 12,992 | 11,444 | 1,666 | 5,376 | 31,478 | |

*Note.* Figures represent 1,000 in 2006 population.

*Source.* U.S. Census Bureau (2007). Table A1. Marital status of people 15 years and over, by age, sex, personal earnings, race, and hispanic origin. *America's families and living arrangements: 2006.* Retrieved March 29, 2007, from http://www.census.gov/population/socdemo/hh-fam/cps2006/taba1-all.xls

potentially available men. Finding them is the challenge, and those setting out in pursuit of love often do so with qualms.

When I talk about love with single women over 50, one of the first questions I get is, "Where is it? Where can I find this late-life romance that you say can be so fulfilling?" I usually respond, "Where have you looked?" Most people are reluctant to actively go out and look for love. Whether widowed, jaded, or feeling adventurous, most of us find that looking for love in later life poses a unique set of challenges. The process is so daunting that many choose not to pursue it, possibly due to an understandable reluctance to be objectified.

## Love and Objectification

Looking for love puts us in a paradoxical position. As Irving Singer explained, appraisal and love are distinct processes.[2] Appraisal seeks to determine the objective value of a person or a thing through careful examination and comparative analysis. When we appraise a house, we list its attributes, compare it to others in the neighborhood, and assign a value. But appraisal is antithetical to love, which confers value quite apart from the person's "objective" characteristics. True love, we are told, is unconditional. It sees value in a person regardless of characteristics. When we say, "I want to be loved for who I am, not what I am," we acknowledge this paradox.

Some find objectification offensive and dehumanizing. Buber might describe it as an "I-it" relationship, in which the other is seen, not as an end in himself or herself, but as a means or an instrument for meeting personal needs.[3] Buber argues that true love requires an "I-thou" relationship, in which the other is not appraised or analyzed as a system of parts but is accepted as a whole person. Of course, as Buber and others have observed, I-it relationships can become I-thou relationships. Couples can move from objectification to love and back again.

Like Candy, many older adults find that looking for love evokes a market mentality that taps into their deepest insecurities. Those who find themselves single in late life are not accustomed to the appraisal process, having last been available decades ago. Most have forgotten how to play the game, and some find objectification particularly uncomfortable. Age is a complicating factor, not only because of the challenges of older bodies and larger families, but also because everywhere we look we receive messages telling us that "old" is unattractive. Who wants to enter into a market with a built-in disadvantage? The people in our study adopted two basic strategies: "Go out and look for it" and "Let love find you."

## Looking for Love

When my great-grandmother died, she left her husband on a ranch in Nebraska with four children and hundreds of cows to take care of. He promptly sent for a mail-order bride, who raised his children and lived with him until his death. The mail-order bride business is an early example of commercial matchmaking. Today, older adults actively seeking partners are more likely to turn to the dating scene, the Internet, or newspaper advertising.

### The Dating Scene

A visitor at any senior center dance would probably conclude that the marriage market of later life is alive and well. Couples meet, pair off, and separate at these weekly events. Several of the people we interviewed for this study were actively dating people met at these dances, where men were judged as much for their footwork as their character. Of course, dating in the later part of life is not limited to senior centers. The people we talked to met potential partners through organizations and churches as well as family and friends. For example, 72-year-old Alicia had met several people since her husband's death. She described her experiences:

> He asked me if I was still married, and I said, "Oh, I'm a widow now." He's got the cutest blue eyes. [Both laugh.] I asked him, "Where did you get the blue eyes?" He's Mexican, and he said, "The milkman," just being funny. His dad had blue eyes. And I met another man . . . the first one I met after my husband died. . . . He had been dead about 4 months, and I went to a class at church, and I met this man. He was 80 years old then, but so . . . I don't know . . . just real easygoing, real young looking, you know, but he wanted to get married right away, and I was not about to get married 4 months after my husband died, and so this other woman wanted him, I could tell. And he ended up marrying her. . . . And then I met this other one. He's from Puerto Rico and he is really close to his family. Sometimes, he tells me he's gonna be here at a certain time, and his family is wanting to do something, and he'll be hours late, you know, and it's really hard to get used to somebody . . . with a family.

The dating scene can be complicated. Barbara, age 83, described a recent dating adventure in glorious detail. Barbara is cautious when dating because she has had unpleasant experiences with men who are either rejecting or mean.

> And a man sat next to me. I puzzled over would I like to go out with him or not, anyhow, he made a few remarks that I couldn't quite figure out. The next day he calls me up and he says, would you meet me for a drink at 3:00? I'll come in and I'll meet you there. So I go and I'm really dressed up too and I'm thinking, look for the red flags, don't just jump. So the first red flag, he says to me, wait for three-quarters of an hour and the drinks are half price. On the first date! . . . Anyhow, we're talking and meanwhile he's stroking my arm, putting his arm around my shoulders. He's stroking my back, but on the first date. I mean, give me some air. . . . He asked me for Friday, Saturday, and Sunday. And I said, you're going too fast. I'm not free till Saturday. . . . And he says well, where should we go now? He says, you know, I've never seen your cat. So I said, well, you haven't seen my cat, you haven't met my boarder, 'cause I have a student. He says, I just meant what's your cat's name? As he covers up.

Barbara was planning to give Match.com a try. She had an active dating life, but thought the Internet might speed the process. She thought she might list herself as a 70-year-old, since 80-something men were really too old for her.

## Internet Dating

Most of us know someone who has met a partner over the Internet. Participants begin by developing their profiles and move on to itemize what they are seeking in a love partner. Some sites allow specification by gender, age, race, physical build, restaurant preferences, and religious affiliation and invite customers to specify whether they want a casual relationship or are in serious pursuit of matrimony.

### Alice's story

At 68, Alice is looking for a casual relationship. She waited for 13 years after her husband of 32 years (and five children) abandoned her for a younger woman. Alice explained her reluctance to enter the dating scene, saying, "I felt that I really needed to feel really good about myself." Though ready for male companionship, Alice is not interested in marriage. She wants to stay home and be single and enjoy her female friends. "If I meet somebody it is frosting on the cake. And I tell these guys that and they just don't get it. . . . Because they're used to . . . my generation of men want to take care of women. And they expect women to want to be taken care of. And so when I tell them that, I've had one guy say, 'I really don't understand that. Explain that to me. Can you explain it to me so that I understand?'" Alice doesn't think she can explain it. She was raised to be dependent on a man, but enjoys her independence and treasures her newfound happiness. She does have some specifications: "I'm not interested in someone who's been married three or four times. And I'm not interested in someone who's going to tell me all about his past relationships, you know."

She sees the Internet as a good way to meet new men. "I haven't had a lot of opportunity to meet men really. And so it's just been this year that I've actually done this, gone online. And that's just been a really interesting experience. But I had to feel ready to do it." Alice tried a couple of Websites before settling on Match.com. "I did a couple of others. I did perfect match and they match you up and I had one person. And he was really old and uninteresting. The Match.com has been, I had like, five e-mails the first day. . . . They wink—they can either wink at you or send you an e-mail."

Like many other people who use the Internet, Alice has relation-ships with men she has never met in person. "I've got one fella that I've been e-mailing for 4 months. So, we've got a really nice e-mail relationship." He wants her to move to Colorado. She does not want to. Alice has not met him in person, but they have exchanged photos of themselves and their grandchildren. "And we get along really well. We have a lot in common, . . . and we both like a lot of the same kinds of things, and we will meet sometime, but I think he's just as capable of coming up here as I am of running down there. . . . Then I've got another one yesterday and he's in Arizona." He wants her to come to Arizona for a meeting.

She has also had quite a few "actual" dates. "On the first date I had, the guy was from Idaho. He's a widower of 20 years. He's younger than I and um, and the only [thing] he kept saying is, 'I can't believe I'm dating somebody who's older than I am.' And I looked probably 20 years younger than he. . . . He was really looking for a wife. You know, and I'm not really looking for a husband. If I meet somebody I'll know. . . . But I'm too early in the process." She met another widower who couldn't stop talking about his wife's illness and death, even though she had been gone for 11 years. Then, "the third guy had been married twice and had a significant relationship for 7 years he [had] just gotten out of. Interest-ingly enough, I knew his first wife." She said that dinner was "all about him." In fact, so many of her dates left her literally speechless that Alice thought about going into business. "So, then I had to think of strategies, because those kinds of things are going to happen. So, I decided I wanted to open a school for men, middle-aged men [to teach them how to listen to women]. They don't have anyone to tell them how to behave socially." Alice said the hard thing about her dates was letting them know she did not want to go out with them again. These days, she just tells them the truth.

Alice's least enjoyable date was a man who made a pass, then told her how long it had been since he had had sex. She was not interested. "I just thought, you know, I don't need that. Which I think is a difference between being my age and being younger. . . . I feel like I have more options. You know, that if I don't want to go out with someone, I don't have to go out with them. . . . Whereas when you're younger I think you feel you might miss an opportunity." Overall, Alice views Internet dating favorably. She is cautious about when and where she meets people, and the Internet helps her meet some interesting male companions. "The nice thing about most of the people I've gone out with is that they're well educated and they've traveled a lot. . . . So, they have interesting stories to tell."

Once she met a man she enjoyed. "He was real easy to talk to. And um, he was athletic. He rides a bike and I ride bikes, and um, he was in very good shape; and he volunteers and I volunteer. So, he's kind of a giving person. . . . He talks about me, asks me about myself and my children. He doesn't have any children. . . . He was very gentlemanly. . . . And we both said that we'd like to see each other again, but I haven't heard from him." She is not sure she wants to call him. "Trust is a big issue."

Like Alice, millions of older adults are using the Internet in their search for romantic partners. So many, in fact, that dating Websites like Perfectmatch .com, eHarmony.com, and Match.com all market to the senior population, as do less well-known sites like ThirdAge.com, Boomerpeoplemeet.com, and SilverSingles.com. Of course, these Websites are commercial enterprises, and most charge membership fees. Their offerings range from the simple chance to meet someone to a "scientifically calibrated" matching system designed to ensure compatibility.[4]

Since little has been written on seniors' experiences with Internet dating, I decided to visit one of the sites myself. I went to a site that advertised free networking for people over 50, and got stuck on "describe your appearance." Was I "below average," "about average," or "good looking"? Imagining myself in search of a partner, I was sorely tempted to choose the category most likely to attract interest. I knew the right answer was "good looking." But the Website cautioned me to be honest. I studied my face in the mirror. It went from "good looking" to "below average" in 2 minutes. I gave up, thinking it was time look into Botox.

The main argument in favor of Internet dating is that it is efficient. Even in late life we are busy, and who has the time to filter through all the duds our family and friends send our way? Plus, the Internet can expose us to a much bigger market. We may discover people thousands of miles away whom we would never have met through traditional means. Besides, the Internet is great for insomniacs, who can cruise the listings at 3 A.M. in their pajamas. Most people recognize the disadvantages—the risk that people lie in their profiles, and the safety concerns.

At the same time, Internet dating (perhaps more blatantly than other approaches) forces participants to objectify themselves—a process that can be dehumanizing, not to mention demoralizing. Beyond objectification, these Websites create the illusion of disposability. They give the impression that there are hundreds of people out there who meet our specifications. This can create a mind-set that mitigates against the commitments and compromises necessary for long-term intimacy.

## The Over-50s Personals

Internet dating seems to have replaced personal advertisements, just as news Websites seem to be replacing newspapers. None of the respondents to our study mentioned using the personals when looking for love, although these ads do afford an interesting glimpse into the way older adults in search of love "market" themselves.

A communications scholar in London named Justine Coupland has studied older adults' experiences with personal ads.[5] She compared what she called strategic self-presentation in advertisements placed in personal sections of British newspapers by people who were over 50 with those placed by younger adults. Her results revealed an emphasis on the positive that, she maintains, is typical of personal advertisements. But in the case of older adults, that emphasis involved age denial, in which the advertiser claims youthful attributes. As Coupland reported, "This strategy, variously realized, is to claim that although the person is older, he or she is not 'fully' or 'normatively' so."[6] As an example, Coupland cited an ad placed by a woman who described herself thus: "UNBELIEVABLY YOUTHFUL, widow, 65+, intelligent, well-traveled, frustrated by local geriatrics, reluctant to miss the good things in life, WLTM [would like to meet] similar man." Coupland also reported that ads placed by older adults revealed less ambitious and less sexual goals than those placed by the young. Seniors are more likely to express interest in companionship than passion.

The findings of her research illuminate one way older adults experience the process of objectification. Whether on the Internet or in personal advertisements, older adults' presentation of self points to internalized ageism. To be desirable in these market settings, we distance ourselves from the attributes of our age. Can you imagine placing an advertisement that reads, "Slightly achy widow, 65+, enjoying the wisdom and quiet comforts of age, seeking a sex slave to share her bed"? Such an ad would violate two important norms of successful self-presentation: (1) deny age attributes; and (2) avoid sexual references that may seem inappropriate in someone of that age. In essence, advertisements demand that we both deny and act our age at the same time.

All of this is not to imply that personal ads and dating Websites do not meet the needs of older adults. Their very proliferation suggests that they can be an effective tool for those who are actively looking for love. Many seniors find companionship and entertainment through them, and undoubtedly some find romantic fulfillment as well.

## Letting Love Find You

Many older people are reluctant to go out and look for love, saying that it feels desperate and a little demeaning. Some are content to let love find them—or not. That does not mean they sit at home quietly waiting for someone to ring the doorbell. Either they do not experience great yearning for romance, or they control their longing through self-discipline and self-awareness. In addition, people who report that love finds them usually have active social lives and spend their leisure time with others who share their interests; they do not bury themselves in work or family concerns, or spend their evenings glued to a television. Sandrine is an excellent example.

### Sandrine's Story

Sandrine and I go for long walks where we discuss life, work, and love while huffing and puffing up and down the hills. Widowed in her mid-50s, for years Sandrine spoke of her deceased husband in the present tense: "Peter loves to go to the cinema" or "He complains when I cook spicy food." From time to time she spoke of love and her dreams for the future. Sandrine's plans focused on travel and grandchildren. She said she was "not at all interested in a new relationship." Not at all interested she remained, until she met Michael at a party. He was involved with someone else, but the chemistry between him and Sandrine was powerful enough to irritate his date. Still, it took months before their first date. Shortly afterward they were in love, and he had moved into her home. It seems love snuck up on my friend, offering the perfect partner at the perfect time.

Sandrine's experience is a great lesson for those hoping love will find them. She is living proof of the possibility, and her actions can serve as a guide. First, she did her grief work. She did not try to rush this process, even though it took several years. Second, she took great care of herself. She exercised regularly, had massages and facials on schedule, ate fresh healthy food, and got plenty of sleep. Third, she kept up her social life. She accepted and issued invitations and introduced herself to people she had not met. Finally, though she did not need to, she remained engaged in her profession, working part time for the structure and interest it provided. Sandrine loved herself and so she was ready when love found her.

## Conclusion

Looking for love is a delicate dance of illusion and reality. Illusion motivates us to get out there and take risks. Then reality intrudes. The romantic marketplace forces us to look at ourselves as commodities. We do the same to others, generating a list of the features we desire in a romantic partner and ticking off the pluses and minuses of each candidate. The process may be rational and it may even be efficient. But it can be cruel. As we have seen in this chapter, it is not the only way to find a romantic partner. Many prefer to skip the search and let love find us when it will. And, in many cases, it will.

The romantic ideal of long-term commitment often spurs the pursuit of romance. Some say, "I am looking for my soul mate!" Others are more prosaic: "My goal is marriage." The following chapters turn to long-term romances to examine the illusions and realities that mark this highly desired experience and the social forces that sustain it.

## Try This

1. Presentation of Self: Write your own personal ad. Whether or not you are looking for love, you might find it interesting to experiment with the process of objectification. What key assets would you emphasize if you were looking for a romantic partner? Would honesty require that some liabilities be disclosed? How do your pluses and minuses stack up? It might be fun to do this with a partner.

2. Noticing Love: Yearning and longing can be a problem for people who are looking for love, creating impatience and pressure that foster self-deception. If you are experiencing yearning—and many people do—try to get it under control. First, acknowledge the longing. Second, allow yourself to receive love when it is offered. Regardless of the source, open yourself to this awareness. You may receive love from a pet, a colleague, an adult child or grandchild, or a friend. Maybe a stranger smiles at you and gives you a compliment. Consider all of these love received. Just by noticing, you will increase your awareness of incoming love. This should ease the pressure a bit. Then consider the possibility that the longing is based, not on what you want in the future, but on nostalgia for something in the past. If you are depressed or unhappy, it will increase the longing. So—love yourself, and do what you can to increase your contentment.

## Suggested Reading

Goldman, C. (2006). *Late life love: Romance and new relationships in later years*. Minneapolis: Fairview. Connie Goldman found love in her later years, and in this book she presents the stories of 21 couples who did so as well. Written in the respondents' words, the stories illustrate many of the themes that emerged in our study.

Zukerman, R. (2001). *Young at heart: The mature woman's guide to finding and keeping romance*. New York: Contemporary Books. Dr. Zukerman was a professor at UCLA, and she draws on her clinical practice in this how-to book, full of specific advice for older adults on looking for love.

Together for 4 decades.

# Part III

# Lived Love

The role of illusion shifts when couples move into long-term committed relationships. The fantasies and pretense of infatuation are replaced by the stable realities and the sustaining illusions of mutual involvement. Romances that survive this transition can supply rich possibilities for personal growth and community transformation. This part of the book celebrates those relationships and the communities and families that sustain them.

When it comes to love, we are all swimming in the same pond. The love lives of older adults have ripple effects on those of future generations. Strong love relationships make for strong families and healthy communities and, at the same time, the health of our romances is determined by family history and the social and economic conditions that surround us. The energy and resources of stable romantic involvements provide a solid base for the growth not only of families but of neighborhoods, states, and nations. These are the realities of lived love.

Community involvement is a hallmark of their relationship.
*Photo by Marianne Gontarz York*

# 5

## A Kind of Settled Bliss: Romance in Committed Relationships

*Marty radiated vitality as he explained to me that his whole life was a love story. He wrote about it in his 250-page autobiography, titled* The Life and Times of Marty C. Gilbert and Ethel Briggs Gilbert. *We talked for a while, and when we were through I asked whether he needed a parking validation—nope. He had thought it would be easiest to find my office on foot so had parked at the V.A. Medical Center and walked a mile to the university. He was looking forward to the walk back. Marty's demeanor, appearance, and energy seemed about right for a man in his mid-60s. Marty was 87 years old.*

*The life and times of Marty and Ethel began at the University of Idaho, where they enjoyed "a wonderful college romance" until Ethel returned home to begin teaching. There she met a dashing young man and began to date him. After a few months, her conscience would no longer permit her to correspond with Marty while dating this man, so she wrote an agonized but extremely tender eight-page Dear John letter and asked that Marty not respond. At the time, he respected her wishes; but over 50 years later, Marty said he wished he had written back to express his deep feelings. He felt grateful for their time together and understood and respected her choice, even though it broke his heart. At the same time, he hoped she would not blame herself for his pain because he wanted only the best for her. Finally he said, "I would tell her that in spite of the present situation, I still love her with all my heart and am consequently registering myself as a ready backup to her plans for future happiness."*

*Marty did not tell her any of these things, resolving instead to wait in the wings. He said his love went deeper. He knew she had not wanted to write the letter and that he would eventually "beat the other guy out."*

*A few months later, when rumor of a breakup reached him, Marty rushed to pen a letter inviting Ethel to renew their correspondence. He did not mention that he had just been accepted to the Harvard graduate school. When he received her delighted acceptance of his invitation, thoughts of going East flew from his mind. He could not be that far away from Ethel. He just "wanted to be with her." Within months the couple was engaged. They married 2 years later, in 1939, and made their first home in a 14 × 16 foot tent in a Civilian Conservation Corps camp. Their first son was born in 1943, and Marty's hardest parting came within hours of his birth. He was called to serve in the Navy and had to leave his wife and son in the hospital and ship out to the Pacific. Later Marty's job took him to Washington, DC, where he served as legislative liaison for a government agency. This time Ethel went with him, giving Marty some much-needed, confidence "'cause I was bashful."*

*Marty feels that his love for Ethel stemmed from their shared experiences. "She was the greatest friend I ever had. I mean even before we were married." He also thinks love changes people, partly by helping them develop empathy and partly by making them more interesting. "Frankly, the majority of bachelors that I've met didn't have much personality."*

*I asked Marty how he expressed his love. He said respect was important. "You also encourage 'em if there are times when they need encouragement," even if it is just small things. "If you're going to college, you find the cheapest bouquet that you can find. . . . You don't have money to spend." Ethel expressed her love in ways he could readily understand, through respect and encouragement, and "not cooking the things I didn't like." Of the relationship between love and sex, he says, "I think that the person that you love, and really love, seriously, then I think sweet sex is a part of that love."*

*Marty and Ethel were together for 59 years. Their four sons are great sources of pride. Marty was successful in his job, and in his later years enjoyed the contrast between the tent in which they began their married life and the comfortable suburban home they were eventually able to afford. His advice about love? "Be responsible."*

*Ethel has been gone for about 8 years, and Marty still misses her. After a debilitating period of mourning, Marty decided that "life goes on; I must live in the present. . . . My memory of our love was too precious to change to a mood of seeing only futility in life and to live the remainder of my days in bitterness and sorrow." Marty expects to be reunited with Ethel in heaven. Until then, he remains a poster child for vital involvement.*

Long-term commitment is a major theme in our romantic landscape—much admired and widely celebrated. Marty described his marriage to Ethel as "the love story of my life," beginning with infatuation and continuing beyond Ethel's death, 59 years later. Marty continues to love her with affection that transcends mortality.

Like Marty, most Americans spend most of their lives in committed relationships.[1] This chapter celebrates the lived love present in long-term romantic relationships, beginning with a foray into census data. Although imperfect as a measure of commitment, marriage rates and demographics enable us to make international comparisons and consider social trends affecting marriage. We then turn to the growing trends of late-life marriage and commitment outside of marriage before focusing on the personal dynamics of lived commitment.

## Love and Commitment

I told my children that when I grow up I want to be just like Marty. I covet his vitality and confidence. Yet when an older adult tells me about an idyllic long-term romance, I sometimes twitch with envy and disbelief. Can such a perfect thing be true?

My grandmother was married to my grandfather for over 50 years. My mother described her father as distant and unaffectionate, saying he was often away and my grandmother always felt she was "less than" his first wife, who died young. But I have a letter from my grandmother in which she wrote that she hoped I would one day enjoy a relationship as wonderful as the one she shared with Pappa. I puzzled over the discrepancy between the relationship my grandmother remembered so fondly and the one my mother described so critically.

I suspect that many readers experience disbelief or skepticism in reaction to Marty's story. Embroiled in the daily struggles and insecurities of married, single, divorced, or partnered life, you may wonder whether your memories will have the pleasure and confidence of Marty's reminiscences. In the next section, I consider what committed love means today, and what it takes to maintain a long-term romantic relationship. In the process, I suggest that commitment in retrospect differs from lived commitment, and that commitment per se is not the point.

Many see commitment as an integral part of romantic love. As we saw in Chapter 1, commitment, passion, and intimacy are the components of

Robert Sternberg's love triangle. This chapter celebrates commitment in love—without intending to disparage casual or transient relationships. Remember that life expectancy in the United States nearly doubled during the twentieth century, so when we expect a modern relationship to last for a lifetime, we are asking much more than we would have in previous centuries. That said, let us briefly consider commitment by the numbers.

## Commitment by the Numbers

Marriage is certainly not the only form a committed relationship can take. Growing numbers of Americans share their homes and their lives in intimate committed relationships that do not have the official sanction of marriage.[2] But at the population level, marriage serves as a convenient proxy for commitment.

Americans as a nation are enthusiastic about marriage, with marriage rates that exceed those in other developed nations. In 1990, for example, our rate of marriage surpassed that in Italy, Germany, Canada, Britain, France, and Sweden. That year, 715 of 1,000 women of marriageable age in the United States were married, compared to a low of 557 in Sweden.[3] Not only do we marry at higher rates than other nations, we express greater enthusiasm for the institution of marriage. Between 1999 and 2001, the World Values Survey asked people whether they endorsed the statement "Marriage is an outdated institution." Only 10% of Americans agreed with this, compared to 22% of Canadians, 26% of British, and 36% of French residents.[4] America's high rate of marriage is accompanied by a high rate of divorce. So Americans experience more marital transitions than people in other developed countries. This is illustrated in Figure 5.1.

Americans are a marrying people. Our nation's fondness for marriage may not reflect a national tendency toward romance so much as it does the power of organized religion in America, which often demands that people marry rather than cohabit. Just as Americans attend church and believe in God more than citizens in other parts of the world, we also marry in greater proportions. When living in New Zealand, I was struck by the widespread use of the word *partner*. Even government agencies referred to my husband as my partner. A colleague explained that "Kiwis aren't as inclined towards marriage as you Americans. Many of us just can't be bothered." She, for instance, had been living in a committed relationship with her partner for 27 years, and saw no need for the sanction of marriage.

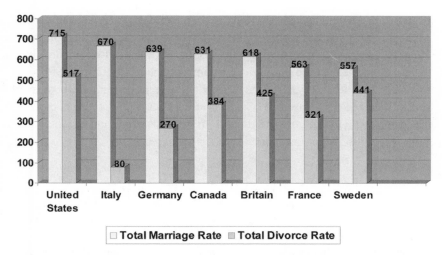

Figure 5.1.   International comparison of marital rates. (From Cherlin, A. J. [2005]. American marriage in the early twenty-first century—putting US marriage in international perspective. *Marriage and Child Wellbeing, 15*(2). Retrieved November 30, 2006, from http://www.futureofchildren.org/information2826/information_show.htm?doc_id= 290321)

## *Late-Life Marriages*

In her comprehensive study of marriage, historian Stephanie Coontz quoted a psychiatrist who wrote in 1953 that "a girl who hasn't a man in sight by the time she is 20 is not altogether wrong in fearing that she may never get married."[5] Attitudes were relatively unchanged in 1986 when, as Coontz explained, *Newsweek* reported that a single 40-year-old woman had a better chance of being killed by a terrorist than of getting married.[6] *Newsweek* was not the only magazine to trumpet these findings. *People* magazine led with a headline proclaiming, "The New Look in Old Maids."[7] In 2006, *Newsweek* admitted that their fear-mongering assessment had been dead wrong. The magazine blamed their mistake on faulty research.[8] Evidently, three demographers at Harvard and Yale had issued a report indicating that the odds of marriage for a single 40-year-old woman were exceedingly low.[9]

Maybe in the 1950s this was so, but marriage practices have changed considerably. The face of the newly married is growing older as age of first marriage has steadily increased for both men and women. In 1960 the median age at first marriage (the age at which half of the population is married) was 22.8 years for men and 20.3 for women. By 2004 these figures had increased to 27.4 years for men and 25.8 years for women.[10] This leaves growing numbers of people in their 20s and 30s who have never married. In 1975, 63% of women aged 20 to 24 years had married, whereas by 1990 the comparable figure was 39%. This trend continues into the mid-40s. In 1975, 96% of women aged 40 to 44 had married. While still high, this number declined to 92% in 1990.[11] If these trends continue, by 2044 the median age at first marriage for both men and women could increase to 33 years. Marriage is aging, and this is moving the institution into uncharted territory with new dilemmas and expectations. These are illustrated in my friend Katie's experiences.

### Katie's Story

After a dramatic breakup with her lover, Katie began to rethink her life. She realized that she had been searching for someone to raise a child with, and that as her biological clock ran down the search had taken on an unhealthy intensity. That sense of desperation had led her into a destructive relationship with a professional colleague. With this realization, Katie decided to stop looking for a mate and adopt a child on her own.

It took some time, but when she was 48 Katie received word from Bolivia that a little girl was available for her. This momentous news came one month after Katie had met Glenn—a delightful companion who even liked giving back rubs! Unfortunately, Glenn, a widower, emphatically did not want children. This set up an agonizing dilemma for Katie. Should she give up the child she had wanted for years? Or abandon the man she was enjoying so very much?

Katie opted for the child. She traveled to Bolivia with her brother and brought her baby home. With support from colleagues and friends, Katie created a life for herself and her daughter. It was hard, being a single parent in her late 40s, but the baby was marvelous and Katie was a master at juggling responsibilities. She even managed to see Glenn from time to time, always being careful to insulate him from her parenting responsi-bilities. Bit by bit, Glenn began to express interest in helping with the baby, and before long he fell in love with her too. Katie married for the first time when she was 50, and today she and Glenn are coparenting their 4-year-old daughter. Together Glenn and Katie juggle the responsibilities of their two careers, their lovely daughter, and their aging parents. Katie cannot imagine a more fulfilling life. She is grateful that she and Glenn found each other when they were mature enough to recognize a good thing when it came along.

Like Katie, more people than ever before are marrying late in life. Thousands delay their first marriage well beyond their 30s. This includes royalty and the intelligentsia. Japanese Princess Sayako was "still single" on her 35th birthday and used the occasion to suggest that marrying late is "a natural trend in a sense, given women's way of life is diversifying."[12] In September 2000, Gloria Steinem married for the first time at 66. Of the occasion, Steinem commented, "Though I've worked many years to make marriage more equal, I never expected to take advantage of it myself."[13]

Those who marry later stay married longer. Age at marriage is consistently recognized as the most important predictor of divorce. In 2001, the Centers for Disease Control reported that 40% of first marriages involving brides at ages 18 and 19 ended in marital dissolution within 10 years. By contrast, only 24% of marriages involving brides over age 25 ended in divorce or separation.[14] This trend toward later marriage may increase the stability of marriages, even as it reduces the years people can spend being married.

## Commitment Outside of Marriage

Growing numbers of Americans are choosing to live with their partners outside of marriage. Since 1990, the Census Bureau has allowed same-sex couples to identify themselves as unmarried partners. For a while, those who identified a member of the same sex as a spouse were disqualified from the census, but that has changed. Today they are counted as unmarried partners. The 2000 Census counted 5.5 million households of unmarried partners, up from 3.2 million in 1990. Although the vast majority of these households are headed by members of the opposite sex, over half a million (594,000) included same-sex partners (301,000 male; 293,000 female).[15] Stanford and Larry maintain one of these households.

### Stanford and Larry's Story

Larry called me when he saw an ad in our local gay newsletter. Ordinarily a more private person, Larry said, "If we don't talk about our lives, how can we expect people to understand?" With snacks and drinks at the ready, we settled into the cozy living room for a delightful long conversation.

Stanford and Larry met in 1968. Larry explained that they attended the same gym, and one snowy night, "I came in late and he was there and he said, 'You were late tonight. Where have you been?' and I said, 'Oh, I've been teaching a piano lesson,' and he said, 'Oh, I teach piano.' And that was the end of the conversation. A little bit later he said, 'Where are you going after this?' I said, 'Well, I'm going home to watch my new television.' I had a new color television. This was when color television was first coming out, and he said, 'I've never seen a color television,' and I said, 'Would you like to come watch my TV?'" Later they laughed about the line. Stanford explained, "We dated for about 18 months and then we moved in with each other and in case it didn't work out we kept his apartment for the next 12 years."

Larry and Stanford come from devout, conservative families. I asked whether the families supported their relationship. Stanford explained, "You know what? It never has been discussed with my nieces or nephews. All my nieces and nephews were born after Larry came to live with me. He was always here. He was always very friendly with them and they just accepted him. . . . My dad was very distraught because Larry called him by his first name—right from the beginning. He went right up to them [parents] and called them by their first names, looked them straight in the eye and talked. He can talk about lots of things so that's where it was." Larry's family was also supportive.

Larry and Stanford have been together for 38 years. Both are handsome and energetic. Stanford is 75 years old, and Larry is 65. I asked whether they celebrated anniversaries, and one of them explained, "Not much. First dates, birthdays, Christmas, and anniversaries. We don't exchange presents. Yesterday we were in the store. I said, 'Look, a Valentine's rack. Should we go over there? I'll pick out the one I was going to give you and you can read it and say, "Oh that's nice," and put it back on the shelf!' We share a lot of fun things together. We travel. We entertain. We are entertained by people. But we don't exchange gifts. That became tiresome after the first four or five years. Writing 'I love you, I love you' and all of that junk." Instead, they express their love by holding and kissing and saying "I love you" many times a day. "When I was a manager at [a local business] 11–12 years ago he had this big bouquet sent to me which wasn't for Valentine's Day or anything, and the girls who work with me said, 'Are those from your boyfriend?' and I said, 'Yeah' and they said, 'Dammit! My husband never does that for me.' And we all had a good laugh about that. But it's just small unexpected things like that."

I asked how they divided household chores, and Stanford explained, "What you're good at and what you like to do. He's a very good cook. So he does all the cooking. I do all the cleaning, and we each do a little of both. When it comes to crunch time I help him get the food together. The yard—I don't care much for yard work. He does the yard work. He is the best launderer there is. He turns out the whitest clothes, the whitest underwear. Never wants to be interfered with. I put my underwear in and it comes out all folded just sitting to be put away. If there is something we share, it's always right down the middle."

Stanford said that the love is very, very deep. And loving is not the gushy stuff. "It's being there when he's coming out of the anesthetic, or when I am coming out of the anesthetic and there he is. We both had back surgery in the last 3 years so it's that kind of thing, . . . love is clean underwear that is just stacked and is white as can be and he did that, he did it for me. And just cleaning up and putting things back where they were, just the way you expect to be, and all of that, he does it because he respects me and he loves me. Respect is an aspect of love. A lot like salt and pepper."

Marriage is not especially important to Stanford and Larry. As Larry explained, "It might be nice to have a paper that said you were married— just a document. It wouldn't make one bit of difference in our relationship." But both men regret that they did not raise children. Larry explained, "I would have liked to have a chance to raise kids and sit and do homework, and you bet those kids would have played [piano] and you bet they would have practiced. I've met parents who want their kids to play and I say, 'Well, you're going to have to sit with them.' It's important that the kid feels the parents are involved. It's important to be involved."

Aging presents some unique challenges to this committed couple. When I asked whether their love had changed with age, Stanford explained, "Probably. Well, I don't know if it's gotten any stronger because I loved him so much right at the beginning. But I think that I have become more dependent on him. Because when it comes down to the bottom line, my siblings have their families and I have Larry, and he's my everything." Larry added, "As we get older, now that I'm retired, the next big thing that happens is death, or getting sick. And we spend a lot of time—we both had back surgery in the last 3 years, I have had two stents put in my heart—dealing with health problems and with prescriptions and that's a whole new aspect you don't have to deal with when you're younger. You have to find the love that is going to encompass medical problems and aging."

I asked, "And how is that? Is that hard?"

"Sometimes, because the doctors say that they don't know specifically how to handle the problem, so you say, well, we're going to have to handle that and find our own way through that."

Eventually, Stanford and Larry plan to move into a retirement community. They're on a waiting list in a nearby city, but hate to contemplate moving away from their home. Stanford explained how they would cope: "Some of the things we have around here we'll have to get rid of but we both decided it would be better. I look at it as a new project—redoing a condo and making it ours. We also want to sell this house and make

enough money, and take our pictures and the quilt and it was done by my
father on his mission, that kind of thing. Something like this, we kind of
look at it as saying oooh, but we've done it. We've done projects here.
Just decorating and redecorating. They'll be projects. That's how you do
it when you're aging."

"Is it scary?"

"Yeah, it is."

Alternatives to marriage are not limited to people in same-sex partnerships. As we have seen, growing numbers of Americans are cohabiting
without marriage. Other arrangements frequently seen among older adults
include "living apart together" and significant friends. These are sometimes
preferable to marriage for those who have lost a partner, and are discussed in
Chapter 8.

## Lived Commitment

We tend to think of commitment as a static force in a relationship—a
promise we make to stay together because (a) we want to; (b) we feel
obligated to; or (c) we have no better alternatives.[16] But lived commitment
is not static or easily measured. Instead, it is a dynamic, paradoxical process that ebbs and flows in unpredictable ways. I like to compare lived
commitment to jazz improvisation.[17] Each player explores a melody that
blends with those of other players to create a listening experience that either
works—or does not.

As we live out our commitments, we experience opposing impulses and
forces: the drive toward autonomy and the desire to be part of a relationship;
a hunger for diverse experiences and a comfort in predictability; a desire for
privacy and a longing for intimacy. These contradictions are part of lived
commitment. They demand recognition, and can inspire personal growth
and enrich relationships

Lived commitment has little to do with infatuation, and everything to do
with love. As we saw in Chapter 1, infatuation involves the projection of the
lover's fantasies and wishes upon the beloved. By definition, it is based on
illusions. Someone once said the best way to cure infatuation is to get to
know the person. Love, by contrast, is based on deep knowledge and acceptance of the other person. Erich Fromm's great insight in his book, *The
Art of Loving,* was that love is a capacity that we can foster and encourage.
Similarly, the "labor of love" consists of the compromises and adjustments
we make as we fulfill our commitment to a relationship.

## What Makes It Possible?

The love that forms the basis of lived commitment does not demand constant sacrifice, but it draws upon our capacity to empathize and identify with the other person to the point where we truly value that person's well-being and happiness. We stop asking them to fulfill our fantasies or to keep us excited and begin to respect and value their unique beauty. When our partners say, "I am not 'in love' with you anymore," we should say, "Hurray! Now we can get on with the business of loving each other."

But how, exactly, do we accomplish that? An enormous amount is written about relationship maintenance and enhancement. In Chapter 2, we heard from respondents who felt that their love had improved with age. It is certainly possible that the cognitive and emotional qualities that come with maturity enhance our ability to sustain a relationship. We looked for other possible explanations of relationship longevity among the 280 Internet respondents to our survey who had been in relationships for 20 years or more.

First, a little bit about these respondents: Most of them (77%) were married to their partners, though some were widowed or cohabiting. Most (96%) reported their romantic experiences had been exclusively or primarily with the opposite sex. They averaged 54½ years of age. Most (79%) were female, and 87% were white. They reflected on relationships that had lasted between 20 and 59 years.

We asked: "What has made it possible for you to remain in this relationship?" This question was answered by 240 people, and their responses are summarized in Table 5.1. No single answer was mentioned by more than 30% of the sample, suggesting that the factors that sustain long-term relationships may be as diverse as the relationships themselves. That said, the answers we received most often were rather predictable: love and caring, commitment and determination, friendship and compatibility, respect and admiration, and tolerance and compromise. In addition, these denizens of long-term relationships agreed with the research literature that children helped maintain their commitment to the relationship.

Kids were mentioned by about 16% of the group, generally married couples, though in one nontraditional situation, a 51-year-old African American woman reported maintaining a long-term relationship with a man to whom she was not married. She said, "We had a child together and have kept coming back to each other even though we have each married other people." Though nontraditional relationships like hers are not becoming common, they are more frequent with the upcoming generation and are likely to reshape the look of late-life marriage in decades to come.

Table 5.1. Long-Term Relationships: What Makes It Possible to Remain? ($N = 240$)

| Theme | Percentage | Illustrative Examples |
|---|---|---|
| Love and caring | 30 | "Our abiding love."<br>"We adore one another." |
| Commitment and determination | 22 | "Mutual commitment to the marriage"<br>"True commitment to each other."<br>"The tenacity of her commitment" |
| Friendship and compatibility | 21 | "He is my best friend."<br>"We are best friends."<br>"Common background and common goals." |
| Respect and admiration | 19 | "We respect each other." |
| Tolerance and compromise | 17 | "We are pretty tolerant."<br>"We are able to put up with each other's idiosyncrasies."<br>"I tolerate her shit, she tolerates mine." |
| Children and family | 16 | "Kids"<br>"4 wonderful children" |
| Partner's strengths | 13 | "My husband is a very good man."<br>"She is very flexible and independent." |
| Enjoyment and fun | 12 | "A good sense of humor. Not taking ourselves too seriously."<br>"We have fun together"<br>"Having feelings of happiness" |
| Communication and honesty | 10 | "We have worked very hard to communicate with each other."<br>"Able to talk and share thoughts"<br>"Honesty with self and my husband, communication." |
| Trust and faithfulness | 9 | "Faithfulness"<br>"I trust him in a lot of different ways" |
| Religion and spirituality | 9 | "I ask God to help me love my husband the way he (God) does."<br>"Spiritual tolerance and the belief that marriage is for life."<br>"Church involvement" |
| Space apart | 5 | "Knowing that while I enjoy being with him, I can live without him."<br>"Having my own life outside the relationship."<br>"He's gone a lot." |

Respondents also sang their partners' praises: 13% attributed their relationship's longevity to a positive attribute of their partners. For example, 43-year-old Beatrice from South Dakota said, "He's forgiving, funny, loving, great with our kids, and would do *anything* for any of us. Example: He knows I spend far too much money on my sister at holidays and birthdays since our mom died and doesn't make me feel bad about it." A few took credit themselves, like 45-year-old Stan from Wyoming who had been married for 21 years. He answered, perhaps jokingly, "My charm and wit."

While the work involved in maintaining a relationship featured heavily, some respondents (12%) emphasized pleasure. These more hedonistic responses emphasized the importance of enjoyment and fun in lasting relationships. Typical was 53-year-old Elsie, who attributed her 32-year marriage to "fun time together doing things we both enjoy."

Several respondents to this question offered hints at the difficulty of maintaining a relationship. One wrote, "Try, try, *try!*" reflecting a recognition shared by Jung when he wrote: "Seldom, or perhaps never, does a marriage develop into an individual relationship smoothly and without crises; there is no coming to consciousness without pain."[18] In the next section we will see what respondents had to say about the challenges they faced in their long-term relationships.

Illusion plays a role in many successful relationships. But it is important to distinguish between illusions that sustain and fantasies that delude. The capacity to idealize our partners by focusing on their positive traits can be very helpful. But, as psychiatrist Stephen Mitchell explained, "It matters a great deal whether the source of idealization is at least partially in the other (highlighted and elaborated through imagination) or purely a figment of the fantasy life of the lover, exploiting the other as an occasion for the projection of his or her own needs."[19]

On the other hand, some illusions can dilute the romance of long-term commitment. Most of us believe that over time a decline in romance is inevitable. We trade this for the stability and security we need from our partners. Mitchell turned this idea on its head in his last book, *Can Love Last?*, where he argued that the notion of security and even the idea that we can really know our partners are themselves comfortable illusions. When we let go of these illusions, we may rediscover the excitement of romance.

## *Challenges to Commitment*

Sustaining interest and romance over time is a significant challenge. Wondering what other aspects of lived commitment were most challenging, we asked respondents in the Internet survey who had been in a romantic relationship for 20 years or more, "What makes it difficult to remain in this relationship?" Their answers are presented in Table 5.2.

Rejecting my assumption, over a third (37%) of respondents said they had not experienced difficulty remaining in their long-term relationships. Those who felt otherwise tended to attribute the difficulty to their partners' failings. Christina, age 48, from Virginia complained, "My husband is not as much a believer (in Christ and the church) as I am. Also my husband is not very sociable." Men had complaints too. Ed, age 66, from Minnesota noted of his wife of 20 years, "She is sometimes moody and controlling." Another man from California, age 53, cited "frustrations about her limitations, particularly in the areas of money, parenthood, and insecurity."

Another widely recognized challenge is difference. During infatuation, we tend to reframe our beloved's idiosyncrasies in positive terms. This cannot last a lifetime, though, and over the decades, "He slurps his coffee so sweetly" can turn into "He is a loathsome slob." Some respondents (16%) in this study reported that differences and growing apart were challenges to their relationships. For example, 77-year-old Carolyn from California cited "emerging incompatibilities of interest." Another emphasized change. This 48-year-old noted, "Any difficulties along the way are easily associated with developmental and social change." Norma, age 53, simply alluded to "personality differences."

Other factors were mentioned by a few respondents. These included normal life stresses, or the ups and downs of a relationship; work and financial problems; boredom; absence of positive attributes like attraction or respect; family problems; and difficulties with addiction or mental illness. Sexual problems and infidelity were fairly uncommon, mentioned by seven respondents each. Only five respondents mentioned the challenges posed by "attractive alternatives," while two said that "falling out of love" posed difficulties for their relationships.

## Personal Growth in Long-Term Relationships

Today we demand that romantic involvements support our personal growth and development. Stephanie Coontz recognized, "Modern marriages cannot just glide down the well-worn paths of the past."[20] She argued that in an era when commitments must stand on their own (rather than relying on financial or personal dependencies, or coercive social norms), couples who remain committed probably have more satisfying relationships than their predecessors.

Table 5.2.   Long-Term Relationships: What Makes It Difficult to Remain? ($N = 220$)

| Theme | Percentage | Illustrative Examples |
|---|---|---|
| Nothing; it hasn't been difficult | 37 | "Na"<br>"Nothing"<br>"Nothing . . . sometimes you just get lucky" |
| Partner's weaknesses | 17 | "He was (is) a jealous person, which contributed much strife and conflict in our relationship."<br>"She is sometimes moody and controlling."<br>"My husband's moods are sometimes difficult, but much less so in the past decade." |
| Differences, growing apart | 16 | "We're different personality types and our approaches to things differ."<br>"Differences and changes in each other."<br>"We just grew apart over time." |
| Normal life stresses | 7 | "The natural fluctuation and wanderings of emotions."<br>"The usual ups and downs of a relationship"<br>"The ordinary strains of marriage" |
| Work/financial problems | 6 | "Financial concerns"<br>"Job changes"<br>"Getting so busy in career that I didn't spend time maintaining the relationship" |
| Boredom/staleness | 6 | "Boredom"<br>"Sometimes those very similarities that make it fun can make the relationship seem stale and not too exciting"<br>"The complacency" |
| Absence of positive | 6 | "Lack of continued attraction"<br>"Only when we forget the respect angle"<br>"Lack of romance" |
| Family problems | 5 | "In-laws"<br>"Problems with teenagers"<br>"Family members that didn't think he was right for me. With time they seem to have gotten over it." |
| Addiction/mental illness | 5 | "He had a drinking problem for a while that was difficult"<br>"Drug use"<br>"My partner developed bipolar II disorder, but it was not diagnosed for over four more years." |

If, as I suggested in Chapter 2, we have an inherent drive for new experiences and personal fulfillment, what prevents us from trading old partners for new, more exciting models? Jung and others argue that social convention is insufficient. Pressure and sanctions do not prevent healthy adults from wandering. When a relationship truly offers no further opportunities for fulfillment or expansion, most people today would be loath to argue for its continuation. Aron and Aron offer two possible solutions for this dilemma. One is to find inner sources of expansion and fulfillment that do not jeopardize the relationship. The other, of course, is to create a relationship that supplies continuous opportunities for growth.[21]

### Commitment in Retrospect

At the end of our interviews with older adults, we asked people, "Do you consider yourself a success at love?" This provided an opportunity to look at their love lives in retrospect. Despite the pain caused by her husband's recent affair, Marilyn, age 38, felt that "I would have to say yes. . . . I think I am a success because if I never loved I would be a failure. I would never know what it was about." Similarly, when we asked 69-year old Jim, he said, "Given the situation, yes. Yes, I do. But I wouldn't want anybody else to try to live through it. It's not been a bed of roses by any means. It has been hell! A wonderful hell." Jim's wife of 42 years suffered from bipolar disorder.

A few respondents did not consider themselves successful in love. In some cases, this reflected their perfectionism. William, a gay man in his early 60s expressed delight with his partner of 20 years. But asked whether he considered himself a success at love, he replied, "No, one can always do better." Similarly, Candy, a 62-year-old lesbian, was optimistic about her search for a romantic partner: "No. No . . . I think I could be [laughs]." Often divorce or long-term status as unmarried led people to describe themselves as unsuccessful in love. Barbara, a woman in her early 80s, explained, "Well, people say, three husbands, wow, you must have something wrong. But to me a success at love means that I had found someone that I could be emotionally intimate with." Though actively looking for a romantic partner, Barbara has not yet achieved her definition of success. And 66-year-old Sally replied simply, "Not really, 'cause I'm all alone."

Many Americans see divorce and relationship terminations as failure. A conversation with 54-year-old Cassie, who was on the verge of her fourth wedding, was illuminating. I asked, "Do you consider yourself a success at love?" "Well, now I do," she said. "Now, not before? Why now?" "Because I think I've got somebody and I think I can make this last." I asked, "So if you make this last, you'll be a success at love?" "Yeah." "And if it doesn't you won't?" "Yeah."

Like Cassie, most respondents associated a successful love life with commitment fulfilled. In response to the question, "Do you consider yourself a success at love?" the most common answer was, "Sure!" Benjamin, age 60, said, "Yeah, because I worked at it. If I hadn't worked at it, I wouldn't have been. You've got to work at it!" And 83-year-old Eunice said simply, "Yes. My husband loved me." Joyce, age 91, was even a little indignant at the question: "What would you say? Don't you think so from what I've told you here? I mean for 50 years and for another 12½ [I had] companionship and only [lost them] because they were both taken from me!" Others, like 72-year-old Maria, just cited their years in marriage: "43 real good years."

Commitment looks different in the past tense because of a relationship maintenance strategy known as positive illusion. Partners in long-term relationships develop beliefs that emphasize an idealized version of the relationship.[22] As a result, the relationship narrative—the story we tell ourselves and others about our relationships—becomes idealized. We maintain this positive illusion through diverse strategies: (1) using *cognitive filters*, we ignore information that contradicts our beliefs; (2) using *downward comparison*, we focus on relationships that seem less appealing than ours; and (3) using *dimensional comparison* when looking at other relationships that are more similar, we restrict our focus to aspects in which our relationship clearly excels.

Aristotle said, "Call no man happy so long as he is alive."[23] We might paraphrase it: "Call no marriage a success until it is over." As we will see in Chapter 8, the loss of a spouse is one of life's most devastating experiences. But it does spare us the possibility of divorce, desertion, and other negative relationship outcomes. In widowhood, the positive relationship narrative constructed to maintain the relationship helps it look favorable in retrospect. So a relationship that seemed fraught with troubles may be remembered as a success. Similarly, researchers have noted a widespread tendency among widows to "sanctify" the deceased.[24]

This is not to imply that there is no such thing as a satisfying long-term relationship. It just helps us understand why relationships can look especially good in the rearview mirror. This may explain the disparity between my mother's recollection of her parents' marriage and the image my grandmother presented me in her letter. When in retrospect we weigh daily conflicts and disappointments against a lifetime of companionship and affection, long-term relationships often come out looking pretty good.[25]

## Conclusion

Lifelong romance is a cherished ideal. Reflecting our general enthusiasm for the institution, Americans tend toward harsh judgment when relationships and lives fall short of this ideal. But extended life expectancy lends new meaning to the phrase "till death do us part." It is challenging to sustain a rich and supportive relationship for life now that most of us expect to reach our ninth decade. Nonetheless, many people do just that, and when we asked our respondents for the secrets of their relationship longevity, their answers were as varied as the individuals themselves; however, some themes did emerge.

Older adults frequently reported that their romantic experiences improved with age. This may be because of individual maturation processes independent of their loving experience. Age alone might make it easier to remain in a relationship. On the other hand, long-term relationships may be love's training ground—the settings where we master the skills required for emotional regulation, communication, and other relationship tasks.

The accumulation of shared experiences may help sustain long-term relationships, becoming a reservoir lovers can draw upon for knowledge and understanding of each other. A shared past enables lovers to anticipate how their partners will behave and to share complex emotions. "This is just like when . . ." can trigger a nod and a pleasant sense of connection.

Supporting actors can also help to bind a couple together. Here we saw couples report that children and grandchildren helped sustain their connection. In the next chapter, we expand the lens to consider the roles of these and other players in the romantic possibilities of later life.

## Try This

Traveling Through Commitment: If you are in a committed relationship, the travel metaphor might be a useful way to describe its trajectory. Imagine that you and your partner came from different lands and are exploring the new territory of your togetherness. Describe the lands you came from. How were they similar? How different? Did you speak the same language? The same dialect? How have your travels been so far? Were there steep rocky places? Is there a trail? What are the meadows like? Any crowded cities? What can you see on the horizon?

## Suggested Reading

Coontz, S. (2005). *Marriage, a history: From obedience to intimacy or how love conquered marriage.* New York: Viking. I have long admired Coontz's thoughtful studies of the history of American marriages. This book is long but well worth the investment. It offers a comprensive, highly readable look at the history of American marriage.

Harvey, J., & Wenzel, A. (Eds.). (2001). *Close romantic relationships: Maintenance and enhancement.* Mahwah, NJ: Lawrence Erlbaum. This academic volume presents theory and research on relationship maintenance from a range of perspectives. It also has a section on applied issues. It is both informative and well written.

Mitchell, S. A. (2002). *Can love last? The fate of romance over time.* New York: Norton. This is the last book psychiatrist Stephen Mitchell wrote before his untimely death in 2000. In it, he argues that romance does not "degrade" on its own but that we actively undermine it through our fear of intimacy. We suppress passion when the relationship matters because it is too dangerous—we have too much to lose. For Mitchell, the feeling of security that we treasure in long-term relationships is as much an illusion as the fantasies of infatuation. His own life offered tragic confirmation. A thought-provoking work.

Schnarch, D. (1997). *Passionate marriage: Love, sex, and intimacy in emotionally committed relationships.* New York: Henry Holt. This is a book on "how to achieve hot sex and deep intimacy" in an emotionally committed relationship. In essence, Schnarch argues that we reach these goals, not through communication or self-abandon, but through differentiation—knowing and holding onto ourselves. A very pleasant read by a talented author.

Wallerstein, J. S., & Blakeslee, S. (1995). *The good marriage: How and why love lasts.* Boston: Houghton Mifflin. Judith Wallerstein and her colleagues interviewed 50 couples who consider themselves happily married. The resulting case studies are interesting, as are the authors' conclusions. For example, they identify four types of marriage: romantic, rescue, companionate, and traditional, and then from a dialectic perspective consider the "anti-marriage" for each type—that is, the negative aspect that can shatter a relationship. This is worth the time, though it is a little prescriptive for my taste.

Learned to love from his parents.

# 6

## Supporting Actors: Family, Friends, and Community

*Warm, articulate, and emotionally complex, at the age of 83 Barbara is a quintessential people person. Like the rest of her life, Barbara's romances take place in an unusually rich social context. Consider what she has to say about the man she married in her early 60s:*

> *What happened is I got a letter from my third husband's wife and I went down. She was a good friend of mine. I went down there and I visited them and at that point something was bothering her. Turned out she had ovarian cancer. And I didn't know it but then somehow I got a letter from Simon that she had died. I couldn't believe it. I decided to stop in to pay my respects. Well, I knew he was a good catch and I also knew that he had had a crush on me when I worked for him. I loved Simon as a friend but there was something about him that was very feminine. So anyhow, I went down and he said would you consider a relationship? I said, all you have to do is whistle. I wanted him to know I was interested. He was an upstanding man in the community and I loved his kids. I really did. He had three kids. His kids were accepting. They wanted their father to be happy, so happy. It didn't take him 6 months to propose. We planned the wedding.*

*Like Simon's three adult children, Barbara's daughter Alicia was thrilled with the match. Barbara and Simon enjoyed the lifestyle they shared. They entertained a great deal, and when Simon's daughter had their first grandchild Barbara was ecstatic. But in time Barbara realized the child had serious problems. One weekend when he was 14 months old, Barbara and Simon flew in to take care of him for a weekend. "This child [was] a beautiful little boy, but he hadn't seen us since he was 6 months old. Never asked for his mother; he never cried; and there were just certain signs that made me realize there was a serious problem." At Barbara's urging, the child was evaluated and diagnosed with severe autism. Thanks to her intervention, early treatment greatly improved his life chances. Then a granddaughter was born to Simon's son. Barbara said, "She was the love of my life for a long time. And I was the love of her life too 'cause I used to go see her almost every day. I adored her."*

*After 5 years of marriage, Simon and Barbara realized that they had, as she put it, "no sexual chemistry." Barbara found Simon less and less physically attractive and other relationship issues eventually resulted in divorce. Simon passed away a few years ago, but Barbara remains in touch with his children.*

*When she was 79, mutual friends introduced Barbara to a man who had just been widowed. Barbara fell "head over heels" for Al. She explained, "I was madly in love with him. He was a marvelous lover, and it was his sense of humor, his personality. Now, he was a house husband for 15 years before I met him. It was like I went from the intellectual extreme, because my second husband and my third husband were both real intellectuals, to this guy who was purely on the basis of personality, physical attraction, strong physical attraction!" And, of course, Barbara just loved Al's adult children.*

*But their early months were not completely straightforward. For one thing, Al was still seeing Nellie. "He had gotten to be friends with a woman whose husband just died, and his wife just died, and they became friends and then they had an affair and then she broke it up because she was religious. But he would see her occasionally and I said to him, 'I don't approve of your seeing anybody if we're in a relationship, but if you still have feelings for Nellie as a friend I don't object to you going out to lunch with her or if you want to have her over for Sunday.' And I don't know what the hell it was with her, but I had the feeling she really wanted him. And I said to him, if she were safety or something. 'Oh, no, no, no, Nellie and I are just friends.'" At Barbara's insistence, Al did eventually tell Nellie about their relationship.*

*He and Barbara enjoyed a passionate 3-year love affair. Barbara said, "And my daughter said, 'Ma, you're like a bunch of kids.' We would tease each other, not tease in a negative way, and I was so happy!" Al moved into a condo in her building and they merged their social lives. Once a week they played bridge with Barbara's friends. They spent time with the adult children. They ate meals together and went out most evenings. Barbara's daughter married during this time, which Barbara says gave her a major case of separation anxiety. Then Al left her. He moved back to the neighborhood he and his wife had lived in and renewed his affair with Nellie, whom he eventually married. Barbara is still close to Al's children, who say*

*they like her much better than the new wife. The couple they played bridge
with says they always thought Al had problems.*

Barbara's experiences illustrate the important role adult children play in
late-life romance. Her daughter is still the most important person in her life,
and the adult children of her partners remain connected and supportive. As
we will see, this is not always the case. Some late-life romances do not enjoy
the sanction of adult children. Barbara has a strong network of friends, both
in the condominium building she shares with hundreds of other seniors and
among her professional colleagues. Like her lovers' children, these friends
remain loyal to Barbara through marriages and affairs, helping her to meet
new people and offering diversion whether she is single or partnered.
Though not central to Barbara's life, religious norms affected her indi-
rectly when Nellie's compunctions forced her to break off the affair with Al.
Likewise, Barbara seems immune to our culture's pervasive ageism, seeing
herself as a sexually attractive woman, and finding men her age physically
appealing.

Most of us are aware of supporting players in our romantic narratives—
the family members and friends who introduce us to potential lovers and
who approve or disapprove of our choices and actions. In this chapter, we
consider the social context of late-life romance, beginning with the interplay
of family members and friends, then moving to the more indirect influence
of social norms and institutions.

## Love as an Intergenerational Affair

The central role of family in our romantic lives is beyond dispute. Most of
us learn to love in families and because of this, loving relationships among
older adults can have ripple effects on younger generations.

### *Families of Origin*

Several studies have documented intergenerational links in the quality of
marital relationships. Adults who report that their parents' marriages were
unhappy tend to have problems in their own marriages,[1] and children of

divorced parents are more likely to have difficult marriages and to divorce themselves.[2]

Research is less clear on the happier side of the equation. The association between happiness or satisfaction in the parental marriage and in that of adult children has been less well established. Nonetheless, respondents in our interviews felt this was an important factor. When asked how they learned to love, 68% referred to their families of origin. Among these, the vast majority (80%) described positive role models in their families of origin. For example, 76-year-old Maria put it clearly, "How did I learn to love? Well, I learned to love through my father, mostly. Because he and my mother . . . well, they . . . course they adored each other, too. But he taught us love and respect. He loved everyone."

Time and again, the people we interviewed explained that they learned to love from their parents. Like Maria, some said that watching their parents' interactions taught them what loving relationships looked like. Others emphasized the way they were loved by their parents. For example, 64-year-old William felt that his parents' love máde him a loving adult: "Well, I think I was lucky. It was just luck I think that my parents were very loving. I always was made to feel like I was secure and loved and could do anything. I think they were unrealistic at times about what they expected of me, but I never for a moment doubted that they loved me." A few people said that the love they felt for their parents and siblings was in itself an important lesson. One of these was 82-year-old Viola, who saw childhood as an opportunity to practice loving the people and creatures around her: "I think you learn to love when you're a child. You love your parents. You love your brothers and sisters. If you have a pet, you love your dog."

Some people we talked to felt that people did not learn to love. Ten respondents saw love as an innate tendency—a capacity that all babies bring into this world. The vast majority of these "love-inclined" babies find their parents positive, loving role models and teachers. But some hone their loving skills on other family members: grandparents, aunts and uncles, siblings, and even pets.

Some of the less fortunate people (17 in our sample) learned to love by using their parents as examples of what not to do. One of these was 64-year-old Rosie. "I'll tell you how. I looked around [my family], saw all these drunks and stuff, and said I'm not going to be like that. I'm somebody. I'm not lowering myself for nobody. This guy I'm going with, he puts me on a pedestal." Like Rosie, 60-year-old Benjamin found counterexamples in his parents: "I suspect that I learned a lot of the wrong things . . . from my . . . just observing my parents. Like I said, my parents weren't good role models, because they fought a lot."

Among our respondents, those who were divorced or single were more likely than those who were widowed or married to report that their parents served as poor role models, demonstrating how not to love. Almost three-fourths (72%) of married and widowed respondents who addressed this topic described their parents as positive, loving role models, whereas under half (47%) of those who were divorced or single offered this type of description.

Sometimes other relatives filled in as loving role models when parents could not. This was 64-year-old Evelyn's experience. She said, "It was always conflictual. We always fought a lot . . . my mother and I, and that made me sad, but I had aunts, and cousins, and uncles that I used to spend a lot of time with on my father's side of the family, and they were very loving . . . gave me a lot of attention. My brothers were older and so they were married." Two women mentioned learning how to love from their grandmothers. One was 56-year-old Anna, who explained that she learned how to love, "From my grandmother . . . from sitting on the couch with my grandmother holding hands to rubbing her back . . . she was so nurturing and unconditional. That was one of her characteristics. She was a totally loving human being." Another woman explained that her mother was an alcoholic, but she learned to love from a sister who loved her tenderly.

Two 90-year-old women reported that their mothers were too busy to provide them with much love as children. First, 90-year-old Gloria observed, "Well, I was 5 when my father died. [Mother was] very gracious and very shy. Shy isn't the word—she was very reserved. But she was left, you know, with five kids, and I'm the middle one out of five." Gloria explained that her mother was too busy caring for the other children to focus on her. Wilhelmina, age 92, described a similar situation: "My father was very loving. My mother was loving, but she was very . . . you know, years ago, women made quilts. They made all of the clothes that you wore, and they washed and they ironed, and they made . . . they worked. It was kind of a hard life where I lived . . . out on a farm." Both of these women spoke fondly of their mothers, and both went on to have long and satisfying marriages. Between them they went on to raise 10 children.

What does learning to love have to do with late-life relationships? There is evidence that the quality of late-life romance can influence the quality of love experienced by younger generations. Two sociologists at Pennsylvania State University, Paul Amato and Alan Booth, did a fascinating study of the relationship between parents' marital relationships and the quality of their adult children's relationships.[3] They surveyed a national sample of 297 parents and their married offspring, collecting data over a 17-year time span, from 1980 to 1997. Their results indicated that discord in the parents' marriage is reflected in their adult children's marriages. But even more intriguing was their finding that change in the quality of parental marriages was also reflected in the subsequent generation. When parents reported greater harmony or less conflict, their adult children tended to report a similar change in their own marriages. Their findings suggest that the quality of romance among older adults affects their children as well.

### Adult Children

Unfortunately, adult children may not see it this way, as some strongly disapprove of their parents' romantic involvements. Pulitzer prize–winning author Robert Butler concludes, "Many adult children continue to be bound by a primitive childhood need to deny their parents a sex life. . . . If one parent dies, children may deliberately try to prevent the surviving parent from meeting new friends and potential new partners in order to protect their inheritance."[4]

Several of the older adults interviewed for this book restricted their romantic involvements out of deference to their children. In her 80s, Ginnie (whom we met in Chapter 3) fell in love with a dashing fellow I'll call Saul, who had three adult sons. After years of agonizing, she and Saul decided not to marry because his sons objected to the relationship. Ginnie said, "I'm sure they're very happy that he's not gonna get married." She attributed the sons' objections to the loss of their mother: "Well, it's only 2 years for them that their mother's been gone." But she sometimes wondered whether Saul's lack of insistence on marriage was a sign that he did not really care. "If Saul wanted to, I'm sure it wouldn't stop him." Ginnie seemed wistful as she contemplated the decision she had made, but nonetheless concluded, "No, neither one of us wants to."

I wanted to tell Ginnie to ignore the children and live the life she wanted. But adult children cannot be ignored. They play a vital role in the lives of older adults, providing tangible support, opportunities to reminisce, and a link to the future. Life appraisal is an important process in later life, and women we interviewed often saw their children's well-being as their life's greatest accomplishment. Among them was 92-year-old Wilhelmina. When I asked whether she considered herself a success, she replied, "Oh, heavens! Ah . . . what could I be the success of? I hope I've been a good mother to my children. That's the most important thing in my life. You bet. I know I must have had something good, because I looked around that group yesterday, and I . . . and I said, 'You know, isn't this great? To have this many of your own family and have them together sitting at the same table and laughing and having fun together.' There isn't anything better than that. There isn't anything better in this world. Money don't buy things like that."

Barbara's experience seems to be more typical than Ginnie's. She "fell in love" with the adult children of her partners, establishing ties that sometimes outlived the romances themselves. So did 91-year-old Joyce. She and her husband of 50 years had no children, so when he died she was very lonely. In her early 70s, Joyce decided to join a senior center so she could learn ballroom dancing and bridge. She met Ray playing bridge. Joyce painted the scene: "I think he was the only man among all of these women. One of my friends called and said the seniors were going to have a bus trip going to the masters and then they're having dinner at the hotel. I only went for dinner. There was 54 on the bus and 52 were single women and I'm sure they're all just dying for a soul mate." Ray was attracted to Joyce because he "liked her spirit," and the two started a love affair that would last for 12 years.

Early in the relationship, Ray introduced Joyce to his children. She remembered the evening vividly: "Mind you, his wife had only been gone 3 months and he decides he wants his family to meet me. I told the family that night felt like being fed to the wolves. . . . I often wondered and they never told me what they thought of [me] . . . after only 3 months that their beloved mother was gone."

Joyce and Ray decided not to marry. Instead they bought a beautiful home on the water and lived together. "And it was a wonderful relationship, a companionship. We did not marry. It was better in my case. I didn't want him to have to support me because he has a family of a son and a daughter and they've been wonderful to me."

At the time of our interview, Ray had been gone for a little over 4 years, and Joyce said his daughter still called her two or three times a week. His older daughter has been especially supportive. "And she's been marvelous to me. On the 90th birthday she hired a beautiful limousine. They came and picked me up. . . . You talk about love!"

## *Friends*

As Barbara's experiences illustrate, friends play an important role in romantic relationships in later life. Like Barbara and Joyce, many people meet potential romantic partners through friends or through organized social activities. Friends provide another set of eyes and ears for evaluating a potential partner. Particularly for women, positive reactions from friends can encourage commitment to a relationship. Among women, the approval of friends is sometimes even more important than family approval in sustaining a relationship.[5]

For some, a friendship network becomes a substitute family. This is particularly true for those who are distanced from their families of origin. At 62, Candy is a good example. She described her community: "Queer people have to have tribes because so many of them have been thrown out by their families. Anyway, I think that a state of love, if you can think of it as an abstract entity, exists within that group. All of us share. We love each other, because we're family. We don't say, 'We are family.' [But] I believe that there are probably 20 people and if any one of us needed help who would come and help. We do it all the time. You say, I've got something I need to— I've got to sell this property and people will give you advice and they'll help each other out. 'Oh, I have a pickup truck. I'll come help you.' Our lives are made better by this kind of love that we have—this loyalty and love. I believe there is a kind of emotional or I might even say spiritual security that I feel in making common cause with other queer people."

Most couples live their lives in some kind of friendship network. It may be a loose one, united by the occasional Christmas card, or it may involve more dense contacts, like a group of people who see each other every week for bowling or bridge. In heterosexual couples, women are typically the glue that binds these networks together.

## Religion and Rituals

Religious beliefs and church activities provide structure and support for a variety of older couples—from partners who find community and meaning in liberal congregations to couples who join more traditional communities. Religion also serves as an instrument of social control, limiting the chaos that unbridled passion might otherwise wreak in our lives. Sometimes, as we saw in Nellie's case, it forestalls intimacy.

Churches provide structure through subtle enforcement of values and norms. We see this in the advice 80-year-old Justine shared at her church. Justine said, "When my father put me on the train to go to Texas to get married, he said—and I told everybody at my church this—'Honey, there's two things I want you to know that will make that sweet man of yours happy in your married life. Don't forget these two things.' I said, 'Okay, Dad, what are they?' 'One. Always keep your dishes done, and the kitchen will look

clean. And always keep your bed made, and the bedroom will look clean.'
And I have never gone without keeping my dishes done and my bed made.
Ever!" Justine probably makes sure that every young wife in her congregation hears this story—probably over and over. As an older woman who has
conformed to traditional gender norms, Justine now transmits those norms
to the next generation through her church.

Beyond this, church activities and services can serve as the context of
romance. Some people meet their partners at church and enjoy the first
public recognition of their coupled status at church functions. Some, like
82-year-old Viola, find that shared religious beliefs and participation in
church activities help sustain a romantic relationship. "I think it would be
very difficult to have two religions. I've always had the same religion as my
husbands. To me it's sort of a drawing thing for you to go to church together
and talk about it when you get home. Discuss it. It holds you together. I
certainly wouldn't advise anyone of two separate religions to get married.
But that's my idea."

Like Viola, 72-year-old Stanley felt it was important to marry within his
religion. He met his wife in Hawaii while he was in the Navy and after a
brief courtship, they married in the Lutheran church. "What was a plus to
me was that I worried what her family was going to think. . . . You know,
they always like to know what religion you are. . . . When we got home . . . I
think the second question out of [her mother's] mouth after we got acquainted was, 'Stan, tell me what religion you are.' And I said, 'Well, I'm a
Missouri Senate Lutheran boy.' I saw this tremendous smile on her face and
she said, 'You know, Molly's Missouri Senate Lutheran, too.' Well, that just
set me in with the family."

From the posting of banns to the wedding vows themselves, religious
rituals serve to establish community support for the marriage. Abby, age 54,
saw her Quaker wedding ceremony as an opportunity to announce to her
community that she was committed to Peter and to seek the help of family
and friends who would nurture and support their relationship. "We were
married in a religious ceremony. So, it took on a different commitment.
Within a Quaker marriage . . . you marry each other in the eyes of God . . .
communal marriage. . . . Someone came to me last week and said, 'Oh, your
marriage certificate isn't legal?' It doesn't matter. It's not that that makes it
meaningful." Abby and Peter have been together for 25 years.

Religiosity and romance are not necessarily related. Researchers have
generally found that highly religious couples are less likely to divorce, but
there is no clear evidence that religion contributes to greater marital satisfaction.[6] Respondents in our Internet survey were evenly split on whether

love had religious meaning. A little over half (55%) said yes, and the remaining 45% said no.

Those who did see a connection between love and religion were asked to describe it. Respondents felt that religion helped secure commitment in a relationship, either through shared beliefs or through adherence to biblical directives. For example, 62-year-old Betsy, from Virginia, wrote, "The Bible speaks of man and woman coming together and the two becoming one flesh. It speaks of man being the head of the house, but it tells man to love his wife as Christ loved the Church and gave himself for it. If man follows this, the wife need not fear. The wife is told to respect her husband as the head of the house. With the husband and wife following the directives of the Bible to love one another and respect and care for one another, their spiritual love will stand a chance." While only a few people shared Betsy's views on the biblical source of gender roles, many felt that either God or religious values made the labor of love easier. For instance, 69-year-old David, from Montana, said, "My faith helps me understand how to put love into action—understanding, patience, kindness, gentleness, sharing." Some saw romantic love as a manifestation of God's love for humanity. As 58-year-old Carrie put it, "Love is a relational characteristic between God and me, and love for my husband has a spiritual dimension to it and is a gift from God." Allie, age 54, from Nebraska, agreed: "Love is a spiritual experience. Not necessarily a religious experience. Blessing of the church is not important to me."

## Gay/Lesbian Couples

Four of the gay men interviewed for this book reported conflict with their religious communities. These men all reported having entered into heterosexual marriages. Daniel, age 59, said, "I was a Mormon. I knew what my life was supposed to be like, so I just did that. . . . After I got home [from a mission], we got married. And I remember I wanted to get married. I wanted to have a family. I would never think about not getting married. I would never think about having a boyfriend instead of a girlfriend because even then I didn't know anyone who was gay." Daniel went on to discuss the hardships of being gay, religious, and married. After he came out, his marriage ended, and Daniel left the church. He did not reject his faith, however, and still considers himself a devout person.

On the other hand, Stanford (age 65) and Larry (age 75) have been together for most of their adult lives. They have also been active members of the Mormon church, enjoying the acceptance of their congregation and their neighbors. As Larry explained, "We are both still on the rolls of the church. Before we moved here, we were active in one of the few wards where there was an organ and a piano. Stanford played the organ and I played the piano and the congregation really liked it. Stanford, being gay, he also had to bring flowers to the ward in the winter. So they liked the flower arrangements and they liked the music. But these people all around here are LDS [Mormons] and they at least consider us friends. All the [neighbors] have been in our house. And at Christmas the bishop and the congregation came and decorated our tree."

Other gay men, like 66-year-old Edmund and his partner Barry, found ways to connect with other religious communities. After leaving a conservative congregation, Edmund and Barry became ecumenical. They held their commitment ceremony in the Episcopalian church and are active members of their local Methodist congregation. Edmund explained that for Easter, he and Barry cook Greek food at church for over 300 people.

In our Internet survey, respondents whose romantic experiences were primarily or exclusively with members of the same sex were less likely to report a connection between religion and love. Only 12 (22%) of the 54 people who identified as gay or lesbian saw a connection. Cassie, age 63, was abruptly deserted by her partner of 16 years. She said, "I think my early learned values in a religious context caused me to be deeply concerned about integrity, honest and open communications, living for a higher purpose than simply self-interest. These sound so idealistic, but they have a profound effect on the choices I make to set aside the unimportant in order to sustain a relationship. Is it self-interest? Probably, but I have found I often suffer misunderstandings by the other in making these kind of choices. Sometimes, people cannot fathom someone who will forgive and go on without vindication. They seem to wait for the other shoe to drop. Right now I'm questioning everything I ever believed about my values and beliefs, so it all sounds like groundless and meaningless intentions." Several respondents shared Cassie's desire to live their romantic relationships in ways that are consistent with their religious values. Among them was 61-year-old Nathan, from New Mexico, who explained, "I believe in honoring my partner, being monogamous, and cherishing my partner. I believe that represents a basic sense of Christian love, but then I and my partner are gay and we do not take it all that far." Others saw romantic love as a manifestation of God's love. As 51-year-old Naomi from Maine quoted, "To love another person is to see the face of God."

## Social Trends and Norms

Dealing with families and romantic partners, most of us see ourselves as actors—agents of our own fates. We seldom realize that even though we may be actors, we are also acted upon by broad social trends and norms. Later life sometimes allows the opportunity to reflect on the way trends and norms have affected our romantic experiences.

William Faulkner said, "The past isn't dead. It isn't even past!" He was right. Trends and norms extending back into our nation's history come to life in the romantic experiences and expectations of older adults. People in their 80s and 90s experienced the Great Depression and a major world war. These events and the norms of the era continue to influence their romantic relationships.

In retrospect, Viola attributed her disastrous first marriage to the effects of the Great Depression. Her father had hired a handsome young man to work as a thrasher on the farm. Though 10 years older than Viola, the thrasher (whose name we never heard) "was thrilling because he had a car and could take me to the movies." The couple had to wait until Viola was 17 because her parents would not give permission for an earlier wedding. Before the ink was dry on the wedding certificate, this anonymous man was off cavorting with other women. Divorce was highly stigmatized in the 1930s, but Viola went after it. "Finally I went to a lawyer to get a divorce and he said, 'Oh, you can't get a divorce! You'd be a scarlet woman . . . an outcast to society. I wouldn't think of giving you a divorce.'" Viola stayed in this marriage for over 10 years, during which time she left her husband and moved to various places where she could work to support her three children. After years of living apart, a divorce was finally granted, freeing Viola to seek a more suitable partner.

Some respondents reflected on the norms of a more recent era. Anna, age 52, talked about being a lesbian in the 1970s: "There wasn't enough support system at the time. . . . Nobody knew I was out. Nobody knew I was a lesbian and so I hadn't come out yet . . . so it was a miserable time. It's hard to get people to understand it's so different now. . . . We felt like we should be able to be different from the heterosexuals, be able to . . . but it just destroyed people. . . . It turned out to be very unhealthy. It's very painful." Anna also recognized the social context of her relationships. "The importance of a community in the fate of a relationship is not definitive, but it seems clear that if you have family, neighbors, and friends supporting you, it's easier to get through . . . whereas when the whole world, including the laws, are telling you, 'This relationship is wrong' . . . that can undermine your relationship."

In Chapter 1 we explored the possibility that unstable social conditions make for unstable romantic relationships. Researchers have clearly documented the effects of stress on the quality of marital relationships. Several studies, including national samples, have demonstrated that financial problems contribute to divorce. Others have shown that stress in the form of either limited resources or excessive demands can impair marital communication.[7] Here we have seen that economic deprivation can make a man with a few resources exceptionally attractive, while social stigma can discourage divorce and marginalize people of minority sexual orientations. Meanwhile, as we have seen, the pervasive stigmatizing of older adults has subtle and enduring effects on late-life romantic possibilities.

*Ageism*

Ageism is a negative attitude toward older people and the process of aging that manifests in subtle and varied ways. Most gerontologists agree that this attitude is widespread in the United States, to the extent that it constitutes a social norm—the notion that people of a certain age are "too old" to do something, or the disapproval we encounter when we do not "act our age." Ageism arises when a mature job candidate is set aside in favor of someone with "more energy," or when a surgeon declines to treat a 90-year-old because people of that age are "too frail," or when anyone finds physical affection in older adults disgusting. Perhaps the most damaging aspect of ageism comes when it is internalized and our notion of the possibilities of late life are unnecessarily restricted.

One need only watch commercial television for an evening to see advertisements designed to persuade us that aging is unattractive. One of my favorites is an ad for men's hair coloring. A handsome gray-haired man is repulsed by a young blonde woman he tries to pick up in a bar. He goes to the bathroom and colors his hair brown. When he returns to the blond as a new man, she greets him rapturously and leaves in his arms. Since they are spending billions of dollars on this ageist propaganda, we must assume the ads are effective. Either they persuade us that age is unattractive, or they tap into our latent fears.

As more people live to an advanced age, the use of age to regulate or limit behavior should diminish. Every day older adults expand the possibilities of later life. We see 80-year-olds skydiving, going to school, and even getting married. Faced with this rich diversity, stereotyped notions of what it means to be "old," "older," or even "very old" may just fade away. In the meantime, constant vigilance will help us shrug off ageism when it surfaces in our daily lives and our romantic expectations.

## Conclusion

Is it an unbearable cliché to suggest that it takes a village to carry on a love affair? Nonetheless, romance does not spring up in a social vacuum. Early lessons in how to love take place in families of origin, and subsequent lessons come from friends, social institutions, and other family members. Beyond the immediate community, society influences the course of romantic partnerships through the stresses and challenges it imposes.

At the same time, love changes families, communities, and even societies. This is why others have a stake in our romantic adventures. More specifically, late-life romances have ripple effects beyond the individuals involved. Researchers have tentatively demonstrated the intergenerational impact of romance in the senior generation of a family. And most of us are aware that when long-term relationships are disrupted difficulties can extend well beyond the immediate family.

Love among older adults changes the social context for everyone. I was reminded of this one night when my husband and I attended an outdoor concert. Settling into my seat, I was delighted to see an older couple necking furiously in the row right in front of ours. Watching their obvious pleasure, my husband and I snuggled in a bit closer than usual, and during the evening physical affection seemed to radiate out from that couple. By the end of the concert, couples in the vicinity were nestling close and having a great time. Perhaps a few went away with an expanded sense of late life's romantic possibilities.

## Try This

1. Love in Social Context: If you have a romantic partner, keep track for one week of the number of times you mention your partner to someone else. Do you find yourself saying, "My husband . . . " at the grocery store? To your boss? Do you invoke the image of "My wife . . . " when you drop off the dry cleaning? At the gym? Do you share stories about what your partner did with a close confidante? Do you share the dilemmas and challenges of

life as a couple with someone you trust? Jot these events down in a "social context" log that you will review at the end of the week. I bet you will be surprised by the variety of people and places that you have drawn into your life as a couple. Now ask yourself what kind of support you drew from each of these interactions. What purpose did it serve vis-à-vis your relationship? What does your log tell you about your own social support network?

2. Love's Village: Map out the "village" in which your romances take place. Where are the stressors? The supports? Where do you look for approval and disapproval?

## Suggested Reading

Deida, D. (2002). *Finding God through sex: A spiritual guide to ecstatic loving and deep passion for men and women.* Austin, TX: Plexus. I could not believe it when I spotted this title in, of all places, our college bookstore. It was a must-have for the title alone. I have to admit that the content is intriguing. I loaned my first copy out to a student and never got it back.

Comforted by forgiveness.

# Part IV

# Love's Disillusions

In the late nineteenth century, Spanish philosopher Miguel de Unamuno argued that the greatest tension man faces is between the reality of death and the desire for immortality. Some suggest that we manage this tension by creating myths about life after death. Love is an integral part of the cruder realities of life and death, even as it inspires some to hope for eternal passion.

The relationship between illusion and disillusion is a delicate balance. Both are essential realities of romantic love. Illusion lures us into relationships that may sustain us for a lifetime. Disillusion reinforces life's bitter lessons. The euphoria of illusion may feel more pleasant than the misery of disillusion, but both are necessary parts of a rich and fulfilling life. Indeed, as we will see in this part, the lessons of disillusion contribute to the direction of our lives and the nature of our personalities.

We tend to associate illusion with youth and disillusion with old age. But as we see in the cases described in this book, life is more complex. Older adults can be ensnared by love's illusions, albeit less frequently and perhaps less intensely than the young. And disillusion poses a challenge at any age.

Part II of this book considered love's illusions, and in Part III we celebrated the realities of long-term romantic commitment. Here we turn to the disillusionment of betrayal and rejection, and the sorrow of loss. This final section brings us full circle to the possibility of new love following the loss of a partner.

Remains close to his children.

# 7

# Betrayal and Rejection

*Mattie's first experience of love was also her first taste of betrayal. Born in Santiago, Chile, in 1934, Mattie fell in love at 16 and was married within 5 months. Their first few months were idyllic, but she became pregnant right away and her husband "start changing, changing, changing. . . . He wasn't anymore my dream love." He started drinking and seeing other women, and eventually he brought home a sexually transmitted disease. When she sought treatment, her care providers assumed Mattie was unfaithful to her husband and lectured her on the sin of infidelity. Mattie went home and slit her wrists. "Blood," she recalls, "there was a lot of blood." Her 8-year-old son went to neighbors for help, and they took her to the hospital. When she woke up and explained to the doctor why she tried to take her life, he assured her, "No man is worth the life of a mother!" Those words saved Mattie: She left her husband, moved her children to Argentina, and opened a successful beauty salon. When the family later migrated to the United States, she met and married Dirk. "In the beginning," she remembers, "I loved my husband with all my heart." But this would not last.*

*A convert to Mormonism, Mattie believed that families are reunited in heaven. A process known as sealing is necessary to ensure that they will be able to find each other. One day she mentioned her desire to be sealed with a child from her previous marriage who had died in infancy. Dirk refused. He did not want to spend eternity with another man's child. As Mattie tells it, this immediately killed her love for the man. He had betrayed her confidence in him as a loving and supportive husband.*

*Mattie's pretty home has been an armed camp for the past 6 years. She and Dirk live in separate bedrooms. "We live totally separate lives. The only thing I do is cook for us." She does not enter his room, "Not even to clean!" Still, Mattie believes she is bound to Dirk for eternity. Divorcing him is unthinkable. "What would my family say? I have my principles." She recognizes that though he no longer loves her, "He needs me . . . for his health, for convenience. . . . It is terrible for me to recognize." Mattie no longer believes in romantic love. She says her only love is for her children and her God. After decades of deceit and isolation, she concludes, "There is no love. . . . Nobody respects anybody." Mattie does love herself, though. She eats right and exercises regularly.*

In some ways, Mattie's experience of late-life betrayal was not unusual. Romantic betrayal often arises later in life. In fact, some researchers have noted that the likelihood of infidelity rises with each year of marriage. Older adults can find themselves abandoned when the partners they relied upon for decades suddenly fall in love with younger people. Some, like Madeleine Albright, grow through the experience to achieve things they had never anticipated. Others, like Ted (whom we met in Chapter 3) find late life brings the bitter aftertaste of past betrayals.

As we will see in this chapter, most people dealing with betrayal are faced with sexual infidelity. The chapter begins with a discussion of affairs, considering their prevalence and asking why people stray. We then turn to betrayal's aftermath to examine forgiveness, revenge, and the outcome of betrayal in relationships and jealousy. A brief consideration of other forms of betrayal closes the chapter.

## What Is Betrayal?

Psychologist Julie Fitness has conducted extensive research on romantic betrayal. She offered a clear definition: "essentially, betrayal means that one party in a relationship acts in a way that favors his or her own interests at the expense of the other party's interests. . . . In a deeper sense, however, betrayal sends an ominous signal about how little the betrayer cares about, or values his or her relationship with the betrayed partner."[1] Betrayal is often synonymous with sexual infidelity, but it also takes more subtle, insidious forms: emotional withdrawal, exposure, and lies. From the betrayed person's perspective, even repeated disappointments may come to be seen as betrayal. Mattie's second experience of betrayal revealed that Dirk valued their eternal relationship less than she had believed. This was a shattering blow to her sense of security and commitment. Forgiveness does not seem to be on the horizon, and the two live in a swirl of revenge and hostility that ironically seals them unhappily ever after.

## *Sexual Infidelity*

Mattie's first husband committed a classic romantic betrayal: sexual infidelity. For most of us, infidelity is the sine qua non of romantic betrayal. Of the 632 people in our Internet survey who reported having been betrayed by someone they were romantically involved with, nearly half (48%) had been cheated on.

As attitudes toward marriage have shifted, our understanding of infidelity has become a bit more fluid. As we saw in Chapter 5, more Americans are cohabiting without the sanction of marriage. These secular relationships are typically based on mutual trust and commitment and the expectation of sexual monogamy. Some couples, including same-sex couples, prefer an approach known as negotiated nonmonogamy. This is what Edmund had in mind when he moved in with his partner, Barry; but he had not anticipated his own reaction.

### Edmund's Story

In his mid-60s, Edmund (whom we met in the last chapter) reflected on the beginning of his romance with Barry. At the time, Edmund was looking for romance, and Barry did not fit the bill. Edmund explained, "He wasn't my fantasy. He wasn't cute. He was infatuated with me right away and would meet me at my apartment in Salt Lake and we would go to a dance together, and we kind of had sex but it wasn't ever the wild pizzazz kind of thing." But over time, Edmund started to wonder. Barry was widowed, raising two teenagers, and Edmund became fond of the children.

The magic finally arrived. "One day as far as falling in love—he has a travel bug, as you can see, and we were in San Francisco and we were in Chinatown in a motel, and he was in the bathtub, and he's always been a big man and he took up this whole bathtub. It was a pink and black bathtub probably from the 50s and I looked at him, and I thought that was the cutest thing I had ever seen, and I finally realized that I was in love with him!"

So they moved in together, but their relationship was tumultuous. "There is no commitment, compared to what I had expected in a relationship because of my parents, and he also had the same kind of parents and so I guess we kind of thought that's the way it should be, just kind of accepted commitment, but I would go out, or he would go out, and we would kind of cheat on each other, and we'd have maybe a little casual sex and we'd talk about it and then we'd find out and then we'd get mad and we'd be angry. Then we'd say, well, we really didn't decide not to do that, so we finally decided that our relationship was an open relationship."

For 7 years Edmund and Barry had an open relationship with sexual partners coming and going. But they didn't bring their partners home. Then Barry crossed this line. He not only brought another man home, he had him move into the guest room. When Edmund objected, the man moved out.

Then, as Edmund explained, "One night when I thought we had gotten back together and this guy came back and he said, 'I guess I'll go downstairs,' so Barry stayed downstairs with him. I was, like, 'Who would you kill?' because I can't take it. I'm in the corner, here. And all of a sudden it's over with. I pushed a chair—I picked up that chair, broke it to pieces. I was just in a rage. I didn't know where I was going, what I was going to do. I ran outside and on the front porch there was a hammer and I picked up the hammer and I was standing like this with the hammer, and Barry came up the stairs and said 'What is that?' And I said, 'You goddamn son of a bitch, I am so angry,' and I could lay bricks. I started taking the house apart with this hammer, and he just said, 'Settle down.' I think he was scared I was going to kill him, and I saw this window, and my piano was there, and I was just about ready to throw the hammer through the window and I saw that my piano was there and that stopped me, and then of course I went all to pieces and he hugged me and said, 'You're okay. Just let me get this part of my life over with—I just have to do this.' Well, a woman wouldn't have stayed with him, not after all the movies I've seen."

After Edmund's epiphany, the couple settled into a comfortable domestic arrangement. They raised Barry's children, cared for aged parents, and became the center of a loving community of friends. A few years ago an Episcopal priest presided over their commitment ceremony, and this year they celebrated their 25th anniversary. Edmund's advice to lovers describes a fluid kind of commitment. He says, "Commit to each other even if you have to sit down every New Year's and write a different thing. Do something, so that both of you have something to hold on to—I promise this, I promise that—and it may change, so let's talk about the change."

Despite the rise in cohabitation and the variety in the structure of intimate relationships throughout the world, disapproval of sexual infidelity appears to be on the rise. In opinion polls taken in the United States and Europe, the proportion of respondents who condemn infidelity has risen significantly since the 1970s.[2] Today, a majority in the United States and Europe feel that sexual infidelity is wrong.[3]

Extramarital sex violates both the immediate contract between marriage partners and the social institution of marriage. Apart from the trauma inflicted on the parties directly involved, infidelity jeopardizes the institution's ability to regulate sexual activity and provide a stable environment for raising children. A man whose wife has been unfaithful can have no confidence that the children he supports through the sweat of his brow are actually his, and a wife whose husband has deceived her may live in fear that he will abandon her and the children for a lascivious life with his new sweetheart. For these very practical reasons, sexual infidelity is widely condemned.

Yet for all that, and for the strict prohibitions that have arisen in secular and religious settings alike, it is surprising how many people engage in extramarital affairs. Of course, it is difficult for researchers to gauge the full extent of sexual infidelity because of the taboo surrounding it. Generally, national studies report that 20% to 25% of Americans who have been or are married have engaged in extramarital sex at one point.[4] In one national study, 25% of men and 15% of women reported having engaged in extramarital sex.[5] This gender difference is consistent. Men remain more likely than women to report having sex outside of marriage, though this gap seems to be shrinking, and among younger age groups there appears to be no gender difference.[6]

With its promise of anonymity, our Internet survey was a useful device for measuring the extent of infidelity among the more technologically savvy. Generally, people are more likely to report having been the victims of sexual infidelity than having themselves committed such an act.[7] About one-quarter of the respondents in our study (25%) reported having been cheated on, while only 16% reported that they had cheated on their partners.[8]

## Predicting Infidelity

Why do people stray? Researchers have puzzled over this question, and the most definitive response seems to be, "It depends." Infidelity probably reflects an interaction of the quality of the relationship, events or conditions outside the relationship, and the characteristics of the individual who strays.

Marital distress contributes, as both a cause and the result of sexual infidelity.[9] Some have suggested that extramarital affairs result from deficits in the primary relationship.[10] So, for example, relationships with low satisfaction, high conflict, or infrequent sex may drive some to seek fulfillment elsewhere. As counselors and therapists worldwide are aware, this does not do wonders for the marriage itself. Indeed, adultery is the single most common reason for divorce throughout the world.[11] Still, as we saw in Chapter 6, it takes a village to sustain a committed relationship. Infidelity cannot be understood without reference to the broader social context that surrounds the relationship.

External forces such as history and culture can also influence people's tendency to stray. In Chapter 1 we explored the possibility that an unstable or highly stressful socioeconomic environment supports frequent, intense romantic attachments. There is also some evidence to support the popular belief that people who have more opportunities for extramarital sex are more likely to stray. Researchers have found that people who are in the labor force and those with higher incomes have a higher likelihood of committing adultery,[12] as do those who have had multiple sex partners before marriage and those who live in a central city.[13] Among young adults, Ann Zak and her colleagues found that infidelity was associated with "a lack of support for the relationship from a partner's family and friends."[14]

The characteristics of an individual also influence his or her tendency to stray, and age is clearly a factor. In part, this is because the longer a couple is together, the higher the likelihood that one of them will have an affair. In 1992, over 2,500 men and women in a national sample were surveyed about their extramarital affairs. The results indicated that for every year couples lived together, they became 1% more likely to be unfaithful.[15] This has led some researchers to suggest that sexual boredom is a leading cause of infidelity.

Some baby boomers are particularly vulnerable to sexual infidelity. In 2001, a group of psychologists examined survey data from over 4,000 Americans.[16] Their results indicated that men between the ages of 55 and 65 were most likely to have had an extramarital sexual encounter in their lives, while among women, those aged 40 to 45 were most like to have strayed. These age cohorts were more likely than either older or younger people to have had affairs.

Other individual attributes that increase the likelihood of extramarital sex include gender (historically men have been more likely to engage in affairs, though that seems to be changing); ethnicity (African American men were typically more likely to report infidelity); a high interest in sex; and a history of cohabitation.[17] The role of religion is a bit unclear. While some researchers have reported that attendance at church was not associated with diminished risk of infidelity,[18] others report that strong religious beliefs coupled with church attendance can reduce an individual's tendency to stray.[19]

In heterosexual relationships, men tend to report that they have affairs because their sexual needs are not met in their committed relationships; women tend to say they do so because their emotional needs have not been met.[20] The observation that lengthy relationships are associated with having higher rates of sexual infidelity suggests that in late life committed relationships may be at higher risk of failing to meet the needs of both sexes. Infidelity may be the culminating response to a series of minor betrayals and disappointments in a marriage. It may be the way some people respond to disillusionment.

## The Aftermath: Confession and Forgiveness

Oscar Wilde is accused of saying, "Always forgive your enemies—nothing infuriates them so!" If forgiveness is the best revenge, older adults are well equipped. In later life we are particularly likely to stray (especially baby boomers). But we may also be better able to forgive, due to our greater capacity for complex judgment and emotional regulation. Advanced age also brings time for reflection and the insights that can lead to forgiveness. Let us consider the aftermath of betrayal.

Part of the pain of betrayal is the effect that disclosure can have on a person's identity or "face." Disclosure can be a major face-losing event, particularly when it involves public embarrassment. As some researchers have demonstrated, the method of discovery may influence the relationship impact of a transgression. The greatest damage to a relationship comes through a public revelation. The least damage (and greatest forgiveness) comes through voluntary confession.[21] Geraldine from Wyoming wrote of her husband's unfaithfulness: "I think another hard part of unfaithfulness is how the spouse feels both betrayed and embarrassed. The embarrassment comes from knowing that others, close to you, knew about it, most likely spoke to others about it, but never spoke to you. It really lowers your self-esteem."

It is still unclear whether disclosure is preferable to keeping the darn thing secret. As Tim Cole observed in his 2001 study, truth telling can be costly, and people tend to act in ways that will minimize relational costs.[22] His research also revealed a tendency for people to believe their romantic partners are telling the truth. In fact, in his study of 128 couples, he found that individuals consistently reported that they were more deceptive than their partners—and this had no relationship to the partner's actual deceptive practices. This suggests that the person interested in keeping a secret may find that his or her partner is a willing collaborator. Of course, for some people the guilt of secret keeping may be impossible to bear.

A student brought the story of a lesbian couple to our weekly team meeting. In the couple's first few months, one of the partners, Anne, became sexually involved with a woman outside the relationship. When Judy found out, she was outraged. Anne apologized. Judy forgave. And they continued to have a fulfilling relationship. Ten years later, Judy became sexually involved with another woman. Expecting Anne to understand, Judy told her about the affair after it ended. In a sense, Judy explained, it was "payback" for Anne's earlier transgression. Judy apologized. But even after intensive therapy, Anne could not forgive her. They broke up. Anne explained that to her it was one thing to go out on a relatively new relationship and quite another to betray the confidence of a partner of 10-plus years.

My student's reaction was, "Judy should never have confessed!" My reaction was, "Judy should have cried!" Another student had just told me one of those after-the-fact stories respondents love to share as interviewers walk out the door.[23] The 78-year-old widower she had just interviewed spoke of his wife's affair. Early in their marriage, she became involved with one of his best friends from the military. She quickly broke off the affair and confessed to her husband. He was shattered, but eventually he completely forgave her. They were married for 57 years. My student asked why he forgave her, and he said something like, "Because she was so abject! She wept and apologized and promised it would never happen again. And then she felt awful for months. She punished herself so much I didn't have the heart to."

Good apologies are particularly effective at restoring harmony following a relationship transgression.[24] Psychologist Julie Fitness asked 90 long-term married and 70 divorced individuals about their partners' marital offenses. Some were forgiven and some were not, and respondents were asked to explain why they had or had not forgiven their partners. The forgiven did not differ from the unforgiven in terms of the nature of the betrayal or the intensity of the pain it had caused. The one exception was that repeat offenses were unlikely to be forgiven. Further, unforgiven offenses were more likely to have involved humiliation and hatred. But the key difference was in the aftermath. Offenders who were "truly remorseful" were more likely to be forgiven than those who were defensive and refused to take responsibility.

Why are apologies so effective? Possibly because they give the person who has been offended an opportunity to restore face. The apologizer effectively rolls over on his back, baring his tummy—giving the offended person power and status in the relationship. A good apology does not say, "I'm sorry you're upset." A truly great apology says, "I did wrong by you. You have every right to be upset, and I'm sorry. What can I do to make things right between us?"[25]

The difference between these two apologies is remorse and guilt. In the first case, the truculent offender shows no evidence of remorse. But the second implies that the offender is suffering, which evens the score. Indeed, an apology may just be the beginning of the long road to forgiveness. Faced with a lover's betrayal, some of us demand restitution. The offending partner may need to take actions, such as breaking off contact with an extramarital liaison or behaving well for an extended period before forgiveness is complete.

## Why Do People Forgive?

Our Internet survey gives those in need of forgiveness cause for optimism, because a majority of reported offenses were forgiven. Among those who were betrayed by a loved one, 78% reported having forgiven the person; and among those who had committed a relationship transgression, 65% reported that they had been forgiven. Indeed, 80% of these offenders reported that they had forgiven themselves. Despite the difficulty, a majority of transgressions in loving relationships are (eventually) forgiven.

We asked the 492 respondents in our study who forgave their offenders to explain what had made it possible for them to forgive. Their reasons are both fascinating and varied. The most common response, given by nearly half (43%) of respondents, was simply "time." Some people mentioned the cliché that "time heals all"; others just said "time"; and others, like one 51-year-old woman from South Carolina, were more specific: "16 years."

Len, age 62, from Hawaii, explained, "It took 20 years to get over the infidelity and abortion, but I remain single and will be until I die." Clearly, as Len illustrates, forgiveness does not necessarily mean that the relationship remains intact, or even that it can ever be the same. Several people emphasized that they might forgive but would never forget the transgression, and that a repeat offense would be completely unforgivable.

Next after time in the list of popular reasons for forgiveness came insight or understanding. Over a quarter (28%) of the people who responded attributed their ability to forgive to newfound understanding. Often, they just needed to understand why the person had betrayed them. The need to understand is not just a desire for empathy or insight. People who have been betrayed once need some assurance that they will not go through this again. For instance, 56-year-old Emily, from Georgia, forgave her husband's cheating. As she explained, "Need to know why he did it so I can have the peace of mind that he won't do it again."

Some found that taking responsibility for the betrayal made forgiveness possible. For example, 57-year-old Winnie from North Carolina forgave her husband's affair, saying, "I took a hard look at how I had contributed to the demise of the relationship, which prompted him to look elsewhere."

Similarly, 56-year-old Tyler, from Kentucky, felt betrayed when his partner allowed the relationship to fall apart. He said he was able to forgive because "I had to recognize that I had faults and did some things I shouldn't have." On the other hand, some people were able to forgive when they realized that the betrayal had nothing to do with them. For example, 52-year-old Annie, also from Kentucky, explained that she had forgiven her partner's infidelity, saying, "My own realization that the infidelity/betrayal was more the result of their personality than of my failures."

Sandra, age 57, from Arkansas, experienced multiple betrayals: "When I was raped, he had a few drinks and accused me of inviting the rapist to follow me. He cheated on me with another woman and lied to me, even in marriage counseling. The other man I'm in love with dumped me when things got too emotionally difficult, and withdrew, leaving me hanging." She explained her ability to forgive, saying, "I would say I've forgiven each of these transgressions, but I think what I really mean is that I've come to an understanding and empathy with the men about why each happened. When you really love someone, you accept their imperfections as they accept yours. Those experiences of betrayal left scars though."

Some people saw forgiveness as a defining characteristic of true love. Even before the movie *Love Story* made the sentiment appear trite, many believed that love meant "never having to say you're sorry." As 78-year-old Jim explained, "If you love people, you forgive them." It's as simple as that.

Henry, age 61, from Virginia, offered particularly insightful comments. He described his experiences of betrayal, saying, "It's happened a number of times with different persons I've loved. I think it's virtually inevitable. Examples include using a personal weakness of mine against me, revealing to another something I shared intimately, having another sexual partner at a time of declared monogamy, etc." Then Henry described forgiveness as the heavy labor of true love: "Sometimes the betrayal ended the relationship. In my enduring relationship, forgiveness required hours of talk, tears, agreements, rebasing the relationship, and a lot of other hard work. The hard work required is really exhausting and may define a true love."

A good number of our respondents (12%) reported that they had simply outgrown their anger and found a mature place of forgiveness. Some (11%) reported that distance allowed them to forgive. Another 8% cited a new love as the source of forgiveness.

The vast majority of these people explain their forgiveness as an individual process, largely due to the passage of time or to their insight or maturity. Only a few (9%) said that their commitment to the relationship or concern for their partner triggered forgiveness. An even smaller number (6%) attributed their mercy to the partner's excellent apology or to communication or "working it out" with their partners (5%).

Generally, forgiveness is a complex process, demanding a combination of the factors discussed here. Adrian, 60 years old, living in New York, was enjoying a 3-month love affair. Adrian explained how she was betrayed: "My husband of 30 years decided that he wanted to be with a woman he had dated in high school. For the last 3 years, roughly, of our marriage, things were going well with us. We had had our rocky times in the past. We were then, when she came into the picture, settling into a lovely routine, enjoying each other fully, and looking toward retirement, marriages, grandkids. This came out of the blue for me, and I was devastated." But Adrian forgave her husband somehow—or, perhaps, sort of: "My bitterness hurt no one but me; it was aging me besides. Not a pretty sight. So, I just decided, hey, he's a good man; he's human; he slipped up; but let's get on with our lives. He married her and got on with his; I went to grad school and moved to NYC and am getting on with mine. Now, this is the kicker: I have never met *her*, but I don't feel like I've forgiven her. At least I don't refer to her as Bitch-Whore anymore. I think that's progress, don't you?"

## *Revenge and Suffering*

Revenge can even the score and may not be as destructive as some would have us believe. Sometimes, respondents enjoyed watching their betrayers suffer, even if they did not inflict the suffering themselves. Only a few of our respondents (2%) were willing to admit that revenge or watching the transgressor suffer set the stage for their forgiveness. Alicia, a 58-year-old Latina from California, divorced her husband of 22 years when he slept with her best friend and lied to her about it. She seemed gleeful in explaining that she was able to forgive him because "I have learned that karma really does work, without my assistance!" In the same vein, 51-year-old Cassie, from Wyoming, explained that her first husband, "whom I thought I was in love with, but actually was more infatuated—had sex with another woman. He said it wasn't sex because she just gave him a blow job and he didn't screw her." Cassie, who is now enjoying a "living apart, together" relationship with her boyfriend, explained her forgiveness, saying, "It took many many years. I did not forgive for a very long time. It took separation and vengeance (I then had an affair with a man) and finally just putting it out of my thoughts."

## *Transgression's Result*

Sometimes the outcome of transgression depends less on the offender's behavior than on the needs and characteristics of the person who has been betrayed. If a person is highly committed to or dependent on a relationship, he or she may simply accommodate the betrayal.[26] Marilyn is a good example of this. When she found out her husband was having an affair, she initially wondered whether she could trust him and continue in the marriage, but concluded, "I had spent too much time and energy on our marriage to let something like that interfere."

This illustrates two types of commitment identified by Michael Roloff and his colleagues.[27] They studied relationship transgressions running the gamut from extrarelational sex and physical abuse to betraying confidences or forgetting special occasions, and argued that commitment was a key factor in couples' ability to remain together. These authors distinguished between commitment that stems from fear of losing the partner and commitment based on mutual involvement in the relationship and suggested that, while both types of commitment keep relationships intact, fear of loss is associated with more vengeful, destructive behaviors whereas involvement leads to more positive coping.

## *Jealousy*

Jealousy is a natural response to someone who poses a threat to our romantic relationships.[28] It can be either situational or personal. That is, everyone has the capacity to become jealous in the right situation, but some of us have a greater tendency toward jealousy than others. On a personal level, jealousy has been linked to feelings of loneliness and powerlessness.[29] Some take the absence of jealousy as a sign of indifference.

Women may differ from men in their responses to betrayal. Research on jealousy consistently indicates that men respond more negatively to sexual betrayal than women, while women respond more negatively to emotional betrayal.[30] This holds across cultures and across settings, and has been so consistently observed that researchers have moved from confirming the phenomenon to explaining it. Some argue that this reflects the different reproductive needs and strategies of men and women, while others suggest that it simply reflects women's insight that emotional betrayal can affect many other aspects of the relationship, including sex. Some have argued that this difference is disappearing as gender roles become less distinct.[31]

## Other Forms of Betrayal

Becoming involved with another, sexually or otherwise, is the most common form of romantic betrayal reported by our 632 Internet respondents. But lying comes in a close second, and rejection deserves consideration as well. Table 7.1 illustrates the range of activities that our Internet respondents considered betrayal.

### *Lying and Exposure*

Honesty is an important value in intimate relationships, and nearly a fourth of those who responded to the Internet survey reported that their romantic partners had either lied to them (20%) or exposed them to a shaming experience (3%). Most of the lies had to do with sexual infidelity, as when 56-year-old Catherine's partner lied to her "about a sexual relationship with someone else." But others were life changing. For example, a 41-year-old woman from Hawaii described her experience with betrayal as follows: "lying to you throughout a marriage about wanting kids then finding out they were sterile and knew it."

Public exposure is a humiliating loss of face and betrayal of trust. Sometimes women betrayed their partners by exposing or threatening to expose their secrets. As 48-year-old Len, from Hawaii, demonstrated when explaining his experience: "My ex-wife knew that I was gay and took advantage of the situation when we separated. I was serving in the Navy and she threatened to out me regardless of the fact that she knew prior to our marriage."

As we saw earlier, 61-year-old Harry reported that exposure was part of a series of betrayal experiences in his life. He described it as "revealing to another something I shared intimately."

Some might argue that telling or threatening to tell a secret is a modest sort of relationship betrayal. Nonetheless, as these respondents have demonstrated, those at the receiving end of this kind of exposure feel that it is threatening in part because of the humiliation or damage of the exposure itself, but more importantly because of what it says about the relationship. If we cannot trust our intimate partners to respect our privacy, the only recourse is to withdraw from the relationship by not sharing vulnerabilities and secrets, a response that is antithetical to intimacy.

Table 7.1.   What Constitutes Betrayal? Answers From Internet Respondents

| Responses From Those Who Had Been Betrayed | Men (n = 106) (%) | Women (n = 526) (%) | Total (n = 632) (%) |
|---|---|---|---|
| Had sex with another ("cheated") | 51 | 47 | 48 |
| Lied to me (or kept secrets) | 16 | 21 | 20 |
| Became involved with another, unclear about sex | 14 | 19 | 18 |
| Left me | 20 | 13 | 14 |
| Left the relationship emotionally | 3 | 3 | 3 |
| Emotionally abused me | 7 | 10 | 10 |
| Exposed me (e.g., by telling secrets to others) | 4 | 2 | 3 |
| Was addicted to drugs/alcohol | 1 | 4 | 3 |
| Was homosexual or bisexual | 1 | 2 | 1 |
| Money problems | 2 | 4 | 3 |
| Physically abused me | 1 | 3 | 3 |
| Other | 1 | 4 | 4 |

| Responses From Those Who Had Betrayed a Lover | Men (n = 66) (%) | Women (n = 283) (%) | Total (n = 349) (%) |
|---|---|---|---|
| Had sex with another ("cheated") | 53 | 51 | 52 |
| Thought about another romantic involvement | 0 | 6 | 5 |
| Kissed another | 2 | 3 | 3 |
| Became involved with another, unclear about sex | 12 | 15 | 14 |
| Left the person | 8 | 8 | 8 |
| Left the relationship emotionally; "fell out of love" | 2 | 1 | 1 |
| Was emotionally abusive or mean to lover | 6 | 2 | 3 |
| Pretended to love or care more than really did | 0 | 1 | 1 |
| Exposed lover (e.g., by telling secrets to others) | 2 | 1 | 1 |
| Other | 10 | 6 | 7 |

## *Rejection*

Betrayal and rejection are closely linked. By signaling devaluation of the relationship, a betrayal can be considered a form of rejection.[32] Among respondents to our Internet survey who felt they had been betrayed, nearly one in five (17%) mentioned that their partners had either rejected them or become emotionally distant. For example, 49-year-old Sam from California described his experience with rejection: "Planned on making a life together, then she decided she wanted someone else instead, then realized he was not what she wanted, then wanted me back, but nope, ain't gonna happen." Clearly, at least from Sam's perspective, the rejection was a mistake on her part. I was surprised by the extent to which men complained of emotional abandonment. But 56-year-old Henry, a Native American from Arkansas, demonstrated by saying his partner "left me emotionally." Another man, 58-year-old Clyde from Wyoming, had newly remarried. He said that his previous wife "fell out of love with me." So much for gender stereotypes.

Apart from the loss of a future relationship, romantic rejection is a powerful blow to a person's self-esteem. It is one thing to be rejected by someone who barely knows you, as might be the case in unrequited love— but quite another to be rejected by someone who knows you intimately. Psychologists Bratslavsky, Baumeister, and Sommer suggested, "The later in a relationship the rejection comes, the greater the negative impact on your self-esteem."[33] This may explain why Judy's betrayal proved so devastating to her relationship with Anne.

## Conclusion

Romantic betrayal may be the inevitable result of life in an individualistic era. It may be a sign of the times, fostered by social instability and the commoditization of American life. Or it may be the natural consequence of having a social life. By life's latter half, most of us have survived and many of us have committed romantic betrayal. Some take joy in observing that their betrayers ended up less well off.

We like to think that we become stronger, better, or deeper because of these experiences. Indeed, the intense disillusionment of betrayal affords us the opportunity to revisit old assumptions and habits. Through this dark experience, love offers important insights into our needs, our weaknesses, and our capacity for forgiveness.

Sometimes betrayal serves an essential function, freeing both partners from a toxic cage. Other times, the fact that a marriage has survived betrayal becomes the hallmark of enduring love. Often, betrayal is just a mistake—a taking for granted or a failure to communicate. Either way, it remains one of love's greatest disillusions and life's greatest challenges.

## Try This

1. Mini-Betrayals: Have you felt disappointed in a romantic partner lately? Is he or she failing to live up to your expectations? Notice how you respond to this mini-betrayal. Do you suffer in silence, telling yourself that you expect too much or if you wait long enough your partner will change? Are you keeping score so you will have ammunition in case of a big blowup? Have you ever wondered why your partner behaves this way? What would happen if you mentioned your disappointment to your partner? Or have you already?

2. Gossip: Think about someone you know who has been sexually unfaithful to a romantic partner. How did you feel when you found out about it? Did you tell someone? Why? What role do you think gossip plays in enforcing social norms?

## Suggested Reading

Albright, M. (2003). *Madam secretary: A memoir.* New York: Miramax Books. "This marriage is dead, and I am in love with someone younger and beautiful." With these words, Madeleine Albright's husband Joe torpedoed a marriage that had lasted for two decades and produced three children. Secretary Albright candidly explains that she would have traded her successful career in a heartbeat to make Joe change his mind. While he did waffle, he ultimately settled on the younger model. Albright's lengthy autobiography describes her efforts to fill the gap he left in her life—mostly with work. It is a humanizing look at a powerful figure.

Bauer-Maglin, N. (Ed.). (2006). *Cut loose: (Mostly) older women talk about the end of (mostly) long-term relationships.* New Brunswick, NJ: Rutgers University Press. Not for the faint of heart, this book presents first-person narratives from women who were "cut loose" by their spouses and partners. Apart from a couple of more theoretical chapters, these are stories of betrayal and rage. No sugar-coating here, just refreshing candor.

Theirs was a marriage of equals. He misses her now.
*Photo by Marianne Gontarz York*

# 8

## Love Lost

*Walking to the front door of Susan's historic home on a chilly fall morning, I breathed in the cozy smells of coffee and fallen leaves. Her living room was furnished in eclectic comfort, with plenty of family pictures—mostly of her children in graduation regalia. One corner held a tender shrine to Susan's husband, Tommy.*

*In her early 60s, Susan reminded me of a sturdy Midwestern farm girl, exuding health and wholesome practicality. She had loved three men in her life, all of them tall, handsome, and passionately devoted to a cause. Best of all, none of them demanded that she conform to gender stereotypes. Susan explained, "The thing that is interesting is that . . . I could be a bold, assertive, intelligent, active woman [and] they weren't threatened by it. It is important and it's highly unusual, especially for that generation. . . . I was proud of all three of them. I think they were terrific men."*

*She met Tommy one summer at a picnic and was immediately attracted to him. "He was tall. He was nice looking. He was fun. He was interesting." But he was not the center of her world. Susan planned to join the Peace Corps in the fall and, while she might enjoy a summer romance, she was not about to turn her life around.*

*When Susan returned from the Peace Corps, Tommy was available and as attractive as ever. They eased into a marriage that would last for 25 years. Susan never questioned Tommy's love for her. "He was able to be with me in my fullness and my assertiveness . . . and we stayed married. There were times when things were hard, but it was mostly hard because I was having a hard time."*

*Tommy had a heart attack when he was 41, but, Susan explained, "He had rehabilitated himself so well and was in fairly good shape when he had it, and then he was a jogger and afterward he modified his diet and went to a cardiac gym class and he was like the poster child for the cardiac gym class. They all wished they were as healthy as Tommy."*

*A few years later, he was at a conference in Chicago and had a heart attack while jogging. Susan described the circumstances of his death:*

*My dad had died 10 days earlier and we had all just been staying at my dad's house and sleeping on the floor and things like that. So my husband's parents had come up from Chicago and so when we were all leaving they took me down to O'Hare and dropped me off. The conference was to start off Friday morning, and he went out jogging near my dad's house, and there was a shopping center on the edge of the suburb and he was there and we are not sure why he was there—we don't know—but right in front of a restaurant and shopping center he just dropped down. Some people saw him and called the ambulance and started doing CPR and took him to the university hospital, which was only about a mile away, and they tried to revive him but they didn't know who he was and nobody reported [him] missing because I was here.*

*So anyway the coroner came the next morning again and moved the body. At that point, the key had fallen out of Tommy's gym shorts pocket and my dad had done something you should never do, which is put the address on the key. So they went to the address and they went across the street to talk with the neighbor and he said, "Well, the man who lived there just died, but his son-in-law is staying there." So then they went in the house and they found Tommy's wallet with his picture ID and everything.*

*So they called the police to come and tell me and I was gone to work. And I'd gone out for dinner with some friends and we were having this room and the living room painted and wallpapered and there was no wallpaper on the walls and I had gotten something from Sears. I don't know what it was. I was on the phone on hold with Sears when someone knocked on the door, and I went to the door and it was the police, and I didn't know what they wanted so I decided to hang up. They told me he had died.*

Susan remembers every phone call she made that night.

*Over 300 people attended Tommy's funeral. It was standing room only. They cremated and buried his remains. Susan goes there "every once in a great while." She says, "It's not where Tommy is. . . . If there's anywhere where Tommy still is, it's on the third floor [laughs]. Well, it looks a little different than it looked when he had his office up there. It's two-thirds of the third floor, so he had a big room. . . . But I had to get all the books out of his office. I had to clear out some space because his research was spread out on the floor [laughs], so it was interrupted. So it is a change, but basically it's the same space that it was when he was alive. I mean someday I've got to deal with his research notes—you know he was right in the middle of a project."*

*Though it's been 10 years since his death, Susan says she thinks about Tommy all the time. She honors his memory by serving on committees that serve causes he cherished. She once had a dream where he came back and she said to him, "Wow, you gave us quite a scare!"*

*I asked Susan whether she could imagine herself in another relationship.*

*"Well, it's interesting. I think I was more open to that right afterwards than I am now. I just got so used to being by myself and do what I want when I want it, things like that. The other thing, I sort of look back on it and I say, you know, these really impressive men loved me and it worked at some point in some way, maybe not as much as I loved them, but I really loved them. Sometimes I look back and think that was truly remarkable." I asked whether Susan thought that was enough, and she replied,*

> *Sort of. What I am thinking of myself is 'fat and gray-haired,' and what I think, if that's all there is, it is enough. . . . One exception—there's a man that took me to the university. He was a nice, nice man. He would drive up and I was just thinking, you know, maybe I'll invite him and a couple mutual friends for dinner or something like that. And I happened to sit behind him at a concert; he was with a woman and I all of a sudden got the feeling that he was engaged. . . . And I was glad I didn't embarrass myself or him either. . . . I think part of it is that here there are so few choices. . . . It's a small town and you want to be with someone who is as intelligent as you are, and then someone who can handle being, you know, with an outspoken, assertive woman. It's not everybody. I'm realizing when I think of the people I have loved very strongly that a commitment to something beyond themselves is part of my criteria. So to find someone with all those things would not be likely. The other thing is everyone, most people around here know Tommy, or knew Tommy, so I'm sure that they think "Do I measure up?" or something. . . . I mean, I've gone out once with guys that I work with. One guy that I knew took me out for lunch and coffee. He met me at my office and kissed me hello, on the lips, which I thought was a little strange.*

*Susan went to lunch with this man and he kissed her good-bye, but they never went out again.*

C. S. Lewis observed that grief is "a universal and integral part of our experience of love."[1] Love does not end with bereavement, but it does change; and just as every love affair is unique, each bereavement follows its own path. Nonetheless, Susan's experiences illustrate some common themes. First, even 10 years after the loss, her grief was palpable but not overwhelming. This is fortunate, and not unusual. Extreme grief reactions can be hazardous. Second, people who lose a romantic partner often have detailed memories of the events immediately surrounding the death. In her memoir of losing her husband, Joan Didion remarked on how tales of a death so often begin with "It was just an ordinary day," suggesting that we can hardly imagine something as unthinkable as death happening under such unremarkable circumstances.[2] Third, like Marty (Chapter 5), Susan is committed to sustaining Tommy's legacy. Where Marty decided to live his life in a way that would have pleased Ethel, Susan expanded her community service to include Tommy's favorite causes. Preserving the legacy is an excellent way of coping with loss and, like other tasks of grieving, can have implications for subsequent relationships. Finally, like many other widows, Susan was not particularly interested in remarriage. She mentioned several reasons why a new relationship might not happen: community pressures, the difficulty of finding a good match, and her tendency to compare men to Tommy.

What Susan did not mention were simple demographics that mitigate against older women finding partners of the opposite sex. Recall that even in their early 50s men are outnumbered by women; and by their mid-80s there are four women for every man. Young women may look upon these figures with dismay, but as we will see, many older widows treasure their newfound freedom.

This chapter begins with grief, describing the process using a typology introduced by William Worden, a renowned bereavement specialist. Departing from his typology, we explore the long-neglected topic of contact with the deceased, asking how many people have this kind of experience and what they draw from it. We then consider the impact of bereavement on immunity before exploring the social context of widowhood and the challenges and rewards of repartnering.

## Grief Reactions

Grief is not a state but a process. In the course of a career that spanned half a century, Dr. Elisabeth Kübler-Ross changed the way Americans think about that process.[3] Based on careful observation of terminally ill patients and their families, she described common grief reactions: denial, anger, bargaining, depression, and acceptance. Unfortunately, her sensitive and insightful descriptions of these reactions came to be understood as a progression of stages that bereaved people "should" go through. Professionals in the helping disciplines memorized their initials, DABDA, and advised those who could not accept the reality of their loss that they were in denial.

Several other theorists have offered their own stage-based approaches to understanding grief. Some draw on attachment theory (introduced in Chapter 1) to explain the stages of loss. John Bowlby observed that when infants are left alone by their caregivers, they respond with shock, protest, despair, and reorganization.[4] We need only imagine a child left alone on the savannah to understand that these reactions might confer an evolutionary advantage. The child is briefly paralyzed by shock, unable to comprehend the reality of the situation. As reality sinks in, the infant protests vigorously and loudly, a response likely to attract the attention of a parent who has wandered a little too far away. When protests fail, the child must conserve energy and avoid attracting the attention of any lions in the vicinity. Despair accomplishes these evolutionary goals, keeping the child still until the parent can return. When, ultimately, the parent does not return, the child must finally reorganize his life to accommodate the loss.

Attachment theorists suggest that our grief reactions follow this trajectory. News of the death may come as a shock, even if we were expecting it, and our minds need time to absorb the new reality. Once that has set in, we might actively grieve until we exhaust ourselves in despair. Only then can we begin the process of rearranging our lives to accommodate the absence of our loved one.

Though the idea of such a tidy process may be comforting to some, the belief that adjustment occurs in predictable stages has generally been rejected in favor of a more nuanced understanding of loss. Instead, we see that people cope with loss using the personal resources, habits, and strategies developed over a lifetime, which remain despite the trauma.

Many find William Worden's approach to understanding grief helpful.[5] Worden draws from attachment theory to identify four tasks for the bereaved: (1) Accept the reality of the loss; (2) work through the pain of grief; (3) adjust to an environment in which the deceased is missing; and (4) emotionally relocate the deceased and move on with life.

Widows accomplish these tasks in unique ways and to various degrees. When Susan received the phone call from the police, she probably experienced a few seconds of disbelief. She may even have said, "No." People often do this when they receive news of a sudden death: "No, that's not possible. He was fine just a minute ago." It can take a while for our minds to absorb such a calamitous event. Widows often report that they keep looking for their spouses, even seeing them in crowds. Where Kübler-Ross might have called this denial, I prefer to think of it as disbelief.

## Accepting the Reality of the Loss

This may be why the events immediately surrounding our knowledge of the death become etched in our minds. We rehearse them over and over, maybe to persuade ourselves they are real. Like Susan, 79-year-old Henry had a vivid recollection of his wife's death. Describing his current love life as "vacant," Henry told his story:

> She'd laid down and I says, "Well, you go ahead and lay down. I'll watch the TV for a minute and keep an eye on you." And she's just sittin' in there like this, and she says, "I think I gotta go to the bathroom." And she was on a walker of course with her bad knee by then. And she said, "I'll probably have to have some help to get up." So I helped her in to go to the bathroom. I said, "I'll just go out to the kitchen and I'll be back." And I says, "Are you ready?" And she says, "No, not for a few minutes." And so she sat there for a little while, then she says, "I think I'm ready," so I got her up and got a hold of the walker and we started to walk back to the bed and she says, "I gotta sit down." And I says, "You've only got about three more steps and you be sitting on the edge of the bed." And all of a sudden just she let go of the walker and just went down and I just had my arm around her holding her, and I could feel she was just limp so I grabbed a pillow off the bed, put it down on the floor, and then laid her down like that and stood up. I turned around and looked like that and she was gone. I mean I could just tell by the color of her face. And I called and I knew all the sheriffs and everybody and the guy come over and of course he listened to her and he said, "No, she's gone." And I said, "Well, she just went that fast." Which was a blessing.

Henry remembered every detail of his wife's passing, and he found comfort in telling the story even though he had probably told it dozens of times. We found this time and again in our interviews: Bereaved respondents drew solace from telling the story of the death, regardless of how long ago it had taken place; the telling seemed to help the event become real.

## Working Through the Pain of Grief

Once a bereaved person has accepted the reality of the loss, she must work through its pain. Susan was still gently working through her grief 10 years after the loss, as evidenced by the tears she shed during our interview. Like

Susan, 80-year-old Justine experienced grief during her interview. Her husband died in 1991, on the day after our interview. I asked how she adjusted to his absence and she replied,

> It wasn't easy. It was terrible. Every . . . every . . . you know, like this chair [the chair she was sitting in] . . . we got. . . . My husband had his stroke about 3½ months after he retired . . . 71, and he was . . . well, he never did get back. You know, his one side wasn't good anymore, and we got him this chair, and for a long time [after his passing] I couldn't sit in it. Just couldn't sit in it. [Begins to cry.] And . . . and, you know, you look at his chair by the table and where he always sat, and it's empty, and it's hard. You know, his pillow at night, there's nobody there. But, you have to . . . you have to find some way to get through it, because you know he's not gonna be there, and I have my children around me. I told my children, I said, "Well, you know what? I got two choices. I can go over in the corner and cry, or I can pick myself up and I can go on." Those are the choices you have. You have those two choices, and my children didn't have a father anymore, and I thought, "Do you know what? I better starch up my backbone, and be . . . at least they deserve a mother, and I'm going to be that." I'm gonna go on, and do the best I can.

Often in the throes of sadness people wonder why they are experiencing such pain. Is there a purpose or meaning in the pain itself? As scientists learn about the physiology of emotions, they have been able to speculate about the ways they improve our lives and enhance our chances of survival. Sadness slows us down and makes us withdraw from the outside world and our social lives. It can force us into a quiet introspection that allows time and space for adjusting to the loss and making necessary decisions. In essence, sadness allows—even forces—us to regroup and become stronger for what lies ahead.

### Adjusting to Life Without the Deceased

Adjustment comes slowly. For the newly bereaved, each day brings new memories and thoughts of the person who is gone. A widow might begin each day with the stabbing pain of loss when she sees that her bed (or his chair) is empty. Familiar places and people trigger memories of time spent together. Once happy, these memories release an undertow of intense nostalgia that can derail plans for the day. But in time, the memories lose their painful associations. We become accustomed to the empty bed or chair or place at the table. In time, we adjust. We reengage with life and begin doing what is necessary to sustain it.

Justine recognized the need to adjust to life without her husband. Susan also reported the need to make emotional, cognitive, and practical adjustments to a world without Tommy. She tidied up his office and has learned to do the things he once did, like managing car repairs and doing their taxes. Henry, too, moved on: "I looked at it that she's been tortured enough. And like we all say, she's in a better place and all that, but when I sit around at the house. . . . Up at the cabin—I have a cabin in Flaming Gorge, and I've got a lot more things to do up there. Got a big yard. I can go get on the riding lawn mower, you know, to occupy my mind, and I get down here and there's really not much to do and the walls just. . . . Oh yes, I enjoy the mountains and the sky and the lakes."

## *Relocating the Deceased*

Traditional Mexican beliefs about death hold that we die three times: first, when our heart stops beating and we lose contact with the space around us; second, when our body is lowered into the ground; and third, when no one is left alive to remember us.[6] Regardless of our beliefs about life after death, a part of us (if only a memory) continues as long as someone who loved us is alive. Widows live with the memory of their loved ones—and that memory must be contained or it will invade and disrupt their daily lives. The process of relocating the deceased allows widows to contain their memories in a physical space or time. This relocation is a metaphor for the boundaries we build to contain grief and memories.

Susan relocated Tommy to the third floor of their home. Many people relocate their loved ones to the cemeteries or mausoleums that shelter their remains. Having physically placed the remains, they find it easier to relocate the emotional part of their relationship with the deceased. They go to the cemetery to commune with the deceased, and the memories and emotions that now make up the relationship are relocated to that time and place. As many of our respondents explained, you do not stop loving the person who is gone. But you relocate the love and the relationship in order to move on. As we will see, the need to relocate (not replace or remove) the deceased can be a real issue for subsequent relationships.

## Contact With the Deceased

Sometimes widows have contact with their deceased partners through dreams or visions. Sigmund Freud wrote about these visions in his essay

"Mourning and Melancholia," describing them as "clinging to the [love] object through the medium of a hallucinatory wishful psychosis."[7] Freud saw this as turning away from the reality of the loss, but many people experience these "wishful hallucinations" as healing experiences that enable them to move on.

Little systematic research has been done on this topic, so we decided to include it in our Internet survey. Partly my students and I wondered how many people had this kind of experience, and partly we wondered how those who did were affected by it.

Among the 108 respondents who reported that they had lost a romantic partner through death, 29 (27%)—2 men and 27 women—reported having contact of some kind with the person they had lost. These bereaved individuals described four types of contact: dreams, a sense or feeling, a visitation, and contact through family members.

The most common type was dreams. Hannah, a 57-year-old widow from Utah, explained that her husband had died suddenly. She saw him in her dreams, and in them she said, "I talked a lot, especially at first, mostly monologues describing how I felt or asking a lot of questions—there was a lot of anger on my part. A couple of times, when I was at a crossroads and needed comfort or answers, he answered me, usually in dreams." She described her reaction to these experiences: "Usually I felt I was just projecting memories, but a few times his answers were out of the blue and totally unexpected, but they really helped me out. Mostly I still feel the contact as confirmation that love has more than one dimension and if it is a true love, it will be never ending."

A simple sense of the person's presence was the next most common experience. Both of the men in our survey reported this. For instance, 57-year-old Harold from South Carolina lost his first wife to illness. Though he has since remarried, he reports experiencing the woman he lost as a spiritual presence, and says it made him feel, "Eventually, great!" Adrianne, age 50, from New Mexico, lost a dear friend suddenly. She has experienced his presence repeatedly since then:

Two weeks after his death—I didn't know he had died. I felt his presence. He was my soul mate. I hadn't heard from him in 8 years but had been thinking about him for 2 weeks and decided to try and locate him. I called information and got a phone number, dialed, and a woman answered (his sister). I explained who I was and she told me he died 2 weeks earlier. I hung up the phone and felt him with me. We had a conversation in my mind. I went to his memorial and saw him as light. He has been with me

ever since—1995. He comes to me when I am doing something spiri-
tually inclined. I don't see him but I feel an energy sensation and an
oscillation in my heart area. It is similar to how I felt when we were in the
same room when he was alive.

Adrianne added, "It makes me feel elated. A sense of awe and wonder."

A few people reported visitations while they were awake. For example,
60-year-old Beatrice, from Massachusetts, lost her partner unexpectedly.
She said, "I believe I saw his ghost in my kitchen." The experience, which
made her feel "comforted and loved, hasn't happened for many years
however." Antonia, age 50, lost her partner about the same time. She described his visitations, saying, "He is my guardian angel. He comes to me
when things are bad. I am not the only one who has seen him. There is no
face but I know it is him." She said these visits made her feel safe.

Finally, perhaps the most easily understandable type of contact happens
when people are reminded of the person they lost through a family member
or friend. I interviewed 94-year-old David at the home he and his wife had
designed in a small town in Colorado. He was surrounded by keepsakes that
evoked memories of Sarah, from family photos to copies of the book they
had written together. David explained that since her death he saw Sarah in
the faces and actions of their children, and that these tangible reminders
kept her alive for him.

The vast majority of people reporting these experiences said they made
them feel good, using words like *peaceful, comforted, loved,* and *reassured*
to describe their reactions. Some reported mixed feelings, "both happy and
sad." Negative reactions are possible, however, as indicated by the experiences of a few respondents. Gerrie, age 42, from Wisconsin, described her
contact with her deceased ex-husband: "Conversations in dreams with this
person. When scattering his ashes, the wind blew them back at me into my
face. I feel that was his last slap in my face." She said the experiences made
her feel disturbed. Also, 50-year-old Tamatha, from Arizona, felt the same
way when she saw her partner in her dreams. She said his presence made her
feel "afraid, then angry."

## Bereavement and Immunity

The past three decades have seen great progress in our understanding of
reactions to loss. This is particularly true in our knowledge of bereavement
and mortality. For decades, those working with the elderly observed that the

death of a spouse was often followed closely by the death of the surviving widow. This observation led some practitioners to conclude that surviving spouses were at risk of illness and death. Some thought this idea was non-sense and argued that the practitioners were being superstitious, relying on folk wisdom. All older adults are vulnerable to illness, and the few times when a widow succumbed were being overinterpreted to support an old wives' tale.

Yet the old wives' tale may have some truth to it. Landmark studies in the 1960s documented a higher rate of death among the newly bereaved.[8] More recent studies have noted that the trauma of spousal bereavement can weaken our immune systems in measurable ways. Researchers in the Netherlands, for instance, found that bereavement interfered with antibody response to the influenza vaccine.[9] Other studies have documented disruptions in immune responses at the cellular level among the recently bereaved. Impact on immune functioning may be greatest among those for whom bereavement is most stressful, with bereaved adults who experience major depression among the most compromised.[10] While the clinical significance of these cellular changes has not been established, these findings alone suggest that severe grief reactions may be hazardous to our health.

Seen in this light, 97-year-old Emma's comments describing her bereavement might be adaptive. When asked about her husband's death, she remembered the funeral:

EMMA: His funeral was the first funeral that the . . . this young bishop had conducted, and there was not one person that cried. Not one person cried, and it was just a jolly, fun time.

INTERVIEWER: Really! How come they were able to enjoy it? Did they just know that they'd see each other again?

EMMA: I don't know whether you know that or not, but what's the use of crying? What's the use of crying? You might just as well be happy about it, because they're out of pain. You know they're relieved from pain, and you should be happy. That would make anybody happy to know they were out of pain, wouldn't it?

Emma's ability to experience pleasure, even in times most people consider sad, might be an adaptive skill that helped her reach advanced age.

Emma was not the only one who found cause for laughter in her spouse's death. Henry also used humor to cope. He explained, "I told the people I probably caused it [her death]." When asked why, he said the night before she died he had told her, "You've got to start getting out of the bed and walk around the room. I says, 'The next morning when you get up and have breakfast, before you go lay down you've got to jump the rope.' And she says, 'Jump the rope,' and she sits there thinking for a while, and she says, 'Jump the rope.' You know she's got a walker. I says, 'Yes, you've gotta start moving your legs and stuff like that,' and she says, 'I couldn't even jump the rope when I was a teenager.' So I told everybody that she decided she's gonna die so she wouldn't have to get up and jump the rope in the morning."

## The Social Construction of Widowhood

Like most phases of our romantic lives, grieving takes place in a social context and, to some extent, widowhood is socially constructed.[11] The death of a spouse confers certain freedoms. In America, widows are allowed public expression of emotions that might otherwise be kept private. They are excused from social and work obligations, at least for a while. And they can expect a degree of solicitousness and care from the people who surround them. But these privileges come with restrictions.

Widows are generally not permitted to be happy—or at least to be seen to be happy—during their bereavement. Neighbors and friends can be shocked by a widow's use of gallows humor, seeing it as a violation of norms that dictate a consistent but gentle sadness on the part of the bereaved. Laughter might be interpreted as a sign of disrespect. On the other hand, extreme venting of sorrow or rage is also discouraged in our culture. Similarly, the bereaved are not expected to begin dating too quickly. In some cultures, widows are never permitted to have romantic relationships.

The role of widow also imposes obligations. Of course, these vary among different cultures, but a conspicuous display of respect for the bereaved is widely prescribed and anything short of this is frowned upon. Imagine how we would feel if a widow stood up at her husband's funeral and complained that he was a selfish slob! At funerals and memorials, widows (indeed, all mourners) are obliged to set aside petty resentments and complaints and celebrate the life of the deceased. This proscription against complaint can become a commitment to maintain the legacy of the deceased throughout the survivor's life.

Helen Lopata coined the phrase "husband sanctification" to describe the way some people idealize their deceased spouses.[12] This probably represents an extreme pole on the continuum of grief reactions that focus on preserving a spouse's legacy. We see a focus on legacy in both Susan and Marty (whom we met in Chapter 5). Susan serves on committees to carry on Tommy's work, while Marty has decided to make his life a testament to the love he shared with Ethel. Like other aspects of the grieving process, the time and energy involved in preserving a deceased spouse's legacy may complicate the task of forging a new relationship.


## Repartnering: A Look at Supply and Demand

Popular wisdom suggests that "women mourn and men replace," a maxim that makes sense given the gender imbalance in the senior population. As we all know, older women significantly outnumber older men. This may change in future cohorts, but today's numbers do not favor widows replacing their deceased spouses. From a market perspective, the supply of marriageable men in the latter half of life is not abundant. Indeed, widowers are 10 times more likely to marry than widows: while only 2% of widows over 60 remarry, one in five (20%) widowers do.[13]

But supply is not everything. The marriage equation in later life is more complex than census numbers would indicate. Things look more balanced when the demand side of the equation is taken into account and we consider whether widows and widowers want to remarry.

At the age of 77, Emily is a case in point. Her husband died 30 years before our interview, but she never remarried. She explained that while her marriage had not been perfect, she had "never met anyone who pulled it out of me." Her love for her husband never dimmed, she was happy spending time with her friends and children, and she felt no need for another husband. Emily was looking forward to being reunited with her husband in heaven since at the time of our interview she had just been diagnosed with pancreatic cancer.

Research in this area has consistently demonstrated that many widows share Emily's lack of interest in remarriage. Deborah Carr, a professor at Rutgers University, surveyed a national sample of 210 widows and widowers and reported that women were about one-third as likely as men to report that they were interested in remarrying.[14]

Women's limited interest in remarriage may stem from a variety of factors. One reason may be the demands imposed by marriage. Marriage has changed since the nineteenth century, when married women could not own property and were subject to their husbands' authority. Nonetheless, modern marriages are still experienced differently by men and women. For women, marriage typically brings homemaking and caregiving responsibilities, while for men it usually brings a helpmate to pick up after them and take care of life's details. Married women usually maintain a network of friends outside of marriage, while men rely primarily on their wives for companionship. Perhaps as a result of these differences, men experience greater health and social benefits from marriage than women.[15]

These widespread gender differences may help explain why women show limited interest in remarriage.[16] Maria Talbott, a social work professor in Oregon, asked widows about their interest in remarriage. One woman summed things up nicely, saying, "For the first time in my life, I have no responsibilities except for myself. . . . In other words, I'm just learning to fly a little bit. And I love it. Selfish, huh?"

Susan illustrated some other reasons why widows may not be interested in remarriage. After a few unsuccessful dating experiences, she concluded that it was unlikely that she would find a partner who could meet her standards. She was busy, working full-time and maintaining an active social life. Her responsibilities for maintaining Tommy's legacy were also inconsistent with remarriage. There is some evidence that widows who engage in the extreme of husband sanctification are especially reluctant to remarry.[17]

Sometimes widows worry that their children would not approve of a new relationship. This was the case for 63-year-old Sari, whose husband passed away shortly after they immigrated to the United States from India. Sari's favorite love story was the film *Andaaz*, which tells the story of a widow with two children who meets a widower in a park. The hero has a child himself, and in the end the couple marries. But she did not expect her life to imitate art. Sari explained, "Even if I love someone I can control it and not have an affair. If I had strong feelings towards anyone I would just move away without saying anything. It would be cutting my children and grandchildren's nose if I did something like fall in love. If I like a man now, my son and daughter will not like it. What will my daughter's in-laws say about me—that I have one leg in the grave and I am doing this. I like to talk to men and go out on senior citizens' picnics, but it is just being friendly in a group situation."

Men, particularly those who have little contact with friends and who relied heavily on their wives for homemaking and care, tend to be more eager to remarry.[18] I am reminded of an 80-year-old friend I will call Michael, who was eager to remarry less than a year after his wife's death. He explained, "I know how to do marriage. I like being cared for. And I don't eat very well when I live alone." Though widowers may be more interested in remarriage than widows, we should keep in mind that only a minority actually find new wives.

Older adults must take into account a complex array of factors in deciding whether or not to remarry. Reluctance may stem from feeling that remarriage would be disloyal to the memory or the legacy of the deceased. Children may discourage remarriage for fear that the change will alienate them from their sole surviving parent or disrupt their inheritance. Marriage in later life brings with it a likelihood of illness and disability that may present the new spouse with heavy caregiving demands. Some people worry that they will lose Social Security benefits or pensions if they remarry. Women in particular may feel that marriage will bring a loss of freedom. Finally, both widows and widowers may feel that no one could measure up to their spouses. On the other hand, it is lonely to live alone, particularly for men who do not tend to maintain extensive friendship networks during their marriages. Remarriage can bring companionship and a measure of comfort to later life. It can improve financial security, particularly for women. A new marriage might also offer stimulating new experiences, like travel and evenings out. And given moral and religious prohibitions, some older adults feel that marriage is the only way to have access to a sex partner.

## Alternatives to Marriage

With these factors in mind, some widows and widowers choose to repartner in ways that do not involve marriage. In a national sample of widows, Sara Moorman and her colleagues found that about 6% of those over age 60 dated, and 1% cohabited without marrying. These researchers also reported that about 7% of their sample reported having a male confidante (a non-relative with whom they shared emotional intimacy).[19] These numbers may change as baby boomers come onto the scene. The romantic expectations of this incoming cohort may be different from those of their parents. A recent survey by AARP found that 70% of single baby boomers between the ages of 40 and 59 dated regularly.[20]

One participant in our study, 83-year-old Anita, whom we met in Chapter 2, preferred cohabitation to marriage. Anita and her husband immigrated to California from the Philippines in the late 1980s, and 4 years later he died. They had been married over 40 years. After years of grief, Anita met Walter, a handsome Englishman whom she described as "a very efficient lover." On top of that, he was an excellent dancer, and he did the driving. They lived together in what she termed a trial marriage for 7 years. Then Walter had an affair. Deeply in love with him, Anita told Walter to "pick her or me." Walter protested, "You have a handsome husband. You have to understand." In her rage, Anita left him and went to San Francisco to visit her daughter. While she was gone, Walter died of a massive stroke. In retrospect, Anita thinks a trial marriage is a great idea for anyone who is contemplating the real thing because you can learn about the man's character, and it is a lot easier to leave him if things do not work out.

Even less committal than cohabitation is another option that has been growing in popularity, a pairing known as "living apart together" or LAT relationships.[21] In these relationships, the couple does not share a household, but they view themselves as a couple and their family and friends do as well. Partners in these relationships report that having their own homes gives them a measure of autonomy and freedom that they could not enjoy if they moved in together. Usually they feel deeply committed to each other.

Several of the widows we interviewed were involved in LAT relationships, though they certainly did not describe them as such. Instead they referred to their partners as friends or sometimes boyfriends. For example, 82-year-old Ginnie and her friend Saul live in separate retirement homes in Los Angeles. They met when she had been widowed for 20 years and Saul had for 2 years, and Ginnie describes herself as being in love with Saul. They try to see each other every day, and talk on the phone several times a day. Ginnie worries about Saul's health and thinks of him often. Though they cannot go out very much, she finds comfort and joy in the relationship.

Evelyn, age 64, is involved in a very different kind of LAT relationship. Two years after her husband's death, she fell head over heels in love with a strong man who, as it turned out, was married. They have pursued a tumultuous, passionate relationship for several years. But Evelyn does not feel that she can ask him to leave his wife: "I'm not asking that, because I don't think I could. As a woman I don't think it's fair." So, as she explains, "I'm partnering with him in this adulterous relationship he's choosing to be in." From time to time she breaks off the relationship. Once they were apart for 4 months. But they always seem to find their way back to each other, and their emotional bond remains strong.

Short of these two extremes are relationships that involve less commitment. A young 82-year-old, Viola spends her nights tripping the light fantastic at senior center dances. Viola has a friend who takes her to these dances. He is a good dancer and a good man, but she has no interest in remarriage. Instead they enjoy their evenings out and call each other from time to time. Viola feels jealous when her friend dances with someone else, which happens rarely since most people at the dances know they are a couple.

## Challenges of Repartnering

Any relationship is challenging, but a repartnered relationship brings unique difficulties. For one thing, there are more people involved. When a widow remarries, she brings the relationship with her deceased husband with her. So the new partnership involves at least three and possibly as many as four people. And that is just in the immediate vicinity. Most new partnerships have players on the periphery as well—adult children, grandchildren, and sometimes even great-grandchildren. As a newly remarried widow put it, "I should have taken a class in crowd control!"

Also, as a widow enters into a new relationship, she does not abandon her grieving. Instead, she brings with her the tasks that remain unfinished and a memory of what it was like to be a widow. Two grief tasks can be particularly challenging for new marriages: relocating the deceased emotionally, and maintaining the legacy.

When you walk into an older couple's family home, photos and mementos are usually on display. I often begin interviews by commenting on photos and asking for the stories behind them. But when I entered the home of Mr. and Mrs. Courtney, I had to find another way to make small talk because there were no family photos at all. As the interview progressed, the reason became clear. Mrs. Courtney could not tolerate the fact that her husband had spent most of his adult life married to another woman. Mr. Courtney explained that he had moved out of his family home at his new wife's insistence because she could not stand to be in the place his deceased wife had lived. He could not even mention his deceased wife's name in the presence of the new Mrs. Courtney. Despite their obvious satisfaction at being remarried, this couple was clearly bogged down in their grief work.

A couple I met while traveling provided a distinct contrast. Ernie and Caroline, both widowed in their 60s, were in their second year of marriage. Early in our conversation, they began telling me about each other's partners. I was struck by the comfort and pride with which Ernie spoke of Carolyn's deceased husband's career accomplishments. It was as if he was helping maintain her husband's legacy. Carolyn seemed less familiar with Ernie's deceased wife but nonetheless was comfortable describing the circumstances of the death and its impact on her new husband. As they shared the joy of a new relationship, these newlyweds also shared the work of grieving.

Although they are—or should be—peripheral to the relationship, adult children often complicate life for widows seeking new partners. We met Ginnie and her LAT partner earlier in this chapter. Ginnie described a run-in with Saul's adult son:

> His family . . . he's got two boys, and when he was in the hospital, I had a run-in with the youngest boy. And it wound up. . . . Well, I had to . . . he was to go home, and his son wouldn't leave. I always takes him to the hospital . . . so he . . . oh, he was to go home the next day, and I had said to the doctor, "He has a lot of trouble with his intestine, and I think he should be evaluated before he goes home," and the doctor agreed with me. Well, the test was one that's generally done on the outside. You don't have to be hospitalized, but he was already there, so why not do it? Well, the son found out and he said, "Who ordered that?" And he found out that I was the one that brought it up, and got so mad, he started yelling in the hospital, and he started out the door, and he turned around, and he said, "And you, lady! You stay out of it!"

There was no question where Saul's loyalties lay:

> Saul told him to leave. He said, "You better leave." So they left, and I took him home the next day. So, anyway, a period of time went by and they said, "We're coming down to see you, Dad." And he said, "No, you're not." And every time they'd say, "We're coming to see ya," Saul would say, "Not until you apologize to Ginnie." And he had to tell 'em that two or three different times. Finally, he called me and apologized.

I said, "Oh, he did? What did he say?"

Ginnie replied, "Oh, just that he was sorry, and I don't accept apologies very . . . very nice, and so . . . but they're a family that everybody hugs and everybody kisses. My family's not like that. I am with Saul, alone, but relatives . . . no. So, it's been . . . I've been very cool towards them, and . . . but now . . . they come at me to hug me and I just turn sideways, and put one arm around 'em, but no kissing."

Fortunately Ginnie's experience does not seem to be the norm. Throughout our interviews, we were more likely to encounter glowing re-ports of couples who successfully integrated their adult children into their lives to the extent that when one person passed away, his children remained close with the second (or third) wife. Sometimes, like Barbara, women we talked to reported that they "fell in love with his children."

## Conclusion

In this chapter we have seen people in the throes of grief, even years after the death of their spouses. We have learned about the tasks and needs that come with grief, as well as the loneliness that widows experience in their newly vacated lives. For most people, the death of a spouse signals a permanent transition into the socially defined role of widow or widower. But a few choose to love again, in partnerships of unprecedented variety. Those who take the more traditional route of marrying their new partners must invent new ways to manage the unique configuration of players that comes with the new relationship. Growing numbers of older adults are adopting less traditional approaches to love in cohabiting and living apart relationships. This should come as no surprise. After all, the very presence of large numbers of older adults is unprecedented in human history. It is natural that these pioneers would redesign social institutions to meet their social and personal needs.

## Try This

1. Being a Friend: Kübler-Ross said, "When we honestly ask ourselves which persons in our lives meant the most to us, we often find that it is those who, instead of giving much advice, solutions, or cures, have chosen rather to share our pain and touch our wounds with a tender and gentle hand. The friend who can be silent with us in an hour of grief and bereavement, who can tolerate not knowing, not curing, not healing, and face with us the reality of our powerlessness. That is the friend who cares."[22] Be this kind of friend, by giving a bereaved person you know some space to share. The person might need to tell the story of the death, and he or she might need to cry. Consider the value of your gift to you and your friend.

2. Imagining Absence: For those who have partners: Look closely at your partner and know for a moment that he or she will not always be part of your life. How does that knowledge feel? Can you imagine yourself alone? Write yourself a letter to read when your partner is no longer with you, then put it in a safe place like your safe deposit box. Share your hopes and fears with your future self, along with all those things you hope you will never do.

## Suggested Reading

Brontë, A. (2004). *The tenant of Wildfell Hall*. Whitefish, MT: Kessinger. Less well-known than Brontë's other works, this novel explores the roles of widows and wives in nineteenth-century England as its artistic heroine, Helen, enters a disastrous marriage with an abusive husband. She escapes and masquerades as a widow, only to attract the romantic attention of another suitor. I love Brontë's vigor, and this book offers a stunning fictional account of the social construction of widowhood and other feminine roles.

Didion, J. (2005). *The year of magical thinking*. New York: Knopf. Didion's best-selling memoir of the year she lost her husband is beautifully written. Friends who have had similar experiences tell me she captures their experiences with insight and depth. The book also offers a peek into the lives of America's intelligentsia. Vanessa Redgrave played Didion in the Broadway play based on the book. Watch for the movie.

Hamilton, D. (Producer), & Mehta, D. (Director). (2006). *Water* [Motion picture]. Canada: Deepa Mehta Films. This unforgettable movie offers a poignant look at the treatment of widows in India during the 1930s. Some have observed that the restrictions depicted in the film are as relevant today as they were 70 years ago. In 2006, the film drew violent protests from fundamentalists in the holy city of Varanasi, who saw it as anti-Hindu.

Kushner, H. (1981). *When bad things happen to good people*. New York: Schocken. One of my favorite comfort books, this small work by Rabbi Kushner addresses the spiritual confusion that can complicate unexpected and overwhelming grief.

Thomas, C. (1957). *Leftover life to kill*. Boston: Little, Brown. If you need an antidote to the spartan elegance of Didion, check out this ribald memoir by the widow of Dylan Thomas. Caitlin is everything Didion is not: fat, messy, lively, and inappropriate. Her romantic adventures in Italy left me laughing and cringing. A delightful romp.

# Conclusion: The Romantic Imagination

In high school I had a crush on a skinny kid named Larry who played drums in our marching band. Naturally this fabulous guy thought of me as a buddy, freely sharing the uncensored details of his romantic adventures. One day he told me about his recurring dream. He said, "Whenever I get close to a girl I might be in love with, I dream that I'm standing with her on a cliff and God gives me the choice between jumping off myself and watching him push her off. I look at the rocks below and agonize for a while, but in the end I always say the same thing: 'Take her.' That's how I know I'm really in love!" We contemplated his paradoxical dream for a while, then life moved on.

I thought of Larry decades later when Mike, a fabulous guy in his 50s on whom I had something of a crush, told me his painful secret. "I have," he confided, "never truly loved a woman." Mike had been married for over 20 years. I suspected that he misinterpreted his own version of Larry's dream—that he equated love with sacrifice. When he told God to "take her"—rejecting the chance to make the ultimate sacrifice—Mike assumed that meant he did not really love the woman. I thought Mike was setting the bar too high.

Clearly Mike needed to figure out what love was for him and how he wanted it to be manifest in his life—an important developmental task at any age, and one that can have a special urgency in our later years.

## What Is Love?

Could love be an illusion? Is it our culture-bound interpretation of random biochemical events? A myth promulgated to keep us subjugated to the needs of the social order? Or a cruel joke that lures us in only to tear us apart? By far the most common response given by hundreds of the people to whom we posed the question was, "Love is a feeling." But feelings

179

change—sometimes by the minute. How can we base our lives and our children's futures on a feeling? Feelings may be beyond our control. Could love be an act of will or a style of behavior? The notion that love is a verb has a certain resonance.

Love may be a philosophy. The *Oxford American Dictionary* defines philosophy as, "A theory or attitude held by a person or organization that acts as a *guiding principle for behavior.*" Love can and undoubtedly should serve as a guiding principle for behavior.

One of my favorite definitions of love came from 61-year-old Henry: "Love is more than fondness or liking or sexual attraction. For me, it's a connection that endures. I think that one of the reasons that love is so hard to define is that love fully reveals that it's love only after a long time."

Love is all these things and more. We redefine romantic love throughout the life course in a way that is consistent with our experiences, our families, our communities, and our cultures. We ask our partners, "How do I love thee?" and find a different answer every minute. But somehow the connection endures. Whether we remain in relationship or not, each moment of lived love is etched into our mammalian brains, and each loving experience changes us.

As we have seen in this volume, late life can be a time of opportunity and growth. By life's later decades, most of us have amassed a rich store of lessons and insights that constitute our personal romantic narratives. Some may be surprised to learn that strategies that were once effective fail in later years. The coquetries through which a 20-year-old attracts attention seem ludicrous when employed by an 80-year old matron. Faced with the physical changes of aging, others may be forced to discover new ways to meet their need for physical intimacy. The reflection afforded us in later life may change our understanding of the past. What looked like a bitter rejection at age 30 may, at 70, be seen as a gift.

Over the years, we revisit these lessons in the process of revising, expanding, and improving our personal narratives. This process may happen organically without our conscious awareness, or it may be triggered by a formal opportunity to reminisce or engage in a therapeutic dialogue. Given its depth, pervasiveness, and power, romantic love deserves a place in professional interventions targeting older adults.

## Love and Change

One of my favorite professors introduced me to a classic dictum: "Every man is in certain respects: Like all other men, Like some other men, Like no other man."[1] Time and again, the results of this research have emphasized the uniqueness of individual romantic experiences. Nonetheless, some generalizations are possible. Romantic love influences not only the direction of life events but also the content and structure of the self. Ultimately, we are what we love, and in later life, to a great extent, we are what we have loved.

I have identified four possible mechanisms for this transformation: First, intense romantic experiences like infatuation or betrayal offer powerful lessons that can translate into personal insights; second, our experiences with love provide opportunities to master the complex skills necessary for healthy relationships; third, love expands our behavior repertoires, teaching us that we are capable of more than we imagined; finally, love's transitions force us to change paths, rearranging our lives and our plans to make room for our beloved. Each of these could be a fascinating area for future research. Other potential research topics that emerge from this work are discussed in Appendix B.

## The Romantic Imagination

Romance blurs the boundary between fantasy and reality. Experiences structure our romantic imaginations, even as fantasies influence the way we perceive the world. Imagination is especially important in late life, when we are free of the pressures of preparing for the future and honed by decades of maturation. Like the proverbial child in the candy shop, we might bask in the delicious possibilities before us. Or we could meander along paths discovered long ago. Some of us may charge off to conquer new territories. Others might cower, afraid to break rules or cause pain. Regardless of the experiences that await you, I hope your romantic imagination will be enriched and emboldened by heightened awareness of late life's romantic possibilities.

# Appendix A: Love in the Literature

Table A.1.  Love in the Professional Literature*

|  | Search Term | Term Alone | Term and "Elderly" | Term and "Young" |
|---|---|---|---|---|
| *PsycInfo* | Romance | 1,626 | 5 (.3%) | 173 (11%) |
|  | Love | 11,172 | 83 (.7%) | 645 (6%) |
|  | Marriage | 32,580 | 524 (2%) | 1,724 (5%) |
|  | Sex | 11,172 | 83 (.7%) | 645 (6%) |
| *Sociological* | Romance | 633 | 3 (.5%) | 91 (14%) |
| *Abstracts*** | Love | 2,882 | 83 (3%) | 555 (19%) |
|  | Marriage | 18,778 | 679 (4%) | 2,546 (14%) |
|  | Sex | 28,078 | 826 (3%) | 3,288 (12%) |

*Searches conducted August 17, 2005, with no language or year limits.
**Peer-reviewed journals.

# Appendix B: The Research in Detail

This research used a qualitative methodology that combined in-depth interviews with a largely open-ended Internet survey. It was organized around four research questions:

1. How do older adults (age 50+) describe and experience romantic love (their lived experience)?
2. How do gender, culture, and age influence the lived experience of romantic love?
3. Is it possible to fall in love at advanced ages? If so, how do adults describe this experience? Do their descriptions differ from those offered by younger adults?
4. How do older adults interpret their lived experiences of romance?

Clearly, the results of this study cannot be considered representative of the general U.S. population. Nor can they be considered definitive in identifying all possible experiences and beliefs in this population. The methods used here are intended to illustrate and interpret a range of possibilities. The results are suggestive and can be used to provide hypotheses and direction in this unexplored realm of human experience.

## Recruiting the Sample

Interview respondents for this study were selected using a purposive recruiting method known as maximum variation sampling. Rather than representing the average or norm, this approach allows us to describe a range of diverse experiences. I sought to include participants who represented a range of possibilities along six key dimensions: race/ ethnicity, age, gender, sexual orientation/identity, income, and marital status. The resulting sample totals 110. This group includes 19 people aged 19 to 49, the under-50 sample; and 91 aged 50 to 97, the 50-plus sample. The under-50 respondents were included to allow a better understanding of age-based differences; however, the work reported in this book is based on the 50-plus sample.

The recruiting process involved several approaches and extended over a 3-year period. When I began the study, I was invited to sponsor a dance at our local senior center. As sponsor, I provided refreshments at intermission and in exchange was allowed to give a pitch during the break. Ten respondents (3 men and 7 women) were recruited through

Table B.1.   Interview Sample: Referral Sources
(50-Plus Only; $N = 91$)

| Source | Percentage |
| --- | --- |
| Friends/neighbors/colleagues | 53 |
| Health care providers | 13 |
| Senior center dance | 11 |
| Senior centers (contest, flyers) | 9 |
| GLBT center | 5 |
| Senior workshops | 5 |
| Respondents | 1 |
| University presentation | 1 |

this process. Through professional contacts, I recruited several hospice clients and residents of care facilities (a nursing home and an assisted-living facility). Friends and colleagues who heard about the study recommended some respondents. A presentation at a local university yielded 8 young adults and one 50-plus respondent. A local pharmacist, aware of my interest in interviewing men, recruited several. One woman was referred to the study by a respondent. For Valentine's Day I collaborated with our county senior centers on an essay contest called Tell Me a Love Story. A total of 17 essays were submitted and judged, with winners receiving dinner for two donated by a local restaurant. I invited everyone who submitted an essay to participate in an interview. I recruited gay and lesbian respondents through a colleague in Maine, herself a lesbian, and through the Salt Lake GLBT Center. Late in the process, I began to offer workshops at senior centers. These gave me an opportunity to test tentative conclusions with an audience of seniors and to recruit additional respondents. Five interviewees were recruited through workshops. Table B.1 summarizes the results of this recruiting process.

A quick note on gender differences in recruiting: Generally it was easier to recruit women to participate in these interviews. Men sometimes felt embarrassed by the topic, managing their discomfort through jokes and sexual innuendo. Some male participants found it easier to discuss the bare facts of their experiences than to explore the meaning and emotional dimensions. Still, with patience, respect, and serious concern, men in this study were able to reveal surprising (to them) levels of emotional depth and richness in describing their romantic experiences.

## Respondent Characteristics (50-Plus Sample)

We conducted interviews with 110 people, among whom 91 were age 50 years or older. Table B.2 summarizes the characteristics of this 50-plus sample. Most respondents (63%) were women. Monthly income averaged $3,233, with a range of $700 to $10,000. Most (86%) were Caucasian. The most common marital status in the group was widowed, which represented 35% of the sample. Another 28% were married at the time of the interview; 22% were divorced. Five respondents had been single all their lives; two

Table B.2.  Characteristics of the Interview Sample (50-plus Only; $N = 91$)

| Gender | | Age | |
|---|---|---|---|
| Female | 63% | Mean = 72 years | |
| Male | 37% | Range = 51 to 97 years | |
| Race/Ethnicity | | Monthly Income | |
| Caucasian | 86% | Mean = $3,233 | |
| Hispanic | 8% | Range = $700 − $10,000 | |
| Asian/Pacific Islander | 5% | | |
| Native American | 1% | | |
| African American | 1% | | |
| Other | 1% | | |
| Religion | | State of Residence | |
| Mormon | 29% | Utah | 75% |
| Catholic | 9% | California | 11% |
| Protestant | 11% | Colorado | 4% |
| Quaker | 3% | Georgia | 3% |
| Other (*Agape*, Pagan, Unitarian) | 4% | Idaho | 1% |
| None/agnostic | 4% | Maine | 3% |
| Baptist | 2% | New York | 1% |
| Buddhist/Hindu | 4% | Texas | 1% |
| Muslim | 1% | | |
| Not given | 32% | | |
| Marital Status | | Sexual Orientation | |
| Widowed | 35% | Heterosexual | 87% |
| Married | 28% | Homosexual | 12% |
| Divorced | 22% | Bisexual | 1% |
| Single/never married | 8% | | |
| Partnered | 5% | | |
| Engaged | 1% | | |

were in committed partnerships; and two were engaged. Most of the sample (68 respondents) lived in Utah, with the remaining living in California (10), Colorado (4), Georgia (3), Idaho (1), Maine (3), New York (1), and Texas (1). These states were chosen for practical reasons (one or more of our research team had funding to travel there). Luckily, we managed to include people from coast to coast, though the sample is clearly biased in favor of the West. Also, 64 people disclosed their religious affiliation. Under one-third (29%) were Mormons, with the remainder of Catholic, Protestant, and other faiths. The vast majority of the group (87%) were heterosexual, with one respondent reporting a bisexual orientation, and 11 identified as homosexual. The mean age of the 50-plus sample was 72, with a range from 51 to 97. Two respondents died within a month of completing the interview and several more have passed away since the study began.

## Interviews

At the beginning of the interview each respondent completed a consent form, which included consent to be tape recorded, as well as measures for disguising identity. I explained that I prefer to change a person's name, and any additional measures the respondent wanted were noted. This was not a concern for most respondents, though a few requested changes in their locations or circumstances, and others chose their own pseudonyms.

I conducted 35 of the interviews myself. The remaining interviews were conducted by M.S.W. students (9 women and 2 men) who enrolled in an independent study course titled Experiences of Love. For the course, the students undertook the study of love, with assignments that included interviews, readings, essays, and data analysis. Most interviews were conducted in respondents' homes. A few were done in rooms provided by local senior centers. Initially I tried to match students and respondents by gender. This system proved unnecessary and was abandoned. Generally I asked students who interviewed respondents of the opposite sex to conduct the interview in a public place or with another student present. The interviews generally lasted an hour and a half, with a range from 45 minutes to 8 hours. Interviewers completed field notes describing respondents and the interview process after completion of the interview. With respondents' permission, all but four interviews were tape recorded. Comments made after the tape recorder was turned off were recorded in interviewers' field notes. Sometimes respondents asked that information be kept off the record, requests that were carefully honored.

The interview protocol was designed to strike a balance between a free-flowing conversation and a more structured approach. For some respondents, the first question was enough to start them telling their story in a free-flowing fashion. Others required more direction. Interviews ended on a lighter note, with respondents reflecting on their successes and considering a whimsical question about the color of love. During the first semester my students and I refined the protocol, which now consists of 21 questions. A copy is included at the end of this appendix. Respondents were offered the opportunity to review their transcripts, and a few did so, offering corrections.

## Data Analysis

Narrative analysis was the leading approach to data analysis in this study. Consistent with methodologist Douglas Ezzy's recommendation, the process included five aspects:[1]

- Compiling the story
- Analyzing the context and content of each story, focusing on insights and understanding
- Comparing and contrasting stories for similarities and differences in content and interpretation
- Examining the effects of background variables, in this case gender, age, and culture
- Identifying stories or content that illustrate themes, insights, and understandings

Graduate students at the University of Utah were invited to participate in a seminar on advanced qualitative data analysis, where they reviewed and debated insights and understandings. Four doctoral students participated in this process.

The data included two types of narrative: field notes and interview transcripts. The transcripts represented the bulk of the material, and early stages of data analysis were focused on organizing this volume of material. NVivo software proved helpful in this regard. Comments in each interview were organized thematically, and early analysis compared and summarized respondent comments around topics or themes such as "What is love?" or "Falling in love." Descriptions of lived experiences were distinguished from interpretation of experiences.

Interpretation of each interview involved review of the transcript as a whole, to identify key insights and understandings unique to the interview. These were listed as either confirmed (interviewer shared the insight with the respondent, who agreed with its validity) or unconfirmed (speculation that was not checked with the respondent). The source of each insight was indicated as respondent-generated, interviewer, or unclear. Insights were organized chronologically and together provide a narrative of the research process. They were also organized thematically and grouped with relevant comments (particularly nonconfirmatory comments).

Comparison was initially organized around the six background variables used in sampling: race/ethnicity, age, gender, sexual orientation/identity, income, and marital status. A few insights were generated in this way, with age and marital history appearing to be the most important distinguishing factors in respondents' description of their experiences. Later comparative work focused on insights generated in the thematic analysis. We asked, for example, whether those who reported unsatisfactory love experiences would indicate that they learned to love differently from those whose experiences were more gratifying. In these more ambiguous comparisons, it was important that more than one person participate in categorization and coding to keep bias to a minimum.

The late stage of data analysis coincided with the early stages of writing this book. The challenge was to identify an organizing framework for the book that would reflect the broad themes in the data. Although not an original focus of the study, the role of illusion emerged from the data. I had a personal inclination to organize the book chronologically, and the notion of illusion, reality, and disillusion seemed compatible with the data and my preference. With this framework in place, the final stage of analysis involved choosing individual interviews to illustrate the broad themes. I made these choices in collaboration with the research team.

## Truth Value or Trustworthiness

All social researchers bear the burden of demonstrating the truth value of their work. In this setting, the pursuit of truth demands, first, that findings accurately present respondents' experiences and perceptions; second, that the researcher's biases and preconceptions are explicit and do not dominate interpretation of the data; and third, that the method is described in sufficient detail that an independent researcher can confirm the results by replicating the work. The third requirement is addressed in this appendix. I undertook several measures to meet the other two.

## Ensuring Accuracy

Throughout the interviews, my students and I used active listening to ensure that we understood what respondents were telling us. With permission, the interviews were tape recorded, and then they were transcribed. Respondents were given the opportunity to review and correct the transcripts of their interviews. However, only a few chose to do this.

## Controlling for Biases

As the work progressed, I became aware of how deeply invested I was in my belief that passionate love as I understood it was possible at very advanced ages. I came to see this as my most problematic bias. Early interviews seemed to support this bias. In each city I visited, I could locate couples who described themselves as being in love. Rather than assume we were talking about the same experience, I asked them to carefully describe what it felt like to be in love. As seniors operationalized this construct for me, I realized that we were talking about different experiences. Despite advertisements seeking people who had fallen in love late in life, I did not find anyone over the age of 64 who experienced infatuation precisely the way I understood it.

Other measures used to control bias included the following:

- An interview process in which insights and awareness are checked with respondents
- Periodic meetings with older adults where I presented my tentative conclusions for their reaction
- Weekly meetings with students involved where we played devil's advocate with our explanations and interpretations
- Presentations at professional conferences
- A personal journal that served as a repository for my subjective experiences and beliefs about the process
- An audit trail that allowed me to track all conclusions to their source in the data
- A constant search for cases that disconfirmed my conclusions
- Maintaining the distinction between speculation and observation

## The Internet Survey

To broaden the base of this research, I conducted an Internet survey using the Surveymonkey.com Website. I expect to use the findings of this survey to elaborate on the themes identified in the interviews. The procedures for the Internet survey were approved by the University of Utah Institutional Review Board. I asked my colleagues in the College of Social Work to pretest the survey, then revised it and began recruiting respondents.

The survey was accessed either through my University of Utah home page or through a link that was e-mailed to members of the Association for Gerontology–Social Work (AGE-SW), participants in the Hartford Foundation Geriatric Initiatives, and colleagues throughout the country.

## Recruiting

Snowball sampling was used to generate responses. Under the subject heading "Request for help with a research project," e-mails were sent through two major gerontological listserves. Then recruiting e-mails were sent to state chapters of the National Association of Social Workers. Recipients of the messages were encouraged to forward them to others they thought might be interested. Approximately 700 responses were received during this period. Then a targeted recruiting effort was initiated. This "Google-based" approach was intended to expand recruiting beyond the field of social work and to increase geographic diversity. A search of each state's name coupled with the word *gerontology* was conducted and 5 to 10 individuals selected randomly from each list. Recruiting e-mails were sent to 400 individuals. The Google-based approach resulted in 47 e-mail replies (30 agreed to participate and pass the message along; 10 declined to participate; and 7 requested more information). Following this recruiting initiative, 327 individuals completed the survey.

## The Internet Sample

Over a thousand (1,035) people living in all 50 states completed the Internet survey. Most of these (80%) were women, and most (93%) identified themselves as either exclusively or primarily heterosexual. The Internet respondents were considerably younger than those interviewed. Their mean age was 42 years, with a range from 18 to 86. Just over a third (34%) were aged 50 and over. Consistent with their younger ages, Internet respondents were less likely to be widowed than interviewees. The Internet sample was predominantly (82%) white, and just over half (55%) lived in Western states. Their characteristics are presented in Table B.3.

## Limitations

About half (59) of the interviews were conducted by M.S.W. students. While all of the students were trained and supervised, their ability to achieve critical subjectivity varied a good deal. A few relied heavily on the protocol, treating the session as a structured interview. Others were able to generate insights on the spot and check them with re-spondents.

Of course, my own interviews were less than perfect as well. Time and again, I would slap my forehead in the car after an interview, wishing I had asked a question or checked

Table B.3.   Characteristics of Internet Sample ($N = 1,035$)

| Gender | | Age | |
|---|---|---|---|
| Female | 80% | Mean $= 42$ years | |
| Male | 20% | Range $= 18$ to 86 years | |
| | | | |
| Race/Ethnicity | | Geographic Distribution | |
| Caucasian | 82% | West | 55% |
| Hispanic | 5% | Northeast | 19% |
| Asian/Pacific Islander | 4% | Midwest | 16% |
| African American | 4% | South | 10% |
| Other | 4% | | |
| Native American | 1% | | |
| | | | |
| Marital Status | | Sexual Orientation | |
| Married | 52% | Exclusively/primarily heterosexual | 93% |
| Single | 17% | Exclusively/primarily homosexual | 5% |
| Committed (not cohabiting) | 12% | Bisexual | 2% |
| Partnered (cohabiting) | 7% | | |
| Divorced/separated | 7% | | |
| Engaged | 2% | | |
| Widowed | 1% | | |

a thought with a respondent. Sometimes I called back, but more often this was not feasible.

Although most respondents were comfortable with the questions and expressive in sharing their experiences and beliefs, some were not. In a few painful cases, respondents simply did not want to go there. In these cases, respect for respondents' privacy dictated that vital areas be left unexplored.

Although the interview sample does reflect variation along the key measures identified (race/ethnicity, age, gender, sexual orientation/identity, income, and marital status), its geographic variation is limited. The majority came from Western states, particularly my home state of Utah, with a few respondents from the Northeast and the South.

Other methodological limitations relate to the Internet survey. Given the recruiting strategy, I have a limited idea of where respondents came from. As in the interviews, most respondents lived in the West; however, the geographic distribution of this group is greater than the interview sample. Given the recruiting method used, professionals, particularly from social work and gerontology, are undoubtedly overrepresented. The Internet survey's anonymity may have allowed respondents to be more open in describing less socially approved aspects of their romantic experiences; or it might have fostered deception. The lack of face-to-face contact makes it somewhat more difficult to judge the validity of the responses, though a careful reading of the data suggests that responses were internally consistent and thoughtful.

## Directions for Future Research

Qualitative research is especially appropriate for generating hypotheses. This holds true in this study, which offered a wealth of testable propositions. The broad theme of love as an impetus for personal development could be an important focus of study, contributing to our understanding of life span development.

I have suggested that experiences with lived commitment enable people to develop relationship skills. What about people who have never been involved in a committed relationship? While they are a small minority, their experiences might provide a counterexample to this claim. Popular wisdom holds that those who have never committed to a love relationship are unsuited to the task. Is this really the case? How do lifelong independents see themselves and their relationship skills?

An emerging body of research, primarily in Scandinavia, looks at the experiences of older adults in living apart relationships. We identified a few in this study. A more systematic look at this population in the U.S. context may be in order. It will be especially valuable to understand how couples in this configuration manage health and financial crises. For older adults who are married, the spouse is typically the primary caregiver. Can the same be said of these couples? Under what circumstances does the romantic partner assume this responsibility? The interaction between the partner and adult children is another consideration in these relationships, as is the broader social context. Some older adults prefer not to marry to avoid tension with their adult children. This proposition deserves consideration in a study that looks at the way adult children respond to and interpret their parents' relationships.

This study is the first I know of to systematically consider the experiences some bereaved people have of contact with the deceased person. Our Internet findings suggested that about one-fourth (27%) of bereaved people have this experience, and that these are primarily women. These observations should be replicated with a more representative sample. Further, it would be interesting to examine the role of this kind of contact in adaptation to bereavement. Is it primarily observed in cases of complicated grief? Does the contact facilitate adaptation?

This study is also the first I know of to explore infatuation among older adults, a fascinating topic that certainly merits further consideration. Brain imaging studies might consider how the aging brain reacts to infatuation. In this work, I suggested that infatuation is less physical among older adults, and possibly less intense. When an 80-year-old says she is madly in love, she may mean something quite different from the infatuated 20-year-old. It would be interesting to recruit an age-diverse group of infatuated adults and systematically consider the similarities and differences in their experiences.

Finally, the clinical implications of this work merit consideration. Romantic love is one of life's profoundest experiences. Is it addressed when older adults seek treatment for mental health or family difficulties? Do clinicians feel comfortable talking about love with this population? My experiences in the field suggest that paraprofessionals, such as staff in senior centers and housing facilities, enjoy discussing the topic but that professionals like social workers consider it unprofessional to ask people about their love lives. We social workers prefer to discuss "primary relationships." When we use euphemisms like this we may succeed only in distancing ourselves from our clients and shutting off discussion of their deepest concerns.

## Experiences of Love: Interview Protocol

ID: _____          Location: _____
Date: _____          Interviewer: _____

---

Sampling Frame (Fill out at the end of the interview.)
Age: _____   Gender: _____ Race/Ethnicity:_____   Religion?_____
Sexual Orientation: _____        Children: Living _____   Dead _____
Monthly Income/Sources: _____
Primary Occupation When Working:_____   Yrs. Education:_____
Current/Past Marital Status: _____

---

Interviewer: Please describe this person "in a nutshell." Include physical and personality traits that are distinctive, as well as a description of the environment in which the interview was conducted.

## Interview Questions

### A. Tell me about your experiences with love.

1. What is your favorite love story (movie/book/real life)? Why is it important?
2. Who was the first person you ever loved? What do you love about him/her? Did he/she love you the way you wanted to be loved? Did you know how he/she wanted to be loved? How did you express your love? How did he/she? Did this love experience change you in any way? How?
3. Repeat above for each loved person.
4. Who do you love most now? What do you love about him/her? Does he/she love you the way you want to be loved? Do you know how he/she wants to be loved? How do you express your love? How does he/she? Has this love experience changed you in any way? How?
5. Have you been "in love"? Describe the experience. When did it happen? Did it include: Sleep change? Appetite change? Obsessive thoughts about the loved one? Emotional roller coaster?
6. Have you ever wondered whether or not you loved someone (at the time—not in retrospect)? Have you ever wondered whether or not someone loved you?
7. What do you look for in a romantic partner?
8. How does love begin for you? Is it immediate? Does it "grow on you"? Tell me about your beginnings.
9. How did you learn to love? Were your parents "in love"? How could you tell?
10. Have you ever been unfaithful to someone you loved? Did he/she know? Did he/she forgive you? Has anyone ever been unfaithful to you?
11. Is love different now from when you were younger?

**B. Now I have some questions that relate to your beliefs about love. Remember there are no right or wrong answers. We would just like to understand what you think about love.**

1. What is love (i.e., a feeling, decision, drive)? Where do you feel it? How do you know it's there? Can you control it? Or does it control you? Is it "rational" or "irrational"?
2. Where do you think love comes from? What is the source of love? Why do people love?
3. Does love last forever? Does it end? Tell me about endings you have experienced. Have you ever "fallen out" of love? Have you ever been "broken hearted?" Have you ever lost a loved one through death?
4. Is love good for people? Has it been good for you? Do you only love people/things/activities that are good for and to you? Is love ever self-destructive?
5. Is there a relationship between love and sex? Tell me about it.
6. Is there a relationship between love and money? Tell me about it. Does having money make it easier/harder to love?
7. Is there a relationship between love and freedom? Tell me about it.
8. Is there a relationship between love and marriage? Tell me about it. Does marriage help/hinder love?
9. Is it possible for people to live without love? Do you think older people who have experienced/shared love are different from those who have not? Happier? Healthier?
10. Do you think love is different now than it was in your parents' time?
11. Do you consider yourself a success? At life? At love?
12. What advice would you give to a young person about love? [For young adults: What are your hopes and expectations for love in your life?]
13. Is it necessary for people to love themselves?
14. What color is love?

## Love in Later Life: Internet Survey

### Informed Consent

This study explores the experiences of love from the perspectives of adults of all ages. It will provide the basis for a book on the topic.

By completing the Internet survey you will be indicating your informed consent.

Most people find the survey takes under 15 minutes to complete, and your participation is completely voluntary. Participation in the survey carries no significant risk to you.

If you find a question objectionable or unpleasant you may skip it.

The survey is anonymous. There is no way to connect your identity (electronic or otherwise) to your answers. After completing the survey you will have the opportunity to volunteer for a phone interview. If you choose to do this you may voluntarily provide your contact information. But this will not be linked in any way to your answers on the survey.

Contact: If you have any questions about the study you can contact Amanda Barusch, at (801) 581-8842.

Institutional Review Board: If you have any questions regarding your rights as a research subject, or if problems arise which you do not feel you can discuss with the Investigator, please contact the Institutional Review Board Office at (801) 581-3655.

1. Do you agree to participate in the survey?
   a. Yes
   b. No
2. Demographics
   What is your age?
   What is your gender?
   What is your race/ethnicity?
   What is your current relationship status?
   What state do you live in?
   Please indicate which of the following best describes your romantic love experiences:
      Exclusively with members of the opposite sex
      Primarily with members of the opposite sex
      About equally divided between same and opposite sex
      Primarily with members of the same sex
      Exclusively with members of the same sex
3. General Background on Love Experiences
   Have you ever fallen in love? Yes, No
      If no: Do you think there's a difference between being "in love" and being "infatuated"? Please explain.
   Have you ever been infatuated? Yes, No
      If yes: What was the experience of being infatuated like for you?
      If no: Do you think there's a difference between "being in love" and "loving"? Please explain.
   Have you ever loved someone? Yes, No
      If no: Thank you very much—go to end page.
      If yes: Who have you loved?
         Would you please describe your experience of loving that person?
   Have you ever been betrayed by someone you loved romantically? Yes, No
      If yes, go to betrayal follow-up questions.
   Background on love experiences (If "yes" on fallen in love)
   Please indicate how many times you "fell in love" at each of the following ages:
      Younger than 10 years
      10–19 years
      20–29 years
      30–39 years
      40–49 years
      50–59 years
      60–69 years
      70–79 years

80–89 years
90 and over
Are you currently "in love?" Yes, No

**If yes (respondent is currently in love):**
How old were you (in years) when you met the person with whom you are in love?
How long have you been in love with this person?
Do you think there's a difference between "being in love" and "loving"? Please explain:
Please indicate the extent to which you currently experience each of the following in your love relationship: (Response options: not at all, somewhat, very much)
  Think about the person all the time
  Experience emotional highs and lows (like a roller coaster)
  Loss of appetite
  Weight loss
  Sleep disturbance
  Wake up thinking about the other person
  Feelings of personal insecurity
  Feelings of personal well-being
  Greater self-confidence
  Admiration of the other person
  Sexual attraction to the other person
  Increased energy and vitality
  New lease on life
  Sharing other person's victories and defeats
  Desire to take care of the other person
  Empathy and understanding for the other person
Do you think there's a difference between being "in love" and being "infatuated"? Yes, No
  If yes, would you please describe that difference?
Have you ever been betrayed by someone you loved romantically? Yes, No (skip betrayal follow-up questions)

**If no (respondent is not currently in love)**
Now, think about the most recent time that you fell in love. We'd like to know what that was like for you.
What initially attracted you to this person?
Do you think there's a difference between "being in love" and "loving"? Please explain:
  Please indicate the extent to which you experienced each of the following in your love relationship: (Response options: not at all, somewhat, very much)
    Think about the person all the time
    Experience emotional highs and lows (like a roller coaster)
    Loss of appetite
    Weight loss
    Sleep disturbance
    Wake up thinking about the other person

Feelings of personal insecurity
Feelings of personal well-being
Greater self-confidence
Admiration of the other person
Sexual attraction to the other person
Increased energy and vitality
New lease on life
Sharing other person's victories and defeats
Desire to take care of the other person
Empathy and understanding for the other person
How long were you "in love" with this person?
What was the outcome of this experience for you?
Do you think there is a difference between being "in love" and being "infatu-
ated"? Yes, No
    If yes, how would you describe that difference?

## Betrayal

Have you ever been betrayed by someone you loved romantically? Yes, No
    If Yes, how did this person betray you?
    Have you forgiven this person? Yes, No
        If yes, what did it take for you to forgive him/her?
        If no, what will it take for you to forgive him/her?

Have you ever betrayed someone you loved romantically? Yes, No
    If yes, how did you betray this person?
    Was the person aware that you had betrayed him/her? Yes, No
        If yes, has this person forgiven you? Yes, No
            If yes, what did it take for him/her to forgive you?
            If no, what will it take for him/her to forgive you?
    Have you forgiven yourself for this betrayal? Yes, No
        If yes, what did it take for you to forgive yourself?
        If no, what will it take for you to forgive yourself?

## Unrequited Love

Have you ever been in love with someone who did not love you back? Yes, No
    If yes, what was that experience like for you? Are you "over it" now? What did
    (or will) it take for you to get over it?

## ReligionDoes love have religious meaning to you? Yes, NoIf yes, please describe the connection between religion and love as you experience it.

## Long-Term Relationship

Have you been involved in a romantic relationship for 20 years or more? Yes, No
    If yes, how long have you been involved in this relationship?
        Are you married to this person? Yes, No
        What has made it possible for you to remain in this relationship?
        What has made it difficult for you to remain in this relationship?

## Second-Time-Around Relationship

Have you become romantically involved with someone you knew during an earlier part of your life? Yes, No
> If yes, were you in love with this person when you knew him/her before? Yes, No
>> How were you reunited?
>> How is the relationship different now?

## After Age 60

Have you become romantically involved with someone after the age of 60? Yes, No
> If yes, how old were you when this romance began?
>> In what ways is this experience different from when you were younger?
>> In what ways is this experience similar to when you were younger?

## Loss of Loved One

Have you ever lost someone you loved romantically through death? Yes, No
> If yes, how old were you when you experienced this loss?
>> Was the loss unexpected? Yes, No
>> Have you had contact of some kind with the person since his/her death? Yes, No
>>> If yes, Please describe your contact with the person you lost.
>> How did this contact make you feel?

## Sex and Love

Do you think sex is an important part of romantic relationships? Yes, No
> If yes, please describe the relationship between sex and romantic love.

## Wrap Up

Why do you think people experience romantic love?
What color is love for you? Why did you choose this color?
Is there anything else you think we should know about romantic love?

Thank you for your participation!!
If you would like to volunteer for a phone interview please send your name and phone number to: abarusch@socwk.utah.edu


## Acknowledgments

This research was funded by the Goodwill Family Foundation. Procedures were approved by the University of Utah Institutional Review Board.

# Notes

INTRODUCTION

1. At the time, Browning was "between relationships." His beloved Elizabeth had died 3 years before and he had not met Lady Ashburton, whom he would later invite to be his second wife. (She declined.)
2. Haley, B. (1978). *The healthy body and Victorian culture*. Cambridge: Harvard University Press; Himes, C. L. (2001). Elderly Americans. *Population Bulletin*, 56(4), Washington, DC: Population Reference Bureau.
3. U.S. Bureau of the Census. (2000). Census 2000 PHC-T-9. Population by age, sex, race and Hispanic or Latino origin for the United States: 2000. Table 1. Available at http://www.census.gov/population/cen2000/phc-t9/tab01.pdf
4. Kastenbaum, R. J. (1973). Loving, dying, and other gerontologic addenda. In C. Eisdorfer & M. P. Lawton (Eds.), *The psychology of adult development and aging* (pp. 699–705). Washington, DC: American Psychological Association.
5. Please see Appendix A for relevant details.
6. Lincoln, Y. S. (2002). Emerging criteria for quality in qualitative and interpretive research. In N. K. Denzin & Y. S. Lincoln (Eds.), *The qualitative inquiry reader* (pp. 327–347). Thousand Oaks, CA: Sage, p. 337.
7. Tappan, M. (2001). Interpretive psychology: Stories, circles, and understanding lived experience. In D. L. Tolman & M. Brydon-Miller (Eds.), *From subjects to subjectivities: A handbook of interpretive and participatory methods* (pp. 45–56). New York: New York University Press, p. 49.
8. Markus, H., & Nurius, P. (1986). Possible selves. *American Psychologist 41*(9), 954–969.
9. Ibid, p. 954.

CHAPTER 1

1. Native Tahitian cited by Fine, R. (1990). *Love and work: The value system of psychoanalysis*. New York: Continuum Press, p. 38.
2. Solomon, R. C. (1995). The virtue of (erotic) love. In A. Stewart (Ed.), *Philosophical perspectives on sex and love* (pp. 241–258). New York: Oxford University Press.

3. Although I focus on love in ancient Greek culture, the interested reader will find many parallels between Greek and Roman myths and ideals. For a closer look at Roman culture, see Grimal, P. (1967). *Love in ancient Rome*. New York: Crown.

4. Halperin, D. M. (2002). Forgetting Foucault: Acts, identities, and the history of sexuality. In M. C. Nussbaum & J. Sihvola (Eds.), *The sleep of reason: Erotic experience and sexual ethics in ancient Greece and Rome* (pp. 21–54). Chicago: University of Chicago Press.

5. Sihvola, J. (2002). Aristotle on sex and love. In M. C. Nussbaum & J. Sihvola (Eds.), *The sleep of reason: Erotic experience and sexual ethics in ancient Greece and Rome* (pp. 200–221). Chicago: University of Chicago Press.

6. Nussbaum, M. (2002). Eros and ethical norms. In M. C. Nussbaum & J. Sihvola (Eds.), *The sleep of reason: Erotic experience and sexual ethics in ancient Greece and Rome* (pp. 55–94). Chicago: University of Chicago Press.

7. Flaceliere, R. (1962). *Love in ancient Greece* (J. Cleugh, Trans.). Westport, CT: Greenwood Press.

8. Faraone, C. A. (2002). Agents and victims: Constructions of gender and desire in ancient Greek love magic. In M. C. Nussbaum & J. Sihvola (Eds.), *The sleep of reason: Erotic experience and sexual ethics in ancient Greece and Rome* (pp. 400–426). Chicago: University of Chicago Press.

9. Morgan, D. N. (1964). *Love: Plato, the Bible, and Freud*. Englewood Cliffs, NJ: Prentice-Hall.

10. Ibid.

11. Price, A. W. (2004). *Love and friendship in Plato and Aristotle*. New York: Oxford University Press, pp. 19–20.

12. Plato. (1956). Symposium. In *The works of Plato* (I. Edman, Trans.). New York: Random House, p. 342.

13. Sternberg, R. J. (1998). *Cupid's arrow: The course of love through time*. Cambridge: Cambridge University Press.

14. Plato, *Symposium*, p. 368.

15. Ibid., p. 369.

16. From Ovid, *The Art of Love Book 1*. See: Ovid. (2005). *The Love Books of Ovid Being the Amores, Ars Amatoria, Remedia Amoris and Medicamina Faciei Femineae of Publius Ovidius Naso* (L. Lewis May, Trans.). Kila, MT: Kessinger Publishing, p. 113.

17. Ibid., p. 136.

18. French books about this phenomenon were called *romans*, which, anglicized, became "romance."

19. In what now seems to have been shocking naïveté, some Western scholars (De Rougemont, D. [1974]. *Love in the Western World*. New York Harper & Row; Johnson, R. A. [1983]. *We: Understanding the psychology of romantic love*. New York: HarperCollins Publishers; Singer, I. [1984]. *The nature of love, Vols. 1, 2*. Chicago: University of Chicago Press; Solomon, R. C. [1995]. The virtue of (erotic) love. In A. Stewart (Ed.), *Philosophical perspectives on sex & love* [pp. 241–258]. New York: Oxford University Press) suggested that intense romantic

attachments were invented by the West—that romance could not flourish in the highly structured, collectively oriented cultures of the East (Jankowiak, 1995). This view has been effectively debunked by anthropological accounts of infatuation and deep passion in a range of cultures, not to mention the modern translations of ancient Persian love poems by Rumi.

20. Walters, L. J. (1996). *Lancelot and Guinevere: A casebook*. New York: Garland.
21. Hopkins, A. (1994). *The book of courtly love: The passionate code of the trou-badours*. San Francisco: Harper Collins.
22. Mason, M. (1994). *The making of Victorian sexuality*. New York: Oxford University Press.
23. Morgan, *Love: Plato, the Bible, and Freud*, p. 130.
24. Fine, *Love and work*, p. 36.
25. Morgan, *Love: Plato, the Bible, and Freud*, p. 137.
26. Some have observed a parallel between Freud's libidinal energy and Schopenhauer's World-Will. Both are uncontrollable forces that determine the course of individual lives. Critics of psychoanalytic theory object to its "pansexualism," or the emphasis on the libido or sexual instinct as a motivating force for a wide range of human behaviors.
27. Indeed, Jung has been described as a disciple of Freud. The two enjoyed an intimate friendship for several years before their estrangement in 1913. See Davis, D. A. (1997). Jung in the psychoanalytic movement. In P. Young-Eisendrath & T. Dawson (Eds.), *Cambridge companion to Jung*. Cambridge: Cambridge University Press.
28. See Jung, C. G. (1966). *The spirit in man, art, and literature* (R. F. C. Hull, Trans.). Princeton, NJ: Princeton University Press.
29. Johnson, R. A. (1983). *We: Understanding the psychology of romantic love*. New York: HarperCollins, p. 63.
30. Ibid., p. 47.
31. Bowlby, J. (1969). *Attachment and loss: Vol. 1. Attachment*. New York: Basic Books.
32. Ibid.
33. Ainsworth, M., Blehar, M., Waters, E., & Wall, S. (1978). *Patterns of attachment*. Hillsdale, NJ: Erlbaum.
34. See Bowlby, J. (1969). *Attachment and loss: Vol. 3. Loss*. New York: Basic Books.
35. Chisholm, J. S. (1995). Love's contingencies. In W. Jankowiak (Ed.), *Romantic passion: A universal experience?* New York: Columbia University Press.
36. Ibid., p. 52.
37. Oppenheimer, V. K. (1988). A theory of marriage timing. *American Journal of Sociology, 9*, 563–591.
38. See, for instance, Coupland, J. (2000). Past the "perfect kind of age"? Styling selves and relationships in over-50s dating and advertisements. *Journal of Communication, 50*, 9–30.
39. Peterson, J., with Hefner, H. (1999). *Century of sex: Playboy's history of the sexual revolution: 1990–1999*. New York: Grove Press, p. xi.
40. May, R. (1969). *Love and will*. New York: Norton.

41. Reiss, I. L., & Ellis, A. (2002). At the dawn of the sexual revolution: Reflections on a dialogue. New York: Altamira.

42. Ibid., p. 37.

43. Thurston, C. (1987). The romance revolution: Erotic novels for women and the quest for a new sexual identity. Chicago: University of Illinois Press, p. 8.

44. Sternberg, R. J. (1988). Triangulating love. In R. J. Sternberg & M. L. Barnes (Eds.), *The psychology of love* (pp. 119–138). New Haven, CT: Yale University Press.

45. Lee, J. A. (1988). Love-styles. In R. J. Sternberg & M. L. Barnes (Eds.), *The psychology of love* (pp. 38–67). New Haven, CT: Yale University Press, p. 55.

46. See James, W. (2007). *The principles of psychology, Vols. 1 & 2.* New York: Cosimo Classics. (Original work published 1885)

47. See Goldie, P. (Ed.). (2002). *Understanding emotions: Mind and morals.* London: Ashgate. An interesting discussion of the relationship among emotion, thought, and behavior.

48. O'Hanlon, B., & Hudson, P. (1995). *Love is a verb: How to stop analyzing your relationship and make it great!* New York: Norton.

49. Lewis, T., Amini, R., & Lannon, R. (2000). *A general theory of love.* New York: Random House.

50. Ibid., p. 63.

51. Fisher, H. (1992). *Anatomy of love: A natural history of mating, marriage, and why we stray.* New York: Fawcett; Lewis et al., *A general theory of love.*

52. de Beauvoir, S. (1995). The woman in love (from *The Second Sex*). In A. Stewart (Ed.), *Philosophical perspectives on sex and love* (pp. 213–216). New York: Oxford University Press, p. 213.

53. LeMoncheck, L. (1995). Feminist politics and feminist ethics: Treating women as sex objects. In A. Stewart (Ed.), *Philosophical perspectives on sex and love* (pp. 29–38). New York: Oxford University Press; Rapaport, E. (1973–1974). On the future of love: Rousseau and the radical feminists. Reprinted in Stewart, *Philosophical perspectives on sex and love* (pp. 18–28).

54. Fisher, H. (2004). "What wild ecstasy": Being in love. In *Why we love: The nature and chemistry of romantic love* (pp. 1–25). New York: Henry Holt, p. 5.

55. See Foels, R. (2005). Learning and unlearning the myths we are taught: Gender and social dominance orientation. *Sex Roles, 50,* 743–757; Handel, G. (2006). *Childhood socialization* (2nd ed.). New Brunswick, NJ: Aldine Transaction; Salari, S., & Zhang, W. (2006). Kin keepers and good providers: Influence of gender socialization on well-being among U.S.A. birth cohorts. *Aging and Mental Health, 10,* 485–496.

56. Datan, N. (1984). Androgyny and the life cycle: The Bacchae of Euripides. *Journal of Imagination, Cognition, and Personality: The Scientific Study of Consciousness, 4,* 407–415; Jacobi, J. (1965). *The way of individuation.* New York: Harcourt, Brace & World; McCabe, J. (1989). Psychological androgyny in later life: A psychocultural examination. *Ethos, 17(1),* 3–31; Neugarten, B. L., & Gutmann, D. I. (1958). Age-sex roles and personality in middle age: A thematic apperception study. *Psychological Monographs, 72* (whole no. 470).

CHAPTER 2

1. Harris, M. (1994). Growing old gracefully: Age concealment and gender. *Journal of Gerontology: Psychological Sciences, 49*(4), P149–P158.
2. Ephron, N. (2006). *I feel bad about my neck: And other thoughts on being a woman.* New York: Knopf.
3. New Age Media Concepts. (2007). The total European and US market for cosmeceuticals currently stands at US$8.2 billion. NAMC Newswire, May 3, 2007. Retrieved June 12, 2007, from http://press.namct.com/content/view/7558/156/
4. Goodman, M. (1994). Social, psychological, and developmental factors in women's receptivity to cosmetic surgery. *Journal of Aging Studies, 8*(4), 373–396.
5. Manton, K. G., & Gu, X. (2001). Changes in the prevalence of chronic sources of disability in the United States black and non-black population above 65 from 1982 to 1999. *Proceedings of the National Academy of Sciences, 98*, 6354–6359; Schoeni, R. F., Freedman, V. A., & Wallace, R. B. (2001). Persistent, consistent, widespread and robust? Another look at recent trends in old-age disability. *Journals of Gerontology Series B: Psychological Sciences and Social Sciences, 56*(4), S206–S218; Wolf, D. A., Mendes de Leon, C. F., & Glass, T. A. (2007). Trends in rates of onset of and recovery from disability at older ages: 1982–1994. *Journals of Gerontology Series B: Psychological Sciences and Social Sciences, 62*(1), S3–S10.
6. U.S. Bureau of the Census (2003). Census 2000 brief: Disability status 2000. Retrieved August 26, 2006, from http://www.census.gov/prod/2003pubs/c2kbr-17.pdf
7. Lewis, C. S. (1960). *The four loves.* New York: Harcourt, p. 100.
8. Cabeza, R., Nyberg, L., & Park, D. (Eds.). (2005). Cognitive neuroscience of aging: Emergence of a new discipline. In *Cognitive neuroscience of aging: Linking cognitive and cerebral aging* (pp. 3–16). New York: Oxford University Press.
9. Cited in Cohen, G. D. (2005). *The mature mind: The positive power of the aging brain.* New York: Basic Books.
10. Maguire, E. A., Frackowiak, R. S., & Frith, C. D. (1997). Recalling routes around London: Activation of the right hippocampus in taxi drivers. *Journal of Neuroscience, 17,* 7103–7110. Cited in Cohen, *The mature mind.*
11. Cohen, *The mature mind*, p. 6.
12. Cabeza, R. (2002). Hemispheric asymmetry reduction in older adults: The HAROLD model. *Psychology and Aging, 17(1),* 85–100. Cited in Cohen, *The mature mind.*
13. Labouvie-Vief, G., & Medler, M. (2002). Affect optimization and affect complexity: Modes and styles of regulation in adulthood. *Psychology and Aging, 17,* 571–588; Ong, A. D., & Bergeman, C. S. (2004). The complexity of emotions in later life. *Journal of Gerontology: Psychological Sciences, 59B*(3), P117–P122.
14. Carstensen, L. L., Pasupathi, M., Mayr, U., & Nesselroade, J. R. (1998). Emotional experience in everyday life across the adult life span. *Journal of Personality and Social Psychology, 79,* 644–655.
15. Carstensen, L. L., Isaacowitz, D. M., & Charles, S. T. (1999). Taking time seriously: A theory of socioemotional selectivity. *American Psychologist, 54,* 165–181.

16. Birditt, K. S., & Fingerman, K. L. (2005). Do we get better at picking our battles? Age group differences in descriptions of behavioral reactions to interpersonal tensions. *Journal of Gerontology: Psychological Sciences, 60B*(3), P121–P138.
17. See Ong & Bergeman, The complexity of emotions in later life.
18. Erikson, E. H. (1968). *Identity: Youth and crisis*. New York: Norton.
19. Ibid., p. 135.
20. Ibid., p. 136.
21. Erikson, E. H. (1976). Reflections on Dr. Borg's life cycle. *Daedalus, 105*, p. 24.
22. Ibid., p. 23.
23. Gilligan, C. (1982). *In a different voice: Psychological theory and women's development*. Cambridge, MA: Harvard University Press. I do not include the work of several developmental theorists here, including Charlotte Buhler, Daniel Levinson, and Klaus Riegel. While their work may illuminate some aspects of psychological development, its relevance to romantic relationships is limited. Kohlber's work on moral development is introduced in Chapter 6.
24. See Bennet, E. A. (1966). *What Jung really said*. New York: Schocken.
25. Campbell, J. (Ed.). (1971). *The portable Jung*. New York: Penguin, p. 19.
26. Aron, A., & Aron, E. N. (1986). *Love and the expansion of self: Understanding attraction and satisfaction*. New York: Hemisphere.
27. Carl Jung believed midlife was an important time for psychological growth but did not endorse the notion of an inevitable crisis. Elliott Jaques coined the term in 1965 to describe midlife changes he observed in the lives of artists. See Jaques, E. (1965). Death and the mid-life crisis. *International Journal of Psychoanalysis, 46*, 502–514. Daniel Levinson incorporated the idea of midlife transition in his theory, which is largely focused on men's development. See Levinson, D. J. (1978). *The seasons of a man's life*. New York: Knopf.
28. Costa, P. T., & McCrae, R. R. (1980). Still stable after all these years: Personality as a key to some issues in adulthood and old age. In P. B. Baltes & O. G. Brim (Eds.), *Life-span development and behavior* (Vol. 3, pp. 65–102). New York: Academic Press; Gould, R. (1978). *Transformations: Growth and change in adult life*. New York: Simon & Schuster; Livson, F. B. (1976). Patterns of personality development in middle-aged women: A longitudinal study. *International Journal of Aging and Human Development, 7*, 107–115; Livson, F. B. (1981). Paths to psychological health in the middle years: Sex differences. In D. H. Eichorn, J. A. Clausen, N. Haan, M. P. Honzik, & P. H. Mussen (Eds.), *Present and past in middle life* (pp. 195–221). New York: Academic Press; Vaillant, G. E. (1977). *Adaptation to life*. Boston: Little, Brown.
29. Trillin, C. (2006). Alice, off the page. *The New Yorker*, March 27, 2006, p. 55.

CHAPTER 3

1. In Stewart, A. (Ed.). (1995). *Philosophical perspectives on sex and love*. New York: Oxford University Press, p. 191.
2. Morgan, *Love: Plato, the Bible, and Freud*, p. 131.

3. See Fisher, *What wild ecstasy*; and Liebowitz, M. R. (1983). *The chemistry of love.* Boston: Little, Brown.

4. Fisher, *Anatomy of love.*

5. The pathologies of love have a rather fuzzy nomenclature. The terms *lovesickness* or *pathological infatuation* are sometimes used to describe this type of addiction. In a related condition, known as erotomania, an infatuated lover experiences the delusion that his or her affection is returned. Erotomania can be extremely dangerous, resulting in stalking and homicidal behavior. See Gaoni, B. & Shreibaum, D. (1985). Love as fierce as death. *Israel Journal of Psychiatry and Related Sciences, 22*(1–2), 89–93; Goldberg, A. (1994). Lovesickness. In J. M. Oldham & S. Bone (Eds.), *Paranoia: New psychoanalytic perspectives* (pp. 115–132). Madison, CT: International Universities Press; Mullen, P. E., & Pathé, M. (1994). The pathological extensions of love. *British Journal of Psychiatry, 165,* 614–623.

6. Liebowitz, *The chemistry of love.*

7. Fisher, *Anatomy of love.*

8. Tennov, D. (1979). *Love and limerence: The experience of being in love.* New York: Stein and Day.

9. Lewis, *A general theory of love*, p. 131.

10. Dutton, D. G., & Aron, A. P. (1974). Some evidence for heightened sexual attraction under conditions of high anxiety. *Journal of Personality and Social Psychology, 30,* 510–517.

11. See, e.g., Stewart, S., Stinnett, H., & Rosenfeld, L. R. (2000). Sex differences in desired characteristics of short-term and long-term relationship partners. *Journal of Social and Personal Relationships, 17,* 843–853.

12. Fine, *Love and work*, p. 38.

13. Fisher, *What wild ecstasy.*

14. The nearly lost art of feminine wiles may have been an attempt to forestall the moment of truth long enough to completely snag the besotted male.

15. Liebowitz, *The chemistry of love*, p. 200.

16. For studies conducted in these and more cultures, see Jankowiak, W. (Ed.). (1995). *Romantic passion: A universal experience?* New York: Columbia University Press.

17. Fisher, *Anatomy of love,* p. 51.

18. Ibid.

19. Ibid., p. 76.

20. Some authors, like Baumeister, consider any relationship in which only one party is in love or loving a case of unrequited love. So a woman whose husband leaves her for another could be considered to have unrequited love as well. The dynamics of this kind of experience are discussed in Chapter 7.

21. Baumeister, R. F., & Wotman, S. R. (1992). *Breaking hearts: The two sides of unrequited love.* New York: Guilford.

22. See, e.g., Walster, E., Berscheid, E., & Walster, G. W. (1976). New directions in equity research. In L. Berkowitz (Ed.), *Advances in experimental social psychology, 9* (pp. 1–42). New York: Academic Press.

23. Bratslavsky, E., Baumeister, R. F., & Sommer, K. L. (1998). To love or be loved in vain: The trials and tribulations of unrequited love. In B. H. Spitzbert & W. R. Cupach (Eds.), *The dark side of close relationships.* New Jersey: Erlbaum.
24. Frankl, V. *Man's search for meaning.*
25. Baumeister & Wotman, *Breaking hearts*, p. 186.
26. See, e.g., Noller, P. (1996). What is this thing called love? Defining the love that supports marriage and family. *Personal Relationships, 3*(1), 97–115.

CHAPTER 4

1. U.S. Bureau of the Census. (2007). Table A1. Marital Status of People 15 Years and Over, by Age, Sex, Personal Earnings, Race, and Hispanic Origin. In *America's families and living arrangements: 2006.* Retrieved March 29, 2007, from http:// www.census.gov/population/www/socdemo/hh-fam/cps2006.html
2. Singer, I. (1966). *The nature of love: Plato to Luther.* New York: Random House.
3. Buber, M. (1958). *I and thou* (R. G. Smith, Trans.). New York: Charles Scribner's Sons.
4. Culbreth, J. (2005). *Boomer's guide to online dating.* Stuttgart: Holtzbrinck.
5. Coupland, J. (2000). Past the "perfect kind of age"? Styling selves and relationships in over 50s dating advertisements. *Journal of Communication 50*, 9–30.
6. Ibid., p. 28.

CHAPTER 5

1. Data from the 2006 Current Populations Survey are illustrative. Even with declining marriage rates, a majority (63%) of Americans 20 years of age and over were married or cohabiting. At present the Census Bureau does not monitor living apart together relationships or engagements, which would raise this figure a bit. Data on marital status from http://www.census.gov/population/www/socdemo/hh-fam/cps2006.html; 5.5 million cohabiting households = 11 million individuals (assumed 20-plus years of age).
2. Cohabitation rates in the United States have increased among all age groups. This trend has continued since the later decades of the twentieth century. In 2001, roughly 8% of U.S. couples were cohabiting, compared to 30% in Sweden (the nation with the highest cohabitation rates). Ambert, A. (2005). Cohabitation and marriage: How are they related? Vanier Institute of the Family. Retrieved January 6, 2007, from http://www.vifamily.ca/library/cft/cohabitation.html#Marriag
3. Monnier, A., & de Guibert-Lantoine, C. (1995). The Demographic Situation of Europe and Developed Countries Overseas: An Annual Report. *Population: An English Selection, 8*, 235–250; U.S. Center for Health Statistics. Advance Report of Final Marriage Statistics, 1989 and 1990. *Monthly Vital Statistics Report, 43*(12). Government Printing Office.
4. Inglehart, R., et al. (2004). *Human beliefs and values: A cross-cultural sourcebook based on the 1999–2002 values survey.* Mexico City: Siglo Veintiuno Editores.

5. Coontz, S. (2005). *Marriage, a history: From obedience to intimacy, or how love conquered marriage.* New York Viking.
6. Coontz, S. (2006). "Three rules that don't apply." *Newsweek,* June 5, p. 49.
7. Levin, E. (1986). The new look in old maids: A study says that single-minded women may end up staying that way, to which some luminous ladies respond, "So, what?" *People,* March 31, 1986, p. 28.
8. Coontz, "Three rules," p. 49.
9. The report was later issued as an article: Bennet, N. G., Bloom, D. E., & Craig, P. H. (1989). The divergence of black and white marriage patterns. *American Journal of Sociology, 95*(3), 127–138, and after the press furor the authors issued a revised article without the figures for late-life single women.
10. National Healthy Marriage Resource Center. Research and trends: Trends in median age at 1st marriage Retrieved April 4, 2007, from http://www.healthy marriageinfo.org/research/?d=%7BECBD272F-E119-43E1-ACBF-B4687E279070%7D
11. Shiano, P. H., & Guinn, L. S. (1994). Epidemiology of divorce. *Children and Divorce, 4*(1). Retrieved November 27, 2007, from http://www.futureofchildren .org/information2826/information_show.htm?doc_id=75524
12. Marrying late "natural for modern women." (2004). *China Daily,* April 21.
13. Feminist icon Gloria Steinem first-time bride at 66. (2000). CNN.com, September 5.
14. Bramlett, M. D., & Mosher, W. D. (2001). Advance data: First marriage dissolution, divorce, and remarriage: United States. Number 323. May 31, 2001. Washington, DC: Centers for Disease Control, Division of Vital Statistics. Retrieved June 16, 2007, from http://www.cdc.gov/nchs/data/ad/ad323.pdf
15. U.S. Bureau of the Census (2003). Married couple and unmarried partner households: 2000. Census 2000 special reports. Retrieved January 6, 2007, from http://www.census.gov/prod/2003pubs/censr-5.pdf
16. See, e.g., Rusbult, C. E., Drugitasm, S. N., & Verettem, H. (1994). The investment model: An interdependence analysis of commitment processes and relationship maintenance phenomena. In D. Canary & L. Stafford (Eds.), *Communication and relational maintenance* (pp. 115–139). New York: Academic Press.
17. I am indebted to Erin Sahlstein and Leslie Baxter for this analogy. See Sahlstein, E. M., & Baxter, L. A. (2001). Improvising commitment in close relationships: A relational dialectics perspective. In J. H. Harvey & A. Wenzel (Eds.), *Close romantic relationships: Maintenance and enhancement* (pp. 115–133). Mahwah, NJ: Erlbaum.
18. Jung, C. G. (1971). Marriage as a psychological relationship. In J. Campbell (Ed.), *The portable Jung.* New York: Viking Press. (Originally published 1925)
19. Mitchell, S. A. (2002). *Can love last? The fate of romance over time.* New York: Norton, p. 113.
20. Coontz, *Marriage, a history,* p. 282.
21. Aron & Aron, *Love and the expansion of self.*
22. Rusbult, C. E., Olsen, N., Davis, J. L., & Hannon, P. A. (2001). In J. H. Harvey & A. Wenzel (Eds.), *Close romantic relationships: Maintenance and enhancement* (pp. 87–114). Mahwah, NJ: Erlbaum.

23. Aristotle. (2003). The Nicomachean. In *Ethics* (J. A. K. Thomson, Trans.). London: Penguin Classics, p. 22.
24. See Lopata, H. Z. (1999). *Current widowhood: Myths and realities.* Thousand Oaks, CA: Sage.
25. The contrast between Grandma's letter and my mother's perception of her marriage may also stem from a tendency for children to react strongly to parental conflict. We explore the impact of parental conflict on children's relationships in Chapter 6.

CHAPTER 6

1. Booth, A., & Edwards, J. N. (1990). Transmission of marital and family quality over the generations: The effects of parental divorce and unhappiness. *Journal of Divorce, 13,* 41–58; Conger, R. D., Cui, M., Bryant, C. M., & Elder, G. H. (2000). Competence in early adult romantic relationships: A developmental perspective on family influences. *Journal of Personality and Social Psychology, 79,* 224–237; Cunningham, M., & Thornton, A. (2006). The influence of parents' marital quality on adult children's attitudes towards marriage and its alternatives: Main and moderating effects. *Demography, 43,* 659–672; Perren, S., VonWyl, A., Bargin, D., Simoni, H., & Von Klitzing, K. (2005). Intergenerational transmission of marital quality across the transition to parenthood. *Family Process, 44,* 441–459.
2. Amato, P. R., & Booth, A. (1991). Consequences of parental divorce and marital unhappiness for adult well-being. *Social Forces, 69,* 895–914; Christensen, T. M., & Brooks, M. C. (2001). Adult children of divorce and intimate relationships: A review of the literature. *Family Journal, 9,* 289–294; Feng, D., Giarrusso, R., Bengtson, V. L., & Frye, N. (1999). Intergenerational transmission of marital quality and marital instability. *Journal of Marriage and the Family, 61,* 451–464.
3. Amato, P. R., & Booth, A. (2001). The legacy of parents' marital discord: Consequences for children's marital quality. *Journal of Personality and Social Psychology, 81,* 627–638.
4. Butler, R. N., & Lewise, M. I. (1988). *The new love and sex after 60.* New York: Ballantine, p. 11.
5. Sprecher, S., & Felmlee, D. (1992). The influence of parents and friends on the quality and stability of romantic relationships: A three-wave longitudinal investigation. *Journal of Marriage and the Family, 54,* 888–900.
6. Sullivan, K. T. (2001). Understanding the relationship between religiosity and marriage: An investigation of immediate and longitudinal effects of religiosity on newly wed couples. *Journal of Family Psychology, 15,* 610–626.
7. White, L. K. (1990). Determinants of divorce: A review of research in the eighties. *Journal of Marriage and the Family, 52,* 904–912; Andersen, J. (2001). Financial problems as predictors of divorce: A social exchange perspective. *Proceedings for the Western Region Home Management / Family Economics Educators 3,* 35–44. Retrieved March 5, 2007, from http://www.csus.edu/indiv/a/andersenj/Research/FinancialProblems.pdf; Conger, R. D., Elder, G. H., Lorenz, F. O., Conger, J. J.,

Simons, R. L., et al. (1990). Linking economic hardship to marital quality and instability. *Journal of Marriage and the Family, 52,* 643–656.

CHAPTER 7

1. Fitness, J. (2001). Betrayal, rejection, revenge, and forgiveness: An interpersonal script approach. In M. R. Leary (Ed.), *Interpersonal rejection* (pp. 73–104). New York: Oxford University Press, p. 73.
2. Kontula, O., & Haavio-Mannila, E. (2004). Renaissance of romanticism in the era of increasing individualism. In J. Duncombe, K. Harrison, G. Allan, & D. Marsden (Eds.), *The state of affairs: Explorations in infidelity and commitment.* London: Erlbaum.
3. Barlow, A., Duncan, S., James, G., & Park, A. (2001). Just a piece of paper? Marriage and cohabitation. In A. Park, J. Curtice, K. Thomson, L. Jarvis, C. Bromley, & N. Stratford (Eds.), *British social attitudes: The 18th report* (pp. 29–58). London: Sage.
4. Atkins, D. C., Baucom, D. H., & Jacobson, N. S. (2001). Understanding infidelity: Correlates in a national random sample. *Journal of Family Psychology, 15,* 735–749.
5. Laumann, E. O., Gagnon, J. H., Michael, R. T., & Michaels, S. (1994). *The social organization of sexuality: Sexual practices in the United States.* Chicago: University of Chicago Press.
6. Oliver, M. B., & Hyde, J. S. (1993). Gender differences in sexuality: A meta-analysis. *Psychological Bulletin, 114,* 29–51.
7. South, S. J., & Lloyd, K. M. (1995). Spousal alternatives and marital dissolution. *Sociological Review, 60,* 21–35.
8. Note that the denominator in this figure is different from the 48% figure. Whereas 48% of those who had been betrayed were cheated on, 25% of the entire Internet sample reported this experience.
9. Previti, D., & Amato, P. R. (2004). Is infidelity a cause or a consequence of poor marital quality? *Journal of Social and Personal Relationships, 21*(2), 217–230.
10. Thompson, A. P. (1983). Extramarital sex: A review of the research literature. *Journal of Sex Research, 19,* 1–23.
11. Betzig, L. (1989). Causes of conjugal dissolution: A cross-cultural study. *Current Anthropology, 30,* 654–676; Amato, P. R., & Previti, D. (2003). People's reasons for divorcing: Gender, social class, the life course, and adjustment. *Journal of Family Issues, 24,* 602–626.
12. Atkins, Baucom, & Jacobson, Understanding infidelity.
13. Treas, J., & Giesen, D. (2000). Sexual infidelity among married and cohabiting Americans. *Journal of Marriage and the Family, 62*(1), 48–60.
14. Zak, A., Coulter, C., Giglio, S., Hall, J., Sanford, S., & Pellowski, N. (2002). Do his friends and family like me? Predictors of infidelity in intimate relationships. *North American Journal of Psychology, 4*(2), 287–290.

15. Olenick, I. (2000). Odds of spousal infidelity are influenced by social and demographic factors. *Family Planning Perspectives, 32*(3), 148–149; Treas & Giesen, Sexual infidelity among married and cohabiting Americans.

16. Atkins, Baucom, & Jacobson, Understanding infidelity.

17. Treas & Giesen, Sexual infidelity among married and cohabiting Americans.

18. Blow, A. J., & Hartnett, K. (2005). Infidelity in committed relationships II: A substantive review. *Journal of Marital and Family Therapy, 3*(2), 217–233.

19. Gore, K., & Yeatman, S. (2005, August). *Church attendance, religious affiliation, and extramarital sex.* Paper presented at the annual meeting of the American Sociological Association, Philadelphia, PA. Retrieved June 11, 2007, from http://www.allacademic.com/meta/p19894_index.html

20. Buunk, B. P., & Dijkstra, P. (2004). Men, women, and infidelity: Sex differences in extradyadic sex and jealousy. In J. Duncombe, K. Harrison, G. Allan, & D. Marsden, (Eds.), *The state of affairs: Explorations in infidelity and commitment.* (pp. 103–120). London: Erlbaum.

21. Afifi, W. A., Falato, W. L., & Weinger, J. L. (2001). Identity concerns following a severe relational transgression: The role of discovery method for the relational outcomes of infidelity. *Journal of Social and Personal Relationships, 18*(2), 291–308.

22. Cole, T. (2001). Lying to the one you love: The use of deception in romantic relationships. *Journal of Social and Personal Relationships, 18*(1), 107–129.

23. Whenever possible, my interviewers and I document these after-the-fact stories in our field notes; however, if a respondent asked an interviewer to keep material secret it was not recorded or discussed.

24. Metts, S. (1994). Relational transgressions. In D. J. Canary & L. Stafford (Eds.), *Communication and relational maintenance* (pp. 217–239). San Diego: Academic Press.

25. See Vangelisti, A. L. (1994). Messages that hurt. In W. R. Cupach & B. H. Spitzbert (Eds.), *The dark side of interpersonal communication* (pp. 53–82). Hillsdale, NJ: Erlbaum; Jacoby, S. (1983). *Wild justice: The evolution of revenge.* New York: Harper & Row.

26. Buunk, B. P., & Baker, A. B. (1997). Responses to unprotected extradyadic sex by one's partner: Testing predictions from interdependence and equity theory. *Journal of Sex Research, 34*(4), 387–397.

27. Roloff, M. E., Soule, K. P., & Carey, C. M. (2001). Reasons for remaining in a relationship and responses to relational transgressions. *Journal of Social and Personal Relationships, 18*(3), 362–385.

28. Rotenberg, K. J., Shewchuk, V., & Kimberley, T. (2001). Loneliness, sex, romantic jealousy and powerlessness. *Journal of Social and Personal Relationships, 18*(1), 55–79, p. 56.

29. Ibid.

30. Buss, D. M., Larsen, R. J., & Westen, D. (1996). Sex differences in jealousy: Not gone, not forgotten, and not easily explained by alternative hypotheses. *Psychological Science, 7*(6), 373–375; Buunk, B. P., Bram, P., Angleitner, A., & Oubaid, V.

(1996). Sex differences in jealousy in evolutionary and cultural perspective: Tests from the Netherlands, Germany, and the United States. *Psychological Science, 7*(6), 359–363; DeSteno, D. A., & Salovey, P. (1994). Jealousy in close relationships: Multiple perspectives on the green-ey'd monster. In A. L. Weber & J. H. Harvey (Eds.), *Perspectives on close relationships* (pp. 217–242). Needham Heights, MA: Allyn & Bacon.

31. Atkins, Baucom, & Jacobson, Understanding infidelity; Treas & Giesen, Sexual infidelity among married and cohabiting Americans.

32. Fitness, Betrayal, rejection, revenge, and forgiveness, p. 77.

33. Bratslavsky, E., Baumeister, R. F., & Sommer, K. L. (1998). To love or be loved in vain: The trials and tribulations of unrequited love. In B. H. Spitzbert & W. R. Cupach (Eds.), *The dark side of close relationships.* Hillsdale, NJ: Erlbaum, p. 314.

CHAPTER 8

1. Lewis, C. S. (1961). *A grief observed.* New York: Seabury Press, p. 58.

2. Didion, J. (2005). *The year of magical thinking.* New York: Knopf, p. 4.

3. Dr. Kübler-Ross was born in 1926 in Zurich, and emigrated to the United States in 1958. She completed her degree in psychiatry at the University of Colorado, and focused her entire career on issues related to death and bereavement. She died in 2004 at her home in Arizona.

4. Bowlby, *Attachment and loss: Vol. 3.*

5. Worden, J. W. (1991). *Grief counseling and grief therapy: A handbook for the mental health practitioner.* New York: Springer.

6. These beliefs are part of the celebration of Los Dias de los Muertos beginning on November 1.

7. Freud, S. (1957). Mourning and melancholia. In J. Strachey, with A. Freud, A. Strachey, & A. Tyson (Eds.), *The standard edition of the complete psychological works of Sigmund Freud* (Vol. 14). London: Hogarth, p. 244. (Original work published 1914–1916)

8. Young, M., Benjamin, B., & Wallis, C. (1963). The mortality of widowers. *The Lancet, 2,* 454–456; Rees, W. D., & Lutkins, S. G. (1967). Mortality of bereavement. *British Medical Journal, 4,* 13–16.

9. Phillips, A. C., Carroll, D., Burned, V., Ring, C., Macleaod, J., & Drayson, M. (2006). Bereavement and marriage are associated with antibody response to influenza vaccination in the elderly. *Brain, Behavior and Immunity, 20*(3), 279–289.

10. Schleifer, S. J. (1989). *Bereavement, depression, and immunity: The role of age.* New York: Plenum; Irwin, M. R., Daniels, M., Smith, T. L., & Bloom, E. (1987). Impaired natural killer cell activity during bereavement. *Brain, Behavior and Immunity, 1*(1), 98–104; Stein, M., Schleifer, S. J., & Keller, S. E. (1987). Immunity and aging: Experimental and clinical studies. In M. W. Riley & J. D. Matarazzo (Eds.), *The aging dimension.* Hillsdale, NJ: Erlbaum; Kiecolt-Glaser, J. K., & Glaser, R. (1986). Psychological influences on immunity. *Psychosomatics: Journal of Consultation Liaison Psychiatry, 27,* 621–624.

11. Averill, J. R., & Nunley, E. P. (1997). Grief as an emotion and as a disease: A social-constructionist perspective. In M. S. Stroebe, W. Stroebe, & R. O. Hansson (Eds.), *Handbook of bereavement: Theory, research, and intervention* (pp. 77–90). Cambridge: Cambridge University Press.

12. Lopata, H. (1996). *Current widowhood: Myths and realities*. Thousand Oaks, CA: Sage; Lopata, H. (1981). Widowhood and husband sanctification. *Journal of Marriage and the Family, 43*(2), 439–450.

13. Smith, K. R., Zick, C. D., & Duncan, G. J. (1991). Remarriage patterns among recent widows and widowers. *Demography, 28*, 361–374.

14. Carr, D. (2004). The desire to date and remarry among older widows and widowers. *Journal of Marriage and Family, 66*, 1051–1068. It is unclear how many older widows would like to remarry. Maria Talbott reported that about 15% of her sample of 64 widows expressed interest in remarriage. See Talbott, M. M. (1998). Older widows' attitudes towards men and remarriage. *Journal of Aging Studies, 12*, 429–444. By contrast, survey results from 259 widows drawn nationally for the Americans' Changing Lives Survey indicated that only 7.3% were interested in remarriage. See Moorman, S. M., Booth, A., & Fingerman, K. L. (2006). Women's romantic relationships after widowhood. *Journal of Family Issues, 27*, 1281–1304.

15. See Bernard, J. (1972). *The future of marriage*. New York: Bantam; Carr, D. (2004). Gender, preloss marital dependence, and older adults' adjustment to widowhood. *Journal of Marriage and the Family, 66*, 220–235; Cancian, F. M., & Oliker, S. J. (2000). *Caring and gender*. Walnut Creek, CA: AltaMira Press; Lee, G. R., Carstensen, L. L., & Gottman, J. M. (2001). Gender differences in the depressive effect of widowhood in later life. *Journal of Gerontology: Social Sciences, 56*, S56–S61; Antonucci, T., & Akiyama, A. (1995). Convoys of social relationships: Family and friendships within a life span context. In R. Blieszner & V. H. Bedford (Eds.), *Handbook of aging and the family* (4th ed., pp. 355–371). Westport, CT: Greenwood Press.

16. Most studies indicate that older widowers are more interested in remarriage than older women. See particularly Davidson, K. (2001). Late life widowhood, selfishness and new partnership choices: A gendered perspective. *Ageing and Society, 21*, 297–317; Davidson, K., & Fennell, G. (Eds.). (2004). *Intimacy in later life*. New Brunswick, NJ: Transaction. One exception is a study by Deborah Carr, which did not find a gender difference in desire to remarry. See Carr, Gender, preloss marital dependence, and older adults' adjustment to widowhood.

17. Lopata, Widowhood and husband sanctification.

18. Carr, The desire to date and remarry among older widows and widowers.

19. Moorman et al., Women's romantic relationships after widowhood.

20. Kantrowitz, B., Raymond, J., Springen, K., Wingert, P., Kuchment, A., & Kelley, R. (2006, February 20). Sex and love: The new world. *Newsweek*, 51–60.

21. Levin, I. (2004). Living apart together: A new family form. *Current Sociology, 52*, 223–240.

22. Kübler-Ross, E. (1991, January 29). Personal communication.

CONCLUSION

1. Kluckhohn & Murray, cited in Runyan, M. (1982). *Life histories and psychobiography: Explorations in theory and method*. New York: Oxford University Press, p. 4.

APPENDIX B

1. Ezzy, D. (2002). *Qualitative analysis: Practice and innovation*. London: Routledge.

# Index